OUR BIG ADVENTURE

PART TWO

ADRIAN & JACQUELINE RIGG

Published by
Jaqade Publishing

Published by
Jaqade Publishing

Copyright © AW & J Rigg

Cover Design
Trina Esquivelzeta

ISBN 978-0-9574885-3-3

First Edition

With love to

Iris Doreen Rigg

&

In loving memory of

Robert Toward

06/06/1933 to 20/07/2014

TABLE OF CONTENTS

Internet Pictures

www.europetastic.blogspot.com

At this website you can view photographs taken during the tour.

MAP

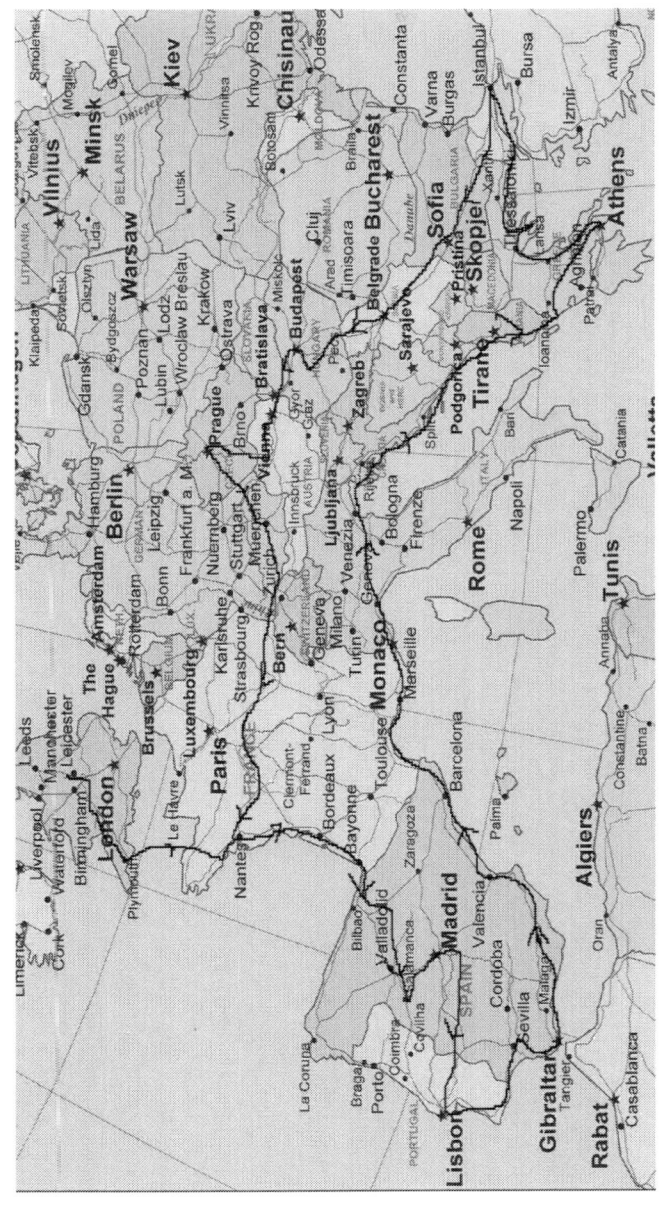

PREFACE

This book is about our experiences, as we take a 'two-year sabbatical' from work, to tour Europe.

Our Second book can be read independently of Part One where we toured Northern Europe and Scandinavia, how the whole idea came about and how we put our plan into action.

Part Two covers the second half of our tour, as we head south through Spain to Portugal and onwards following the coast to Turkey. Then following almost the route of the Orient Express to Vienna and finally through Germany back to France. We hope you enjoy reading about it as much as we enjoyed doing it, and we hope it inspires you to take the plunge in whatever you choose for your life adventure!

This book is not intended to be a tour guide as such, listing museums and sights to see, there are plenty of other books on the shelves for that. This is basically a travel log, chronicling our journey and experiences along the way. You will find a list of the books we used during our tour in the appendix along with other items which we hope will be of interest to you.

...

Most of us are waiting for that 'one day' to arrive when we will do that thing we have always promised ourselves. We tell ourselves 'one day' we will do it, but days go by that turn into weeks and then years and still that 'one day' does not arrive. We read about others doing it, we hear about it on the radio and see it on the telly, and yet somehow ours never turns up. But we keep telling ourselves we will do it 'one day'. Then for us, our 'one day' arrived unexpectedly and not quite how we envisaged it would happen!

In Part One we explain, what motivated us to decide to give up everything that we had worked for, to go on a life adventure. Jackie and I married at the tender ages of 16 and 17 and we soon had a lovely daughter to make up our family. Life was hard going to start with, as we watched our friends going out enjoying themselves, while we scraped by on my apprentice wages. That's not to say we were not happy with our lives, because we were.

However, it's at this time we made ourselves a promise, that 'one day' our time would come and we too would have that quality time to ourselves, doing exactly what we wanted to.

Time wandered on and we were actually living a lovely life and by then had a son who completed our family. Then before we knew it, the kids had flown the nest and it was just the two of us. But still that 'one day' eluded us, as our life style had its own routine and demands. We were actually frightened by the prospect of doing something else. Then the company I worked for closed overnight, making me redundant. After a while and some debate, we realised that our 'one day' had arrived. Even more of a surprise, it arrived while we are both still alive and well!

Having done some serious calculations of where we both wanted to go on our life adventure and how much it would cost, we realised it could be done. Then, after much soul searching and debate, we decided to sell our house in the UK to finance our life adventure. To be fair, we still had a holiday home in France to fall back on.

Having sold our house and after much research, we bought a motorhome, a bit of a challenge as we had never used one before.

We will be travelling in our motorhome, the lovely 'Belle'. Belle is an Autotrail Apache 634U which is 7.2 metres long, with a bike rack on the back carrying two electric bikes. The layout is a rear U shaped lounge, with picture windows to three sides, that can be changed to a dining room with a table, or a made up queen sized bed. She has a second 'over driving cab' double bed area, which we mainly used for extra storage. She is equipped with a cooker, fridge, toilet, shower, heating, TV and plenty of storage space. She has her own electricity, gas and water, which will last a few days independently of a top up. Most importantly she has cruise control, which is proving essential for resting the right leg while driving.

For part one of 'Our Big Adventure' we headed North through France, Belgium, Holland, Northern Germany, Denmark, Sweden, Norway, Finland, Russia (almost), Estonia, Latvia, Lithuania, Poland, Germany, Luxembourg and finally back to France. It was a massive step for us, could we live together in a confined space? Would we like the life on the road? Suffice to say we loved it that much we could not wait to start the second part and *voila!*..... Here we are.

On a personal note, living with someone 24/7 in the close quarters of a motorhome, could prove daunting and I am sure would put most people off. For our part, both Jackie and I are very passionate people, so sparks do fly from time to time. We are also guilty of bickering, which if you listened, is usually over nothing and you would think we are a couple of school kids. In this book, if we mention an argument, then it certainly will have been one.

On the first part of our tour, we quickly identified areas of annoyance. After a while we talked these several minor issues through. Some had to be left and we found a way to work through them, while others would be avoided or the attempt made not to repeat them. The main thing is we are happy in one another's company, most of the time. You have to have a certain amount of personal discipline, to help you identify and avoid friction points. When you feel a mood coming on or something upsets you, fight it, do not retaliate. Most importantly, take the time to listen and talk things through, not necessarily at the time things happen. It's called self-control.

We have developed rules to get us through most events, the 'golden hour' and 'logs on the fire' being just two. The 'golden hour' is to leave an hours silence or the injured party alone for an hour, to let things calm down. Then to offer a drink or something to break the ice, if the answer is no, then leave it a while longer. 'Logs on the fire' is how things escalate, you have to add another line or word to an argument. This then escalates from minor into a major argument, as you add more logs onto the fire, so to speak. So, we both make conscious efforts not to add logs onto the fire, better to leave it alone and let it go out. We all know what burnt fingers feel like. If you have none of these issues in your life, then lucky you. Although for us, a bit of passion adds to the spice of life.

This book started out as an internet blog and a journal, created by Jackie, to which I added my bits and altered as I saw fit. Then Jackie went over it again, added a few more bits that I had missed and gave it a good polish. We realised we were not gifted enough to write the book from a dual perspective. So, although it sounds like me writing all the time, some parts are Jackie, while other parts are mine, but most is a joint effort. Hopefully you will find this easier to read, rather than to keep switching from me to Jackie, or vice versa all the time.

Finally, having made such a good job of correcting Part One, we asked our friends Christine Battelle and Alyson Sheehan, to do the same for Part Two. We would like to give them our heartfelt thanks for being so supportive in getting this second part completed.

Last but not least to friend and a very talented lady, Trina Esquivelzeta for her input and help in designing and creating the second cover artwork to compliment part one.

Sadly, Jackie's mother passed away in between Parts One and Two of the tour and whilst we were back in the UK over the winter. Then, more sadness for us as Jackie's father passed away whilst we were writing Part Two. Fortunately, Jackie was able to spend time with both her mother and father during their final days and hours. These events reinforced our commitment to 'Our Big Adventure'. To do it now, rather than later.

Chapter One

France

February 5th - March 11th

Moëlan Sur Mer - Blaye - Bayonne

There is nothing quite as exciting as setting off on the open road, with the prospect of an adventure of a lifetime ahead. All those places to see and people to meet, food to taste and wine to drink. Oh, and did I mention no work! On the downside, it's always sad to say goodbye to family and friends, but some things just have to be done, if you want to get on with your life. There is never a right time, only now.

We have all the necessary travel insurance, for each country we plan to visit and we have also had the motorhome fully serviced at Leisure Kingdom. This is where we bought Belle from 10 months ago, as a new vehicle. We were given a three year warranty, very important for us, because of what we planned to do. Plus, full roadside assistance in Europe from Fiat who make the cab, engine and chassis our 'home' sits on. She is insured to be out of the UK for nine months and we intend to use this time to the full. Belle is now fully laden with our clothes and enough food for the first few days of our trip, so we are all set to get on the road again.

Having wintered in our home town of Derby, in the UK, we headed off for our holiday home in Moëlan Sur Mer, Brittany, France. We took our usual route to Plymouth, to catch the overnight Ferry to Roscoff, in Brittany. From there it is an 85 mile drive to Moëlan Sur Mer, which is located on the south coast between Quimper and Lorient.

Upon our arrival in France, the weather was fine but chilly, warmer by a few degrees than the UK though. It was great to see all our friends again. We have English friends who live a few miles away and our French friends and neighbours in our little hamlet. For us it's home from home, having been in the region for holidays for the past fifteen years. At the end of February, our son Howard and his girlfriend Amy, came out to spend a few days with us. We had a great time, lovely warm weather, breakfasts on the patio in February and walks along Brittany's beautiful beaches and rugged coastline.

Wednesday, March 7th was the big day! We were so excited. This is when the adventure starts for us properly, as we head off for places new. We set off mid-afternoon, for the drive down the Atlantic coast of France, towards Spain. En route, we planned to stay on the 'Aires' (overnight parking areas specifically for motorhomes) in France, most are free of charge. Many campsites in this area are closed in the winter. As on last year's tour, we were armed with many maps, guide, campsite and aires books, for our eight month journey. We also took our Kindle and iPad, so that we have a constant supply of new books to read, with no additional weight. Weight management in a motorhome is a vital issue, as we only have about 300kg to stow all our living items, which keeps the vehicle within its legal kerb weight.

The weather was cloudy with squalls of rain as we journeyed south past Nantes. Our first stopover was on an aire at a place called St Gilles Croix de Vie. Surprisingly, there were other motorhomes there, so we felt very safe. We really didn't expect to see other motorhomes about, as it was so early in the season. It was free to park at this particular aire and a good place to stay if you want to go into the small town, very pretty and on the coast. That evening we walked along the coast and into the town. It was a one street affair, with not much happening this time of year. The houses were painted white or cream, with different coloured shutters to the windows. The coastal views were very pleasant and the weather very mild. Thankfully, that chilly wind had gone elsewhere.

The following day, we continued south, driving through the Vendee. Although the Vendee is not that far from Brittany, the houses here are very different. Quite a Spanish look to most of them, whitewashed walls and red tiled roofs. It never ceases to amaze us, how in just a few miles, the feel of a place can change so dramatically. We drove past La Rochelle, as we had been there before, it's certainly well worth a visit, but not for us this time.

We had good weather for the drive and the scenery is very pleasing to the eye. For miles, we travelled through rolling countryside and fields of perfectly aligned grape vines. We reached our next chosen aire for the night, at a place called Bourcefranc le Chapus. Again, located on the coast and very scenic, no facilities though. There was a pay machine but it was taped up. On speaking to a French guy in the next camper, he said you didn't have to pay until April. We spent a pleasant early evening sitting outside, looking out to sea. We were soon into our routine again. We cooked pan fried duck breast for our evening meal, a departing gift from Marie, our good friend from Moëlan. This was accompanied by potatoes dauphinoise, and after a few glasses of wine, were ready to take to our bed and were sound asleep in no time.

Onwards, through yet more rolling countryside, we pass row upon row of bare vines, awaiting the warm sunshine. By now we are in the Bordeaux wine region and the very heart of French wine making. As you will have gathered we are partial to a glass of wine, both red and white. Some of the vineyards are magnificent affairs with walled Chateaux, built for the wine making grandees of the area. We recognise a few names from the plaques on their entrances. These appear on the bottles that grace our supermarket shelves, in both France and the UK. This prompted us to stop at a Cave (wine shop) along the way, selling the local produce. Even though we are only buying a couple of bottles they insist we taste the wines of the area. "Go on then.... if you insist!"

This area used to belong to the English Monarchy and was much fought over during the 100 year's war, from 1336 to 1436. It's probably from this time, if not the Romans, that we English developed a taste for Claret and other wines of the Bordeaux region. We used to import gallons of the stuff way back then. So, not much has changed over a few hundred years. Wine is now more accessible to everyone, and more popular than ever. They are even talking of a world shortage in the future, as the Chinese 'Red Passion' for wine escalates.

We soon reach the lovely town of Blaye, having purchased a baguette along the way, for our lunch time snack. We parked up by the large Citadel alongside the river, across from the town centre. The Citadel was built in 1689 by a chap called Vauban, a very famous military engineer and fortification designer of the time. It was to protect the coastline from those pesky English and house the garrison there. It is an impressive grey structure and well worth a visit. Jackie had a happy time snapping away and took some great photos. I was a bit tired and grumpy by then, so I stayed back at Belle.

Our next stop was to be Arcachon. This was a place we had visited a few years ago, whilst touring in one of our little sports cars. It is a very popular seaside beach resort with its lovely bars, cafés and restaurants.

We found the aire, no problem, but it was only very small, not that nice and full of vehicles already. Where do all these motorhomes come from? We drove around the town for a while. It was really very busy and we couldn't even find a place to park our 7.2 metres of motorhome, so that we could have a little stroll round.

We quickly found another aire in the book (All The Aires in France from Vacarious books) and so drove on to Biscarosse Plage, about 25km south. The aire was in dense woodland that backed onto sand dunes and long wide beaches. By the time we arrived at the aire, it was late afternoon and the wind had picked up, causing quite a stir in the tall pines we had parked amongst. We were soon out and taking a leisurely walk to the beach through the sand dunes. The Atlantic coast can be quite dramatic at times. This was one such day as the waves were huge and constantly rolling in, the sound of them crashing onto the beach was deafening. It was very bracing and nearly blew us away. You can easily understand why the area is popular with surfers. We could even hear the crashing waves back at Belle, along with the added sound of the wind through the tall pines, it made for quite an eerie atmosphere.

The next morning dawned bright and sunny for our journey onwards to Spain. We drove into Biscarosse looking for a place to fill up our gas tanks and also do some shopping. Luckily, we managed to find an Intermarche, just outside the town, so stocked up with food and gas. Our final camping stop in France was at Ondres Plage. We were parked in a hedge screened car park for motorhomes next to the beach. Again, the ocean was as noisy as ever, it sounded like thunder, as we were parked only a few metres away from the beach. We were quite safe as there were plenty of other motorhome's there too.

Whilst we were setting up, we met a couple from England, who had cycled up to the beach from another camp site close by. They were from Lancashire and were returning from a few months stay in Spain, also in a motorhome. More interestingly for us, as we chatted, they told us they had camped all over Australia. When they arrived in Oz they bought a car and tent, toured all around, before selling it and returning to England. They had been all over Australia, from west to east and north to south and said it was a fantastic experience. This was very interesting for us, as our daughter lives in Brisbane. It has certainly given us food for thought. There might be a third tour, you never know!

Another sunny day dawned as we set off excited at the prospect of visiting Spain. We decided to go into Bayonne on the way, as according to our travel guides, it was supposed to be very nice. As we headed in, we passed through the area of Ondres, with its very upmarket houses. We soon managed to find a parking place and were off exploring Bayonne. We went straight to the old part of town and port by the river. The Cathedral with its cloistered courtyard was delightful. The rest of the town was archetypal French, with its shuttered four storey terraced streets, with picture windows in the roofs and cars parked anywhere. It was surprisingly busy for a Sunday and very picturesque in places.

After a short stop we were back on the road cruising towards the Spanish border, passing through St Jean de Luc. We would not be visiting Biarritz, as again we had been there on a previous tour. As much as we would have liked to go there again, we had to tell ourselves, we can't do everything and Spain was beckoning.

So France has got us off to a good start, it's such a motorhome friendly place. We were amazed at the amount of motorhomes about for the time of year. We expected to be on our own on the aires, but we weren't, and that for us was great. We feel there is always safety in numbers. We would meet up with many of the motorhome fraternity in the coming weeks, as quite a few Brits were returning from sunning themselves during the winter months in the Algarve or Spain. The budget is also off to a good start, we are way below, thanks to no overnight camping fees. Our trip along the Atlantic coast has reinforced our love affair with France. It has also whetted our appetite for 'Motorhoming' again, as we are now well and truly back in the swing of things.

Chapter Two

Spain

March 11th - March 23rd

San Sebastian – Pamplona – Burgos – Salamanca – Madrid – Toledo – Caceres

We were so excited, it seemed ages since we were last in Spain. We had never explored the interior of mainland Spain, only ever having stopped on the Costa's or holidayed on the Balearic islands. The last time we visited for a holiday, we took the ferry from the UK to Santander. We toured through the beautiful Picos de Europa, then drove into France and up to Brittany, in another of our little open top sports cars. We could remember how much we liked the area and so had looked forward to going back to see what else it had to offer.

We will be travelling on a more or less straight route, from San Sabastion to Madrid and then on to Lisbon, in Portugal. As we cross into Spain, the scenery is breath-taking and very mountainous here, being the start of the Pyrenees, that separates France from Spain. In this beautiful mountainous region, the houses look very similar to those in the Alps. We wonder if steep sloping roofs are necessary to keep the snow from accumulating.

Our first stop was Donostia San Sebastian, a very large city with good beaches, backed by high rise buildings. The old narrow streets are lined with five and six storey blocks, each level fronted with wrought iron balconies. They are mainly apartments with shops below, and are a delight to walk through. It is early Sunday afternoon and everyone seems to be out and about, filling the streets and tapas bars with a cacophony of sound. There is a really nice feel to the place and it is obviously a very popular seaside resort for the Spanish. We spend a pleasant few hours exploring, before heading off to find our camping spot for the night.

We chose a campsite to stay at for a couple of nights, about 10kms west of San Sebastian. We were both looking forward to spending a few nights in one place, to catch our breath! Our Sat Nav, who we have nick-named Sheila, as we have selected a lady with an Australian accent to give us directions, took us straight there, no problem. At times her pronunciation of some of the street names can prove hilarious and adds a little bit of mirth along the way. Unfortunately, the campsite was closed, even though in the book it said it was open from the 1st March. It was late afternoon and although there were other motorhomes parked on the nearby car park, by the sea, we decided to go back to an aire we had spotted, in San Sebastian. One of the reasons we decided to leave, was that bizarrely there was a large chicken coup right next to the car park. We certainly didn't want to be woken up at five in the morning. Cock-a-doodle-don't..... thank you very much!

As we came out of the campsite, Sheila directed us up a different road than the one which we had just driven in on. Before we realised it, we were ascending a mountain. Jackie was getting a bit worried, to put it mildly. We just climbed and climbed, our ears were popping and the road became narrower and narrower, winding and steep. There was no room to turn back, so it was onwards and upwards. We were so high up, we were looking down on some of the other mountains. As we travelled along, we passed what I'm sure was the usual mode of transport on the mountain, a horse and cart. Thankfully, we didn't meet anything coming the other way. Even I was relieved when we eventually reached the top and saw the road snaking back down.

I could not get over how well Belle coped with it all, as some of the turns on an incline, should only have been undertaken by a mountain goat. Of course, the views were stunning, but Jackie daren't look half the time and there was no way we were going to stop and take photos. This was to prove once again, do not just trust the Sat-Nav, you should also consult the map as well. We should have gone around the mountain, not over it. Even the Spanish looked surprised when they saw our motorhome coming from the direction of the peak of the mountain. "Conchita come look, looney English Sat-Nav people are lost again..... aahchiwowa".

We soon found the Aire (10 euros) and a good spot, close to another Autotrail motorhome, one of Belles long lost relatives. I had a little chat to the owner, while I filled up with much needed fresh water for our tank, this facility isn't always available on Aires. He and his wife were from Grantham in the UK and had been to Spain many times. They were on their way back, having spent the winter in Portugal and Spain. He gave us lots of advice on Aires in both countries and wrote down a few co-ordinates, for some particularly good ones.

The following day we were woken early by huge earth moving vehicles, on a site next to the Aire, bring back the chickens said Jackie. Another high rise place going up, we assume.

As we drove inland and south towards Pamplona, the landscape was stunning. We had chosen not to go on the toll roads and so had to drive through the mountains. It was still a motorway, so quite wide, but there were plenty of bridges, tunnels and winding stretches. The views were quite spectacular and there were viewing spots to pull into along the dual carriageway. We stopped at one for a photo shoot and could see down to the tiny houses in the valleys below.

Thankfully, the campsite at Oricáin called Ezcaba Camping was open. We were the only ones there to start with. The young lady at reception was very friendly and welcoming. She gave us a Spanish Campsite guide book, as it was last years and they had a new one. It was to prove very useful, now how nice was that? It was in a lovely location, on the top of a hill, we could see for miles around. The weather was so good too, blue skies and sunshine, we couldn't believe how good it was for the time of year.

It had only taken us an hour and a half to get to the campsite, so we had a quick snack and set off to catch the bus into Pamplona. We had to walk into the nearby village of Oricáin to get to the bus. It was a twenty minute walk, along a pretty riverside path, to the village. We took the torch with us for our return, as we knew it would be dark by then and the path was unlit. It was a very nice area, so we felt we would be safe to walk after dark. The bus arrived on time and we were in the centre of Pamplona within half an hour, one euro each.

We were a bit surprised to find that it was so very quiet. All the shops were closed. It was 4.00pm in the afternoon, so we went straight to the tourist information. They told us that all the shops open at 4.30pm. What a relief, it was like a ghost town. We made our way to one of the main squares 'Plaza Castilla' and had a coffee. As we sat there, we began to see people appearing from all the entrances to the square, the whole place was coming back to life. Siesta time was over. Another thing we noticed was the dress, they were all in winter clothes, with scarves and gloves. We thought the weather was quite mild, but obviously they are used to far warmer weather. In the UK we are used to temperatures below freezing in winter.

We walked around the old streets, looking for a shop where we could buy a more detailed map of Spain, and a little dictionary. We had suddenly remembered, we didn't know any Spanish, except for Hola and Gracias! There is plenty to see in Pamplona, which is famous for the 'Bull Run' through the crowded streets. The old town is especially picturesque, while the newer part is modern but quite nice. We came across the street where the 'Bull Run' starts from, it is very narrow at one point, what a sight that must be and the atmosphere too. We think we would like to return one day, to witness the spectacle of it all.

We were so looking forward to having Tapas. We were spoilt for choice; there were lots of places to choose from. We chose the bar 'Mandarra de la Ramos' on the street San Nicolas, with its hanging hams over the bar and an extensive selection of tapas. So, armed with a glass of Rioja, we set off to work our way through sampling everything on display, from tortilla to goats cheese and walnut tapas. The ambience was perfect, with the sound of Spanish chatter for background noise and good food and wine before us. Several glasses later and only just being able to walk, because of the extra weight now on board, we headed back to the campsite. This tapas bar was to set a very high standard, by which we would measure others, only one was to equal it and that will be revealed later.

When we arrived back at the campsite, there were another two motorhomes parked up, one French and one from the Netherlands. As it was dusk we could see the lights on, but not the occupants. Still, it made us feel we had company for the night.

The following day we woke up to a really thick misty morning, it was also a bit chilly. Had the weather changed? As Pamplona was only 9km away and there was a reasonably flat cycle path into the centre, we decided we would ride back in that afternoon. Jackie went to fetch some fresh bread from reception and asked if the mist would clear? "Oh yes, the sun will be out in a couple of hours", the guy said. True to his word, it was glorious weather again, and only just a short time later. After lunch, we rode along the cycle path, which followed the course of a river and into Pamplona. We didn't want to go in to the centre again, we just wanted to get a bit of exercise and see more of the surrounding countryside. We really enjoyed it, it was very clean and we rode through well looked after parkland and some of the villages were really pretty.   There were lots of people walking and jogging along the pathways. Also, there were many picnic areas, where people could sit and eat, most had bbq's too and we saw quite a few people setting up for their evening meal.

When we got back to the campsite, we were invited to have a drink with the couple from the Netherlands. Dirk and Nella were so nice. They spoke perfect English and were so much fun to be with. We sat chatting for a couple of hours outside, until it got a bit too chilly and by which time we were ready for something to eat. Spaghetti Bolognaise for tea tonight, not Spanish we know, but quick and tasty.

Overnight, Dirk and Nella had a bit of a drama. Their motorhome, a Volkswagon Carado, had decided to go to the toilet, dropping all its water. They had only just bought the van a few weeks before, so they had to get their instruction book out to find out what had happened. It turned out to be the freezing point protection system, which when approaching freezing point, dumps the water to protect the pipes. Just like us blokes after a drink then!

No mist the following morning, just blue skies and sunshine again. We said goodbye to Dirk and Nella, although we were all heading west towards the Rioja region. We hoped we would see each other again as we got on so well. They were touring northern Spain for one month, before returning home. They had travelled extensively throughout the world and had some wonderful stories to tell.

We travelled through some stunning scenery, as we drove along the plain, between distant mountains. There was hardly any traffic on the roads, which were very well maintained and looked new. The snow peaked mountains were beautiful and all around us in the distance. We drove alongside vineyards, where the soil was an earthy red. We were also driving close to one of the pilgrim's paths, which leads to Santiago de Campostila (Way of St James). This is where the shrine to St James is located, who's remains are allegedly buried there. There were many hikers on the path, laden with camping gear, slowly walking the route. This can be up to 500 miles, dependant on where you start from. We could see the path stretching out for miles and rising steadily to the distance hills.

Our good friends the Storks were back with us, (the large black and white birds, with long thin legs and neck) their huge nests, were on top of every available structure, that had a reasonably large flat surface. This was similar to those we had seen in the Baltics, the previous year.

Our next campsite 'Camping Navarette' is located near to the village of Navarette. It is in the Rioja wine making region, just west of Logrona, the regions capital. It was a very good site and had excellent modern facilities. We were soon settled in and had a quick chat to an English couple, who were just about to leave the site. They were on their way back to the UK having spent the winter in Spain. They told us they had walked into the village via a path, that ran along the back of the campsite, through the fields, a very pleasant walk. We thought we would do the same, but on our bikes. We were just getting ready to leave, when Dirk and Nella pulled in next to us. We were really pleased to see them again.

Navarette had one old street. The rest of it was quite modern, but all very nice and clean. The church was very old and the interior was absolutely amazing, it had a golden altar and huge gold statues, backed by art work. The sight was totally unexpected for us, being situated in such a small town, it was a very moving experience. We rode back down the main road to see if we could go into one of the Bodega's there. Bodega's are where they sell wine, usually from their own vines and relatively cheaper than from a shop. Unfortunately, they were all closed. So we bought a couple of bottles of the local Rioja, from the reception at the campsite, both red and white. Normally, I associate Rioja with red wine made from the Tempranillo grape. It has an instantly recognisable caramel twang to it, which is quite unique. It is one of our favourite wines.

When we got back, Nella was preparing a whole flat fish on their bbq, she had bought the fish that day. They had no idea what it was, although they thought it was Turbot. It was a stunning looking flat fish, with grey skin and white flesh that fell off the bone when cooked. We were having a chicken curry, so we said we would try out each other's dishes, when they were cooked. As the weather was so good, we were both cooking outside again. The fish was delicious, so was the curry. The wines, our Rioja and their Malbec, were very good too. Good food and good company in beautiful surroundings, what more can you want?

We said goodbye to Dirk and Nella very late that evening, as they were staying another night at the campsite. We would be setting off to travel west again, to Burgos in the morning. The guide books said the Cathedral was a must see.

The scenery remained the same, spectacular, as we travelled west on the almost traffic free roads. Our next campsite was only a few kilometres from Burgos and again on a bus route, which was ideal for our trip into the town. The Cathedral was fabulous, being of twin spired Gothic design. We don't normally pay to go in these places (they are usually free to enter), but felt we just had to have a look inside this one. Apparently, it took over 300 years to build 1226 to 1567. It is the burial place of El Cid and his wife. There were several chapels within and as you can imagine, it was gold everywhere, absolutely resplendent in frescoes, statues and crucifixes.

Burgos is a large city, with some nice areas in the centre. As is the norm with Spanish cities these days, the outskirts are full of high rise residential areas. We were surprised to see how many new buildings there are. Most look as if they have been built in the last ten years.

At this time Spain is struggling with financial debt in the European Union, having borrowed so much and now struggling to pay it back. You can see where the money has gone though, with all the new buildings and infrastructure. As we travel through Spain, it will be the same everywhere we go. We were impressed with the new roads, even in some of the backwater places and all of the new high rise accommodation. Spain's economy had been booming for the last ten years and no one could see it coming to an end.

From Burgos, we made for Salamanca. A longer drive this day, but the weather remained good for us. The scenery gradually changes from undulating green red earth fields, to flat for as far as the eye could see, with dark shaded mountains in the distance. We drove through Salamanca to get to our campsite at the back of the 'Hotel Regio', which was quite full. The campsite looked run down and well used, the toilets were a bit smelly, but clean. It started to thunder and rain that afternoon, so we stayed put in Belle for the rest of the day.

Up bright and early to a grey cloudy day. We had wanted to visit Salamanca for such a long time, we just love the sound of the name, it sounds mystical. There is a bus from outside the hotel, which cost 1.2 euro each. The old part of the city is really beautiful, with lots of fine buildings, a magnificent central cathedral and main square 'Plaza Major'. We sat outside in the square while having a coffee at the 'Café Novelty'. Inside, there was a piano being played and the lovely sound wafted outside, to add to the ambiance. There are plenty of cloisters, squares, statues, churches, shops and streets to browse. This is also the major university city of Spain, so plenty of young students about. There is a nice hustle and bustle to the place. Later, we stopped at one of the many tapas bars and had another fine wine and food tasting session to finish off another perfect day.

From Salamanca, we drove to Avila, a famous walled fortress town, situated 1132 metres above sea level and the regional capital. There are 88 cupolas around its complete surrounding wall, a very imposing sight indeed as you approach. There is a viewing point on the approach road, from which you can take in the grand spectacle of the walls and medieval structure. You can also get some great photographs...so we did. We didn't hang around too long though, it was such a biting cold wind we soon rushed back to Belle.

We were able to get a parking space just outside the walls and walked into the old town. Not a great deal to see here for us, although there are many historical buildings, the old castle centre is quite small. However, Jackie did manage to buy a little rosary of St Teresa, who famously had visions here and had gone on to open many convents. Jackie's mother was a Catholic and loved Rosary Beads, so it was a nice homage to her, as she had recently passed away. Jackie would later place it at her grave side.

After a quick look around, we drove on to Segovia, famous for its Aqueduct and Alcazar. We had chosen to stay at a campsite here for just one night and thought we would take a look the following day. Unfortunately, the campsite didn't open until April. We very nearly drove on without looking around Segovia, as finding street parking yet again, proved difficult. Thank goodness, just as we were about to give up, we found a parking spot. Otherwise, we would have missed an absolute gem. We parked by the cemetery, close to the centre. I think we were illegally parked, but no one said anything (certainly not the dead) and there were no parking tickets on our return.

We are so glad we did make the effort to look around, as it really is a beautiful city, especially the old town. The aqueduct which dates from Roman times is the longest and most complete and is an absolutely stunning piece of architecture. It dominates the whole valley. The old town is full of lovely old narrow streets, a beautiful cathedral and the fabulous Alcazar palace, which looks like it came straight out of a fairy tale. The cream stone structure has high peaked cupolas and stands magnificently perched on a hillside. Jackie offered to hang her hair out of the tower window, like Rapunzel, so I could climb up and save her. Wishful thinking, I'm certainly not that energetic nowadays.

On the way back to Belle, we found an old traditional Spanish bakery. Here, they sold a speciality from the region called 'Yermes', a lemon sugar-coated sponge cake. It was a bit sweet and sticky and not really for eating in the street without a plate, as we did.

It was late afternoon by now, so we decided to head back to Belle and onwards to Madrid. Unusually for us, we chose to take the toll road as the day was getting on. Normally, as we have plenty the time, we prefer to take the non-toll roads, as this helps our finances. Also, it allows us to see more of the local way of life, as we pass through towns and villages, which is what this tour is all about.

It was only a 45 minute drive down the motorway to the campsite north of Madrid, so we were there early evening. We chose to stay four nights, as we knew we wanted to go into Madrid for at least two days, lots to see. Our campsite was 50km from Madrid, but very nice, at a place called El Escorial, very famous for the huge monastery there. Surprisingly, it is called 'Camping El Escorial', had very nice facilities and is very large. There were not many other campers on the site as we arrived, which meant we could pick our spot.

The next day we decided to take a day of rest and plan our trip into Madrid. The receptionist was very helpful and gave us lots of information and a street map, which we used that night, to plan and mark out our route around the city. The campsite was surrounded by mountainous countryside, it was so pretty. We walked to the bus stop to see how long it would take, as it turned out, it was 20 minutes from the campsite. We had a lovely view of the Sierra De Guadarrama mountain range ahead of us, as we walked. Added to all this splendour, our old friends the Storks were nesting on one of the telegraph poles. That evening it was roast chicken and potatoes cooked in our little oven. We were also able to pick up UK TV on our satellite system, so it was quite home from home that night.

The coach ride into the outskirts of Madrid only took half an hour, as it didn't stop after picking us up. We then had to get the metro, which was excellent, into the centre. We bought a two day ticket, at 10 euros each, so we could hop around the city. Madrid centre has two distinct parts, Old and Bourbon, so we had decided to split our visit into one part each day. We have some distance to cover, as it is the third largest city in the European Union, after London and Berlin with Paris not far behind.

The Old district of Madrid is nice, but the centre didn't really enthral us, perhaps the grey day and cold was affecting us. The Palace was impressive, as was the main square the 'Plaza Mayor'. In summer these main squares do come to life at midnight. We thought we would come across many authentic tapas bars, we were wrong. Most were modern and there were lots of fast food places. We did try one establishment where the Spanish locals frequent 'Casa Labra' and they serve a speciality of battered fish, croquet potatoes and a glass of wine, suffice to say we had one and left, not that appetising at all. Later that day, we did find a very nice Spanish tapas 'Villa Rosa' with tiled walls and decorative porticos that had flamenco dancers performing in the evening. We had a nice meal topped off by a free drink called 'Crema de Aruja', and as we liked it very much, we went straight out and bought a bottle.

It was very busy and there were a lot of people about, especially at the tourist attractions. Everywhere we went, the people were very amiable, always smiling and willing to help, which is unusual for such a large city. However, we were continually warned to keep our bags securely under our arms, as there are many pick pockets. Some areas were in need of an upgrade and we thought a bit scruffy.

When we got back to the campsite, it had been raining. Luckily, we missed the downpour, but it had turned quite chilly by then. What a surprise the next day, when we opened the shutters to find snow falling! Ok it was only light, but we couldn't believe our eyes. What was even worse, there was some poor soul in a tent a few pitches away, who looked absolutely sopping wet. We later found out that he was from the UK. I went over and chatted to the guy and before I knew it, he was enjoying a hot cup of coffee, toast and marmite and a packet of biscuits with us in Belle. Poor Sid was freezing and his clothes were damp. He was travelling alone and didn't have much money left, so was roughing it a bit, but he was enjoying himself, a lovely likeable character.

Sid was from Liverpool and had retired after having a heart attack, at the age of 60. He lived with his cousin in Cornwall and liked to travel for months at a time, on his BMW motorbike and side car. He had recently walked (a few hundred miles) part of the way along the pilgrims trail to Santiago de Compostela, and had enjoyed it very much. He had taken the seat out of his side car to accommodate his camping equipment. Sadly, he discovered the Spanish do not like wild camping, so that had scuppered most of his plans. He had managed to find a secluded beach for a few weeks, but as he pointed out, there is only so much of your own company you can take. Thankfully, the snow and rain cleared up and the sun came out. Off he set on his motorbike and sidecar to visit the monastery at El Escorial, as he had been told it was free entrance on a Wednesday.

We caught the coach into Madrid for a second day and into the Bourbon area. The architecture was much better, wonderful fountains, statues and a beautiful park. This part of Madrid was much more to our liking. We decided that we would have a meal there and found a really nice restaurant called the 'Acayforal Café'. We chose to try the 'Suckling Pig' the delicacy of the region, which was a surprise, because earlier that day, we had seen the little suckling piglets dressed up in a butchers shop window and had both said how on earth could anyone eat such a lovely little thing. Well, several hours later and being slightly famished, we couldn't resist. It was absolutely delicious, consisting of a thin crispy skin and very lean meat that melted in the mouth. Of course, it was accompanied by a good bottle of Rioja.

Luckily for Sid, the sun was out again the following day and the snow had gone. He had a smile on his face, his clothes and tent had dried out too. We said our goodbyes, as we were off to our next stop on the tour, Toledo. Sid came across as one of those lovely loners, who is getting on with his life, no matter what it threw at him. He told us that we ought to visit General Franco's Mausoleum, just up the road from the campsite. He said it was set up high in the hills with spectacular views, all very impressive. Had it not been for Sid, we would have missed it, as no one had mentioned it to us at the reception or Tourist Information. There is still a legacy from the Civil War, where Franco's harsh regime has left mixed feelings about him.

What a sight to see, Franco's epitaph to himself, as he had had it built. It was not only built for Franco, but as a memorial to all those killed during the Spanish Civil War. It was carved into the mountainside, fronted with its pencil pines, a semi-circle of Romanesque arches and a 150 metre high cross, overlooking the valley below. It was free to enter the giant hallways carved inside the mountain. As well as a Mausoleum, it is a Monastery.

A service was in progress as we entered. This did make us stop and think of all the death and suffering this place commemorated, not just how spectacular it all was.

We had the place more or less to ourselves, even the service only had a few people attending. The stigma of the Civil War is obviously still in attendance with the local people, who suffered greatly at Franco's hands. Outside again, the views from the terrace down the valley, are truly breath-taking. Franco or not, the place is a fitting place of remembrance to the fallen.

We then drove the short distance to Toledo and found our next campsite 'El Greco'. It was very pleasant with good facilities and just a short bus ride to the centre. There were quite a few British motorhomes on site, so we said our hellos. The weather had remained sunny and was now quite hot, so we found a bit of time to sunbathe, before setting off into Toledo. Toledo is a small old historical town, surrounded by a medieval wall, set on top of a hill. Again, famed for its cathedral. It has quite a nice feel to it, although a bit touristy in parts. We spend a pleasant hour walking around, interrupted by a coffee at one of the road side bars.

On our way back to the campsite, we met up with our neighbours from the next pitch, Peter and Juliette from Wolverhampton. Needless to say, after tea, we got together and had a good evening chatting and exchanging experiences and information. They had been to many places we had been and also on the same cruise ship the 'Rembrandt'. We said our goodbyes just after midnight as they were off to Valencia, while we would be heading for Caceres. What lovely people we meet along the way. For us this is a big part of the tour, exchanging information and experiences, giving much needed advice and generally having a bloody good laugh.

We set off for Caceres, a three and a half hour drive, renowned for having the most beautiful complete medieval old town. Our drive was mainly on dual carriage ways, through some rugged countryside, with some stunning views along the way. Our normal maximum speed is sixty miles per hour, as this returns us our best miles per gallon (about 25 mpg) and gives us time to take in the views.

At Caceres we stop on an aire, recommended by just about everyone we had met so far. When we arrived, it was full of motorhomes, with several parked in places that were reserved for coaches. As these were the only spaces left, we did the same. The aire parking was located in a municipal complex for young people, who stop over while enjoying various sporting activities, as well as visiting the old town.

It was a short walk up the hill and into the main square, then up the steps and through the wall into the old town, which is to one side of the university city. It feels really old Spain, with its slightly different take on architecture. Most being straight sided, with either square or Moorish style windows. Some are made from small multi-coloured stones with light cream mortar, while others are large block stone buildings. It is quite a compact area dotted with palm trees and is old style impressive. But, as we do, we are soon around and out of the place and so pleased to have seen it. Because we are visiting so many of these type of places, we only breeze around some, there just is not time to see and do everything.

At the entrance to the aire we noticed a little GB camper. We stopped for a chat with the owners, two elderly ladies, who were on their way back from touring Morocco. They said it had all been a fantastic experience and they felt very safe. How brave are they? Anyway, they advised we should move our motorhome, as the police had moved vans on the previous night, for parking where the coaches should park. Back at Belle we waited for a space to become vacant in the car park. Luckily for us, someone moved out, so we were in like a shot. That night was lovely and warm, so we lounged about inside Belle, taking in the chatter and laughter from the young people and campers outside enjoying themselves.

It's been just three weeks since we set off, and yet we feel we have seen so much and come so far. Just one or two observations to make at this time. The wide central Spanish plains and mountainous sierras, present some truly stunning scenery to travel through. Apart from Caceres, most of the old towns are intermingled with new buildings and some are quite out of character, usually apartment blocks, which is a shame. We think perhaps the reason for this, is that as each old building crumbled, it was replaced by a new one, instead of restoring the old, much the same as we do in the UK.

Another disappointing sight we encountered from time to time, was lots of graffiti, even in the small villages. This did not detract from our overall pleasure as we travelled through, it is just sad to see. Having said that, we have still enjoyed every minute so far. Also, it was surprising to meet so many Brits heading back from spending winter in the Algarve. One last thing, we can now truly understand where the saying 'The rain in Spain falls mainly on the plain', comes from. As the plains are incredibly vast flat areas, we experienced that the rain does fall mainly on the plain, having passed over the surrounding mountains.

Also, just to mention security. We had heard lots of bad stories of things that can happen to you in Spain (and Italy). Such as, on secluded roads, people in other cars point at your vehicle as if something is wrong, then when you pull up, they rob you. The same can happen at petrol stations, whilst the man goes in to pay these rogues have even been known to rob the lady. Another example is, if you park in remote parking spots at supermarkets you can go back to find your motorhome has been broken into. And so on... Well, we remained vigilant all the time and were always on the ready. We also never parked over-night on our own, unless on a proper managed campsite. This will apply to pretty much everywhere we go by degrees, dependant on how safe we feel.

Our motorhome has a good alarm system, which can be armed while you are in it. It has a panic button key fob that can be pressed to set off the alarm. There are alarm warning stickers in several languages located at all the weak security points. We also have a very powerful torch, similar to those used by the police, that when shone directly in someone's eyes, will temporarily blind them. All this gives us some comfort. Needless to say, we didn't experience any threatening situations, but perhaps this was because we had heeded the warnings. So, happy and well and still on budget, our next stop is Portugal.

Chapter Three

Portugal

March 24th - March 31st

Lisbon – Quarteira – Vilamoura

We visited Portugal for a holiday with friends several years ago. We stayed in a beautiful hilltop villa not far from Faro, hired a car and toured all along the Algarve. However, on this occasion, Lisbon was to be the highlight of the Portugal tour for us.

The drive to Lisbon would take a good few hours, so we decided to break it up with an overnight stop along the way. Finding a place we both felt safe and happy with was to prove frustrating. We were up early (well for us anyway) and away for 9am. The sun was out and the roads were good and reasonably quiet. We are still avoiding the toll roads where possible, sticking to the main 'N' roads. We were soon across the unmanned border crossing from Spain into Portugal. The scenery began to change almost immediately to whitewashed houses, with red tiled roofs and much greener surroundings.

As we drove along, we passed some horse and carts with people going about their farming business, fields of trees with the new blossom and grape vines. Because we were ahead of time, we did not stop at the first aire we had intended to, and drove on until mid-day. The next aire was by a dam and some distance from both houses and main roads. To get there, we drove through pretty little one street villages whose inhabitants stared at the strange looking vehicle passing through. We also passed some lovely orange groves, the trees laden with ripe fruit. When we arrived, we were alongside a manmade lake by the dam and it was all very pleasant. It was however, very secluded with just a few men fishing. Jackie did not want to stay at all, there was something she did not feel happy about. We had agreed before the tour, that if one of us didn't feel safe, then we would go and find somewhere else. So, after a mid-day snack and a rest, we moved on.

We drove on to a place called Seixel, which had an aire on the estuary across from Lisbon. It looked great, we were close to a ferry terminal for Lisbon and there were plenty of people about, no motorhomes though. Just one small problem, Belle was too big to go through the entrance! Well, by now it was late afternoon so we consulted the books again. This time trusting our good friend the ACSI campsite book, we headed off for our new destination.

We drove towards central Lisbon across the imposing toll bridge dominated by the statue of Christ. The roads were extremely busy and we got lost several times, before finally heading out the other side of the city, on the right road. The suburbs of Lisbon looked quite run down in places, with the usual scrawls of graffiti. The sky line was made up of off white and stone coloured high rise buildings, all shapes and sizes and festooned with satellite dishes. There was also a tram system running alongside some of the roads. You really did have to have your eyes everywhere, as the traffic was very heavy, fast and taking no prisoners. Not for the fainthearted. We stopped along the way at an Intermarché (French supermarket chain) to stock up with provisions.

It was 5pm by the time we reached 'Guincho Camping' on the outskirts of a place called Cascais, to the west of Lisbon. It was well laid out and reasonably full, with both caravans and motorhomes. Each pitch had shade provided by flat topped pines and the ground was quite uneven, as it was very sandy. It was still sunny, so time to get the chairs out and have a beer. Phew, what a day. This was just the type of day we try to avoid. Too much driving becomes a trudge and not a pleasure at all. We made a mental note to try and not repeat a journey like that again.

The next day we just chilled out by Belle and chatted to some Brits who were close by. Ray and Carol had just retired, bought a caravan and so were on their maiden journey. They were enjoying it, but were a bit shy and seemed to want their own company. We met Brian and Jean who hailed from Lancashire and were seasoned motorhome travellers and only too pleased to provide us with a wealth of information. They had driven a motorhome around New Zealand and Canada, and were the sort of people that inspire you to do more. We whiled away another day. There are always a few chores to do, so Jackie did some laundry and then sunbathed, while I made spaghetti bolognaise for our evening meal. This was more like it, rest and relaxation in the sun, not a bad life after all?

The next day we said goodbye to Brian and Jean, as they were off to northern Portugal, before crossing Spain and back home to Lancashire. We caught the bus just outside the campsite, a five minute ride to the centre of Cascais, which is a very pretty little town, buzzing with locals gossiping or busy shopping. From here we took a twenty minute train ride along the coast to Lisbon. This is how we get a feel for a place. There are lots of people on the public transport systems going about their daily business. We observe how they dress, greet one another, how courteous they are and if the young ones give up their seating for the elderly. On this occasion, we were able to take in the lovely views of the coast, as we travelled along.

Lisbon, our kinda town! The main centre is set out on a grid pattern, with uniform five and six storey buildings lining the beautiful boulevards. Some of the streets are pedestrianized. The place is full of shops and bars and all very cosmopolitan. It's a beautiful warm sunny day, so the streets are alive with people of all nationalities. There are some very old style trams as well as the ultra-modern, plying the main thoroughfares. We pass some impressive facades, arches, squares, statues and fountains, as we meander through the centre. There is a castle on the hillside, street vendors, street music, all hustle and bustle, such a great atmosphere.

We eventually stop at a restaurant which has cod (white fleshed fish) displayed on the menu, so I ask is it fresh. "Of course", says the French waiter. Jackie chose the salmon and I have what turns out to be Norwegian salted cod. Nice, but not quite what I call fresh! Still, it's all very pleasant sitting outside watching the world go by. The French waiter told us he was from Paris and had been there for two years just enjoying himself. Our other waiter came from Nepal and was raising money to continue his studies to become a doctor. He was also supporting his family back home. What a contrast.

We soon took up a conversation with a lovely German couple sitting on the next table to us. They were on a cruise, so had come ashore for the day to visit Lisbon. They were from Munich and like so many Germans we met, could of course speak perfect English. Their next stop port of call was Cadiz. Now, if we had lots of money, this would be how we would see the world. We have cruised the Mediterranean and Caribbean in the past and from our experience, it is the perfect way to travel.

After a pleasant few hours, we were sufficiently fed and watered thus enabling us to move on again and explore some more of Lisbon. Sometime later, we mosey on down towards the sea front and sit on the harbour wall for a bit of a rest and sunbathe. We watch as a cruise ship departs and muse over sipping cocktails on the aft deck, while watching Lisbon slip over the horizon. We wonder what the great discoverers of the world such as, Magellan, Dias, Gil and Vasco Da Gama, who also set off from Lisbon, would make of it now.

The following day we travelled south on a four hour journey to Quarteira, on the Algarve. The journey was again through some rugged countryside. We drove past hillsides full of unusual trees, which we were subsequently to learn, are grown for producing cork, which is harvested from the bark. Some of the trees we pass look like huge sprigs of broccoli sticking out of the ground, dark green against the beautiful blue sky.

We arrived at Quarteira Camping and were soon set up, having moved from our first pitch due to soggy ground. The campsite is full of Brits, most having holidayed there for the winter. A few had been there full time for a year or two. The latter appeared to be both the 'have and have not's' from the appearance of their dwellings. Some were luxury caravans while others looked squalid hovels. We got the impression they could not give a 'Tossa del Farto' for returning to the UK. They were the 'brown as a berry brigade', who walked around in cut-off denim shorts, exposing their wrinkled leathery torsos.

Most were in caravans with awnings pitched outside that looked like semi-permanent fixtures. We were to stay here for four nights. We felt that most did not want to make friends with us, because we were only there for a few days. It may sound strange, but there was a little community here and we were outsiders. That's not to say they were not helpful or would not stop for a chat. One chap said that most Brits arrive in November and stay until March. The reason being is that the weather in Portugal becomes very changeable in early spring. This explained why we had met so many Brits returning to the UK, on our trip through Spain.

We chilled out around Belle for two days and took time to read and catch up on some emails and phone family and friends. We also had our general housekeeping duties to do again and to wash our clothes and linen. I hung a line up between the trees, so everyone could see our smalls and mediums! I had become tomato man again, my face is bright red from spending just a little too much time sunbathing, without any protection. Silly me, I'll have to cut my jeans up at this rate. Our next door neighbour gave us tips on where the shops were and how long it would take us to walk to the beach and on to Vilamoura, which is the next resort along the coast. That night we watched a few episodes of the old BBC production of 'War and Peace' which we had bought as a boxed DVD set. This was accompanied by another kind of 'war and peace' outside, as the heavens opened up and it threw it down with rain. The next day we had a thunderstorm, which eventually cleared to sunshine, so it was back out on the loungers for more rest and relaxation.....

We walked into Quarteira along the well set out promenade. It had been partially sectioned off, for people taking part in the 'Iron Man Europe' contest that was being held there. We arrived mid event, with the cycling coming to an end and the running race about to start. There were all sorts of colourful flags fluttering and quite a crowd watching. We strolled along taking it all in, as participants limbered up while others crumpled to the ground exhausted. There were people from all over Europe taking part. We did not stop, but continued on our way to Vilamoura.

We passed a large fresh fish market along the way, where they were selling some fabulous looking fish. Unfortunately, as it was only about 11am, we couldn't buy any, as we were out for the day. We walked on alongside the lovely coast, then followed a dirt track, eventually turning a corner and into Vilamoura. The large harbour at Vilamoura is surrounded by whitewashed buildings, hotels and apartments. This pretty harbour is where some rich and famous people berth their yachts and cruisers, and there are certainly enough of them for us to view. It's all very attractive and touristy, with plenty of shops, bars and restaurants to keep people occupied.

We stopped for a breather, as it was getting hot by now. We sat under shade at a harbour-side bar for our mid-day gin and tonics, and as ever to watch the world go by. It's amusing to muse over who are the 'haves' and who are the 'have not's' and who is just pretending. Anyway, for a while we are with the 'haves', after just one more gin and tonic of course. We guess at which yacht we would each like. Sadly, Jackie does not like sailing, so I chose the biggest in the harbour for her to feel safe in. A long time ago I passed a dingy sailing course and gained a certificate. A friend and I then bought a vagabond two-man sail boat, which we had for a while. I once took Jackie out in a hired sail boat in Devon, which ignominiously we had to be towed back to the jetty in, as Jackie panicked and refused to allow me to sail close to the wind any further. But then again, she often accuses me of sailing too close to the wind, some of it on my own bluster!

We mosey on and around and eventually end up in a very trendy bar, near to a huge hotel by the harbour. There we watched Manchester City play Sunderland in a 3-3 draw, a very entertaining match for both of us. We enjoyed the day in Vilamoura, but as it was quite a walk back to the campsite, and we hadn't eaten, we set off back to Quarteira again, taking in the sea views along the way. Close to the fish market we had passed that morning, we spy a restaurant, which is displaying some very nice looking fresh fish, in an ice cabinet in the window. Our appetites already whetted by that mornings viewing at the fish market, we decided to go in.

We soon have a table under a covered awning overlooking the sea and are taken by 'Le Patron' to view the fish on offer for us to eat. He talked us through each one, with its merits and way of cooking. I would point out, that both Jackie and I, do not take many risks when it comes to fish. Normally for us we opt for boneless cod or haddock, but on this occasion it all looked so nice, we chose a sea bream, which is sold on weight and will be cooked with herbs on an open flame grill. Soon after, the cooked fish arrives on a silver platter and is boned by the waiter at the table. It is absolutely delicious. Needless to say, we while away a couple of hours talking about our experiences so far and enjoying the food, the wine and the vista out to sea. I can't think of a better way to finish off Portugal.

Chapter Four

Southern Spain

April 1st – April 30th

Seville – Cadiz – Gibraltar (UK) – Granada – Benidorm – Valencia – Tarragona –Barcelona

As we had a long drive ahead, we decided to take the Autopista (motorway) into Spain. Even though the signs advised it was a toll road, for some reason it turned out not to be, and so we drove all the way to Seville for free.

Our next chosen campsite is 'Villsom' in Dos Hermanas, a bus ride from Seville. The site is surrounded by a high wall and there is wonderful smell from the orange grove, just the other side of our pitch. The pitches are very small and shaded by palm trees. Still, it's all very nice and the campsite personnel are very helpful. Our next door neighbours are a young German couple, with a baby and young daughter. The pretty little girl reminded us of our own granddaughter Rose, who lives in Australia.

That night around 2.00am we were awoken to the sound of a right old racket, with fireworks and music from a Spanish band playing trumpets. We both thought it must be morning and looked at our clock for confirmation of the time. We found out from reception the next morning that it was a church procession, with Easter celebrations to mark 'Holy Week'. 2.00am? Only the Spanish!

Having gathered all the necessary travel information from reception, we caught the bus to Seville the following morning. We made sure before we got off the bus that we knew where it departed from for our return. It dropped us off right on the side of the Plaza de Espana, which is a magnificent crescent shaped, arched brick building, adorned with ceramic tiles depicting famous events and cities of Spain. It has a central water feature, fountains and ceramic blue and white balustrades. It is very impressive indeed.

We walked from there to the river Guadalquivir and the Moorish tower 'Torre de Oreo' and along to the Plaza de Toros de la Maestranza (Bull Ring) before turning into the city proper. We enquired about the bullfighting, but sadly (and perhaps gladly) we would miss it, as the season starts after we have left Spain. There are one or two special events before, but we would miss them all. It was a shame, as we would have liked to judge for ourselves, as part of our Spanish experience, what all the fuss was about and then pass our verdict on its rights and wrongs.

Seville is split into two parts, 'El Arenal' - with its views of the river and 'Santa Cruz' - with its cathedral and Moorish bell tower. As we enter El Arenal it starts to rain, so the brollies are quickly put up. We are greeted by street preparations, for the Easter processions from each of the churches, with temporary barriers being erected. We had wondered what the young people were doing, all dressed up in what looked like, Klu Klux Klan outfits. Well, that's what it looked like to us, with their high peaked head masks with slatted eye ports and gowns that flowed to the floor. Each church has its own coloured robes, from deep purples to crimson reds. From time to time we would see them walking about, but somehow we managed to miss the festivities.

El Arenal is the more modern part of the centre, with its wide boulevards and five and six storeyed buildings. We are soon at the cathedral in the Santa Cruz area. It is here you can truly see the Moorish influence, with its maze of closely compacted streets and the palatial residence, the 'Real Alcazar'. We wander through the narrow bustling streets, which are awash with tourists. The rain had stopped and at last and so we strolled up and down, around, back and forth, then to and fro. There are so many wonderful sights to see, from gated walled courtyards to the Alcazar itself and its jewel box patios and hallways. We found Seville very pleasant, but wouldn't rush back there any time soon, perhaps it was the rain.

Back on the road again, we rolled along listening to our favourite tracks on the stereo, as we journeyed towards Jerez, famous for its sherry and then onto Cadiz. We drove along some winding hilly sections, which eventually became fairly flat with mountainous backdrops. There are wide fields with rows of olive trees in rich red soil. Old style white villas surrounded by palm trees, contrasting with fields full of solar panels. Surprisingly, as we entered Jerez, there is a housing estate, that except for the plaster clad walls, look just like those we have in the UK.

We are not big sherry drinkers, but do like a glass now and again for a change. So it will be no surprise to learn that we intend to try some, now we are in the heart of the sherry producing region. Our first difficulty is finding a parking spot, once again 7.2 meters is proving difficult to place. We have just about given up, after half an hours fruitless trying and about to leave when we turn a corner as if by magic, there is a row of wide parking spaces. To top that, it's just a short walk to the premier sherry producer 'González Byass' who have the 'Tio Pepe' brand. He's the guy on the bottle with the red Bolero and matching red Sombrero.

We entered (not intentionally) by the exit, which as we have observed, us English very often do. We went into an old building which had traditional dark wood furniture and white walls. Here we are greeted by a very elegantly dressed Spanish lady, who quickly explained that we needed to go to the main entrance. We asked, "Dónde es?" Easier to show us rather than give directions, she relented and proceeded to take us on a guided tour (not intentionally) in reverse, through storerooms housing neat rows of wine casks, lounge areas with wonderful portraits and fine furnishings, eventually arriving at the Entrada (entrance) and gift shop. While passing through the factory grounds, we noticed trees with both oranges and lemons on the same tree. She told us they have been cross-pollinated and are very special. They certainly looked it. We gave her our thanks, "muchas gracias", and she left with a smile. We both agreed how fortunate we were, we didn't need to pay for the tour of the place now! Actually, it did look as if it would have been very interesting to see how the famous sherry was made.

We spend the next hour in the shop, tasting various types of sherry, from the cheap to the expensive and from the dry to the sweet. We did not realise there were so many. We also struck lucky, being between coach party tours, as we received uninterrupted attention and expert advice from the assistants. The shop had displays explaining how each sherry is produced and which one would best complement each type of food. In the end we find one to our taste called 'Cristina' an Oloroso. As it is only sold in half bottles we have to buy two! We also bought two rather nice Tio Pepe sherry glasses to drink out of and a little tapas recipe book, all adding mucho lotto to the taste of the sherry!

Afterwards, we chose to take a little walk around Jerez whilst we were there. You could hear a pin drop, the place seemed to have entered siesta time, not a soul in sight, even though it's still morning, so it's not long before we are back to Belle and off for Cadiz.

On our way we pass orchards of ripening oranges and lemons, all very colourful and a wonderful sight to see in the blazing sun. We approached Cadiz over some low lying flat land, lakes and an expansive bridge. Cadiz is almost completely surrounded by water. Luckily for us, we managed to park up just outside the fortress gates, which enabled us to walk directly into the city.

People's opinion varies so much. Quite a few folk we met said there was not a lot to do and see at Cadiz. Well, I have to report we disagree and really liked the place. It has some nice walks along the fortress walls, a harbour with cruise ships in, magnificent cathedrals, palm lined squares and to top it off, the weather was perfect.

We struck lucky here again. We managed to take in one of the 'Holy Week' processions. We watched as the youngster's gown up in their purple robes and assemble in the square, near to one of the many churches. A little later, there emerged from the church and in one long processional line, priests, adults and children carrying gold crosses, a military uniformed brass band, followed by the ranks of the purple clad participants. Then a float appeared from out of the grand church doors, to the cheers of the waiting masses. It consisted of a large carved platform, on which was set a life size Jesus, carrying his cross, along with his persecutors standing around him. Beneath this heavy moving spectacle, all you could see were the feet of the bearers. It resembled a centipede with shoes on, the rest of their bodies were hidden by purple curtains, with gold edged viewing ports. However, it would have looked so much better if some of the bearers had taken the time to clean their shoes.

Off into the narrow streets the whole ensemble walked very slowly led by the brass band. The float swayed Small children handed out sweets to the crowd from their little hand held baskets. It was all marshalled in ranks and rows, interspersed with purple and gold robed men or women, holding metal rods surmounted with crosses. These were stamped on the floor to signify one for stop, two for move and three for turn. We followed the procession for a while, as did the rest of the crowd of onlookers. It was quite a spectacle and very moving. Apparently, all the churches in the city were doing the same, at the same time. All were slowly making their way to the central cathedral, where there was to be a 'Holy Week' service.

We made our way back to the sea front and along the wall, back to where we had parked. As we walked, I gazed out to sea and thought of Nelson, for it was said that people had watched the battle of Trafalgar from vantage points along these very walls. It was also here, that the flotsam and jetsam from the battle had been blown in by the storm that followed.

We had enjoyed Cadiz, with its narrow streets, bars and cafés, and are so glad we made the effort to go and see it for ourselves.

We travelled 45 minutes along the coast for our overnight stop at 'Camping Roche' at Conil de la Frontera. It's a lovely campsite and the lady at reception gave us lots of information. We had a nice grassy pitch and the shower block and facilities were excellent. That night we had home-made Spanish omelette and Rioja wine followed by coffee and a favourite of ours, 'Frangelico', an Italian hazelnut liqueur. Next morning Jackie said she had not slept well because of the cows mooing, dogs barking and early morning cockerel. I pointed out that we were situated by a working farm. I also told her that I hadn't slept that well either, to which Jackie retorted, "Rubbish, you must snore when you're awake then!"

Anyway, we awoke to clear blue skies and it was lovely and warm outside. Soon the bikes were off the back of Belle and we went for a ride along the coast and into the nearby town of Cornil. The winding traffic-free back roads took us to the pretty white washed town. There were some very nice villas interspersed with scrubland and litter. The coast line was rugged with little sandy inlets and brush covered cliffs. We did some shopping in the local supermarket, picking up some fresh veg and salad along with some spare ribs for tea. Then back to Belle to give our legs and derrieres a rest. It was hard going on the way back, something you don't always notice when it's downhill on the way.

Spanish Tortilla a la Señora Rigg

Ingredients:
6 large eggs
2 tbsp. milk
1 medium onion
2 medium potatoes
1 tbsp. Olive oil
Grated cheese (optional)
Salt and black pepper

Method:
Peel and slice the potatoes. Simmer until cooked but still firm. Drain and leave to cool slightly.
Peel and chop the onion and fry gently in the olive oil until softened, but not browned.
Beat the eggs and add a little salt and black pepper, if desired.
Add half the beaten egg mixture to the onions in the frying pan and cook gently for a few minutes until the egg mixture begins to set. Layer the potatoes onto the egg and onion mixture and then pour over the remaining egg mixture. Sprinkle with cheese (optional)

and put under a hot grill to set the egg mixture and melt the cheese.

Serve with a crispy green salad.

We are up early for the off, eager to see Gibraltar. We drove along the coast road, beneath dark clouds, which made for some very dramatic views. The cloud formations covered the tops of the mountains we now snaked around. We were high up and could see Africa on the horizon across the sea at one point. At times, the scenery was spoilt by the sight of giant wind farms covering the hillsides. As we drove over one peak we were confronted by the magnificent view of Gibraltar dominating the bay ahead. We stop at a viewing point to take in the fabulous sight.

We eventually wind our way down and head along the coast road towards Gibraltar. As we approach, we can see a long line of slow moving traffic making its way to the border crossing. As we neared the border, we spied a wide harbour wall that had a space where we could park Belle. There were other motorhomes there too. It was a fairly busy parking area with cars coming and going, so we felt relatively safe about leaving Belle. After a quick brew and observing who was about, we set off for the short walk across the border.

Gibraltar has a very imposing presence being a massive lump of grey/white green topped rock, jutting out of the sea in the bay that dominates all around. As we cross the border through the Spanish customs, we have to wait for a British Airways passenger aircraft to land as the runway literally bisects the crossing.

The old fortress gate forms the entrance into the touristy shopping streets beyond. The shops are Tax Free! We hadn't really done our homework with regard to Gibraltar, so this came as a surprise. We missed a good opportunity to buy a few bargain luxury items as we dithered over prices. Gibraltar is steeped in British history and it shows everywhere. This was the home of the Mediterranean fleet and Nelson stopped here on many an occasion. It was extremely windy, so unfortunately for us the cable cars had stopped running to the peak and we missed our opportunity to see the famous apes. You could take a taxi-cab tour for 25 euros each, but we decided not to, and to be honest by then we were a bit disappointed with it all. We did spend time taking in the sights and reading about its history on the many plaques on houses, guard posts and fortress walls. It's a tad scruffy in places, nice in others and very Colonial British, but not somewhere we will be rushing back to.

After afternoon tea and biscuits back at Belle (the old colonialism was coming out), we were soon cruising along to our next campsite just past Malaga. It was a pleasant drive along the Costa del Sol. There really are some magnificent views of the resorts as you drive along the dual carriageway that runs along the coast. We tried to drop into Puerto Banus for a look, as we passed by, it's supposed to be a very nice place but again we couldn't find a parking spot for Belle. We travelled on driving through Marbella and finally Malaga for a whistle stop sight-see. When we arrived in Malaga the main road leading out to our campsite was blocked by both road works and another religious procession. We had to do a major detour to get to the campsite around the ring road. This all takes time and by then I'd just about had enough of travelling for one day, even though Belle is very comfortable and a pleasure to drive.

The Campsite 'Torre del Mar' was out of the ACSI book and did advise it was part Naturist. But it was ACSI, so we thought it would be segregated. Well, as they say in our neck of the woods, "You know what thought did?" The receptionists were fully dressed and so we sheepishly booked in. We thought it would be a 'no-no' at this time of year, there was quite a chilly wind blowing in from the sea. The parking pitches were surrounded by high privet hedges to three sides, so very private. Quite undaunted, we drive slowly in. "Jackie don't look"......but it was too late. The first sight we saw as we made our way to our pitch was a man wearing just a tee shirt and flip flops. The next sight was of two men who were totally naked and with completely shaved bodies. The two kindly gents then proceeded to direct us on to our pitch, using not only their hands but also their protuberances. I kept my eyes on the road ahead, but I suspect that Jackie peeped at their directional equipment!

Joking apart, we are not prudes at all, although the first sighting was a bit of a shock, it was quite comical to us. Everywhere you looked there were people of all ages and sizes either in the nude or in just tee shirts. We were soon in our pitch, which was really quite private and for which we were very grateful. I went back again to the reception and asked if it was obligatory to take ones clothes off? "No it isn't, and they won't mind if you don't, but it's better if you do". So, back in Belle we decide to take it as it comes as we have booked to stay for two nights. It was late evening by then so we thought we would see what the morning would bring.

The next morning our blinds are open and we are setting up for breakfast in Belle. There are nude people of all ages walking about with nice brown bodies. As it is sunny and warm outside I set off for the shower block in just my shorts along with my towel and bag of toiletries. I arrive at the shower block without incident, keeping my eyes front. I notice the ladies entrance is blocked off so I nonchalantly wander into the gents and come to an abrupt halt. My gad, there's a naked lady at one of the wash basins putting her make up on in front of the mirror! I retreat outside and look at the sign, yes it was the gents. I make a hasty retreat back to Belle and undertake my ablutions in complete safety.

When one thinks about it, it's obvious if you are nudists, why would you need a Gents and a Ladies? Well, call me old fashioned or what, I certainly do, as I like to make my own noises in the loo along with all the other lads. The thought of ladies listening would inhibit me somewhat. I was just getting over the toilet incident, when Jackie points to an oddly shaped lady passing by our window dressed in only her high heel ankle boots....gosh whatever next? After breakfast we settle outside to sunbathe and relatively speaking it feels a relaxing place. Jackie in her swimsuit and me in my shorts...a right pair of chickens!

After a while and once we got over the nudity, we find our fellow campers are all very friendly and I think because we are partially dressed, they realise we are not nudists. Actually, I did decide to sunbathe in the nude at the back of Belle but Jackie would only go topless. We are out of sight of others except for the birds, who I suspect have been eying up a little morsel. It's all very releasing and I suspect that given time we could adjust to it. We do respect that if that is what makes you happy in life, then that is what you should do. Later that afternoon, we walked (fully clothed) through the campsite to the private beach. It wasn't that nice at all, it was grey shingle and not very inviting. Everyone was enjoying themselves and of course had no inhibitions.

We also reconnoitre outside the campsite and walk down the track to the main road, but there is not a lot to see. On the way back and just outside the campsite we meet up with a British couple from Liverpool and have a quick chat. They said they had been coming to the campsite for years because it was so friendly. Apparently, the guy had been in the armed forces serving with the Commandos!

Our journey next day took us along the coast towards Motril and then inland north through the Sierra Nevada mountains. We are en route to Granada and to visit the Alhambra Palace. The road winds its way upwards and through the mountains. Some of the views are absolutely amazing. The motorway is a feat of engineering, with long bridges that crisscross ravines. Here and there we see snow covered mountain tops. We eventually reach our campsite, named after the nearby village of Beas de Granada, a five minute walk away. The young chap at reception spoke perfect English. He told us his father was from Liverpool and his mother was Spanish. He gave us lots of advice about Granada. The views from the campsite of the snow covered mountain tops were stunning, we were so high up. We were told that only a few days previous, the campsite itself, had also been covered in snow.

We had been advised to book ahead for the Alhambra Palace as there was limited access per day, so our first job was to go on the internet and book our tickets. What a disappointment, it was fully booked every day we planned to be there. I phoned up tourist information, who said it might be possible to find a personal guide who could get us in. We were very upset with ourselves, as Dirk and Nella had warned us to book well in advance, which of course we didn't.

After tea, we decided to walk down the steep hill into the village below. It was a lovely little place, but not as old as we imagined it would be, unless we missed something. Most of the houses and apartments were fairly new builds, with a couple of little shops on the main street. We bought some eggs, bacon and some of the local wine. On our way back we called into reception, to check on the times of the buses to Granada. It was the same guy who booked us in, so we told him about our sadness at not getting tickets for the Alhambra. He asked us to wait at the desk whilst he made a couple of calls. Within minutes, he had booked the tickets for us. Apparently, they had a quota at the campsite. How lucky are we? Spirits lifted and back at Belle, we took in the stunning view of the snowy peaks and had eggs and bacon for tea.

The next day we relaxed around Belle and met Alan and Fern from Lyme Regis. Alan had just retired and they had a new caravan, which they are touring Spain in. Behind us there is another young British couple in a caravan, but who are resident at the campsite. They teach English at a school in Granada. Who said life's dull?

Next morning, after a hairy scary bus ride down the narrow winding back roads, we are soon in Granada centre. The weather is clear blue skies, with no wind and warming up nicely as the day progresses. The city is a mixed bag, some of it is very nice, while other bits are just plain ordinary. The old city centre, at the foot of the Alhambra, is by far the most attractive part. However, the jewel in the crown is the Alhambra Palace itself. It was the seat of power of the Nastrid Moors, from 1298 to 1492, until their ejection by King Ferdinand and Queen Isabella. It is a truly magical place. Set high on a hilltop, with its views over Granada and the old Jewish quarter.

The palace itself is stunning and a tribute to the artisans of the past, as they tried to create their idea of paradise right here on earth. They had done a good job, truly creating somewhere magical. From beautiful gardens and water features, to buildings with magnificent mosaics and light features. As we walk around, every view had something to reward you with. It's both haunting and alluring, as it conjures up minds-eye pictures of a past way of life. We spend the afternoon being enchanted by its beauty and history. It is one of the highlights of our tour.

On the final morning at Beas de Granada we woke up to another beautiful day. We decided to take a pleasant walk through the foothills close to our campsite and get hopelessly lost. I swear somebody had pinched one of the paths and moved a village. We were also facing the wrong way, the sun was setting in the wrong direction and my compass was not showing true north. "Admit it" says Jackie, "you just got it all wrong". "No" I said, "it's the map and the town planners moving things again!" "Hold it the other way round then!" After much searching, we finally came across Brigadoon, on the way back to our campsite.

Travelling southeast the following day, we made for the Costa Blanca. This route takes us back through the mountainous Sierra Nevada and out onto the arid plain. The landscape is so interesting at times, and at others quite featureless, miles and miles of rough ground. We stopped at a Lidl supermarket, which is a motorhome magnet, as it has some good value food and wine. This was to be our main shopping store on the tour as they could be found in most of the countries and places we visit.

We arrive at Marina Camping at a place called Marjal around 4pm. We were soon set up on a nice large pitch surrounded by the international community of Brits, Germans, Netherlanders, Norwegians, French, Italians and Spanish. There is even a hairdresser on site, so Jackie is soon booked in for a colour and trim. Everyone is friendly and we have a bit of a chat with our Spanish neighbours. The facilities here are excellent and wifi is free, so we decide to stay for a few days.

Tired from all the sight-seeing and travelling, we spent most of the time just sunbathing and catching up with emails and the blog. Jackie went to the resident hairdresser one morning and came back pleased with the result. Angie had a small awning on the side of the caravan, which she used as her salon and where customers could catch up on the campsite gossip under the driers! That afternoon, we went for a bike ride along the coast to Guardamar. The sun is still with us, although there is a cool breeze. Unfortunately, as we road close to an inlet, where the water looked quite stagnant, the mosquitoes started to bite. It was still relatively early in the season, but the little blighters were on the loose. On another day we had visitors, Alan and Fern, the couple we had met at the campsite in Beas de Granada. They were with some friends they had been staying with at a campsite close by. They were inspecting the campsite when they had spotted our motorhome. What a pleasant surprise, drinks all round then, coffee and Spanish Liqueur '43'... very nice!

Batteries recharged and relaxed we are off again, this time heading for Benidorm. On the way, we took a detour, to stop and have a quick view of our friend's holiday villa, at La Marina. Dave and Maureen (our good friends and neighbours from Derby), had had the villa built ten years ago, the same time we had bought ours in France. We had talked about it and seen many photos, so could not miss the opportunity to see it, as we passed by. We met their neighbours Robin and Gill (Dave and Maureen were back in the UK), who gave us a guided tour. It was lovely and just as we imagined it, with its pretty terraces and nice big swimming pool.

After another pleasant drive along the coast, we were in Benidorm by lunch time. It was now raining. Our campsite 'Amanello', was situated on a hillside on the outskirts and had beautiful panoramic views of the resort, especially when it was lit up at night. The toilet facilities were brand new and the staff were very nice to us. After a while the rain stopped, so we set off for the twenty minute walk into the centre.

We had been to Benidorm to celebrate our friend Dave Coley's 60th birthday, some 10 years back. We had driven there in our first sports car, a brand new MX5. That was a wonderful experience too, but not to be told now. There were six of us altogether, David and his wife Georgina, their daughter Victoria and her husband Ian. They had flown in and were staying at a five star hotel. We stayed in a hi-rise apartment block, on an urbanisation area, at 'Los Pinos'. Jackie had trouble pronouncing that at times, especially when telling the taxi driver, in order to get us home! We had spent a wild few nights on the town, taking in such sights (not for the faint hearted) as virginal magician 'Sticky Licky Vicky' and comedian Mike Curtis. His best line for me was when he spotted someone crossing the floor and said "I can tell you've got plenty of money" to which she smiled nicely. He then continued by saying "because you've spent bugger all on clothes!" The smile quickly disappeared and the audience were in hysterics. One tip.....Never get up and walk about if a comedian is on the stage, you are asking to be the butt of his jokes.

One day we came across a tapas bar, that I have since made legend among my friends, by saying it was the one place I would teleport them to for its atmosphere alone. It was in the old town and called 'La Cava Arogonesa'. I was so looking forward to returning and having a tasty lunch with all the locals. What a disappointment. It still had the hams hanging from the ceiling and the glass fronted display chiller cabinets showing off the tapas. But the atmosphere had gone, as had the arched drinking/eating area, which had been turned into a walkway leading to more shops. We did have some tapas, which was ok, and we reminisced about how it had once been all those years ago. Back then, after eating each tapas, you wiped your mouth on a serviette provided and then threw it on the floor. After a while the floor was totally covered with them. It sounds terrible to want to do that, but that was the norm at this tapas bar and somehow it added to the ambience of the place.

Benidorm has also changed, although it still has its excellent promenade along the sea front, most of the bars it was famous for have gone. However, the lovely sandy beach remains, with its magnificent sand sculptures. The back streets are now filled with shops rather than bars. The only saving grace is the old town, which still retains its original character. We had heard the Spanish had had a bit of a clean-up, trying to attract a different type of clientele, which we can understand. While Jackie and I will admit to being choosey on the holiday front, not wanting the young 'lager lout' type of holiday. Benidorm had definitely lost something. It was like going to Blackpool or Skegness, without a kiss me quick hat or candy floss in sight!

From Benidorm it was north to Pedramala, near Benissa, to visit the sister of our friend Clive. It was the first time we had met Judith, who has lived here for the past eighteen years. Judith lives alone since her husband passed away a few years ago. A lovely lady and another beautiful villa, which Judith and her husband had had built to their own design. It had stunning views of the surrounding area and down the valley to the town of Moraira. We could fully understand why Judith was loath to give it up, as it held so many memories for her and her dearly missed husband. As a hobby, Judith's husband took a great interest in clocks and had collected some beautiful examples. I took time to admire those which still adorned the villa, as I had the same taste in clocks.

Judith prepared lunch and we then proceeded to chat, drink and eat our way into the evening. Judith also insisted we sleep in a proper bed, so we stayed in one of her lovely guest bedrooms. It made a nice change not to have to make up the bed before we got in it.

After breakfast, we waved goodbye to Judith and headed off for Valencia, travelling the coastal road again. The traffic was somewhat heavier around here, but the roads are still excellent. There was a beautiful blue sky, with a few powder puffs of cloud about and quite warm for April. As we reached a little town called Oliva, we could see young ladies dressed in very short skirts sitting at the roadside. They were at every pull-in, alone or in two's. One very attractive young lady, in a tight white dress that left little to the imagination, was draped over a red BMW bonnet. A sight for sore eyes really, as it was only just mid-morning. I asked Jackie what she thought they were up to, she said she thought they were selling pears and grapes and other fruity items, not. I did admire some of the melons on display. One young lady had just got out of the cab of a lorry, with her little bag of tricks and was adjusting what little clothes she had on. Fruit was obviously selling well that day!

Along the way, we stopped at a few beaches, to take in the lovely views of the coastline and the sea. We finally pulled in at 'Coll Vert Camping', just a short bus ride away from Valencia. The facilities were clean but not that nice. A walk to the nearest beach revealed views of the container port and nothing much else. You just have to take the rough with the smooth sometimes.

After a lazy morning round Belle we set off for the bus ride into Valencia. We had an entertaining chat on the bus to a young guy from Lancaster, who lived near our campsite. He had been there for three years. He worked for a theatre group, who performed locally and at schools. A young Spanish chap joined in our conversation. He had been to Birkenhead, Liverpool and also Blackpool. He was out of work at that time and was going for an interview. As we got off the bus they both wished us a good holiday. It always amazes us how easy it is to strike up a conversation with someone and how interesting it can be.

We walked around Valencia, which is a big city with plenty of hustle and bustle. Having now visited a few Spanish cities, it takes quite a lot for us to feel any kind of 'Wow' factor. That's not to say we don't enjoy visiting new places in Spain, because we do. Valencia is a beautiful city with some fine architecture, a Basilica, parts of the fortress wall, a lively shopping centre, fountains and some historical sites. Also, we finally get to visit our first proper bullring. Guess what? It's free entry.... to a German Beer Festival. Bratwurst – tastic.

We visit a large shopping store called 'El Cortes Engles' where there is 10% off sale prices if you hold a foreign passport. Luckily for us, we had ours with us, so we bought a few items. Now, which one of you said, "I thought you were on a budget?" As the bus pulls away from the busy city centre, we both agree that Valencia is our kind of city.

Rolling on, we pass miles and miles of ripe orange groves, on the way to our next stop Peniscola, a tourist resort further along the coast. It was to be one of our gem finds of the tour. It is here that they filmed part of the film 'El Cid' with Charlton Heston. At the end of the film, the Spanish ride out of the castle on horseback and fight the Moors along the beach. The splendid castle is used as the backdrop to the fierce scene.

'Eden Campsite' was located a few steps from the seafront. It was quite busy, but there were a few good pitches to choose from. We chose one that was quite tight to manoeuvre into, but it was very private. A kind gent started to give me assistance as I backed Belle into the space. Jackie was at the rear doing the same. I had noticed a high kerb to the front, so was taking great care. I gesticulated to my guide at the front, as I reversed slowly into position, to show my concern about the kerb. He assured me all was well, until I heard 'crunch'. I had hit it. I got out and Jackie raced to the front. The kindly gent had disappeared, never to be seen again. Thankfully, not too much damage appeared to have been done, only a scuff that would probably cost us £200 to repair. We were really upset. After some of our torturous escapades in Belle and not a scratch, to be felled by something so simple, was very frustrating........aagghhh.

More lazy days spent around Belle as the weather is warm and sunny. Peniscola has a fortress at the tip of the resort, which is shaped like a hook. It has a wide sandy beach, lovely promenade and is quiet and relaxed at this time of year. I decide to take a bike ride along the coast alone, as Jackie's knee is giving her some pain, as it sometimes does, since she twisted it badly back in February. We just hope it heals soon. The area at the end of promenade turns out to be nothing special, but I do spot a Spanish supermarket for us to use later. One evening we walked along the beach and to the fortress. It's a nice warm evening, so just trousers, short sleeves and a jumper for later. We make our way to a bar at the foot of the fortress and order a jug of Sangria. The bar has that feel good factor, with trendy elegantly dressed Spaniards laughing and chatting away. The sea is lapping at our feet and some relaxing music adds to the atmosphere. We also have a panoramic view of the sandy bay and resort. The bar is heaving and so obviously the place to be and be seen at.

Later Jackie suggests we go into the fortress. I am not so sure, as it does not look that inviting close up.

Jackie pointed out that as we'd come this far, it would be sad not to see it. Good job she did, or we would have missed the best part. Inside the fortress walls, the cobbled streets take you up to the summit and then back down and around. There are craft shops, bars and restaurants housed in the white washed buildings. Palm tree court yards and a magnificent red sunset. The lights inside the buildings gave out a yellow hue, which added something special to the already beautiful evening.

Later, as we walk back along the beach in the dark there are vehicles parked on it, some with their headlights on. It's a fishing competition with about 30 participants, each in an allotted space. They are all equipped with two or three long pole fishing rods. Looking back, the fortress was all lit up in the bay, as were the lights along the promenade. What a view. All of this added to our feel good experience of this charming place.

As we left Peniscola to travel east to Tarragona, we called in at the Mercadona (a popular Spanish supermarket), the one I had spotted when I went for the bike ride. There was a good choice of food and it was a lot cheaper than in the UK. At the deli counter you could buy freshly sliced Parma ham, which tasted absolutely delicious.

En route to Tarragona, we pass more orange groves and even more ladies by the roadside, sitting on fold up chairs under sun parasols with their handbags on their arms. We were shocked to see so many, but we surmise there is safety in numbers.

Onwards to Tarragona and camping 'Torre de la Mora'. The campsite is in the small town of La Mora, about 10km east of the city. Again, the campsite was located at the back of the beach on a beautiful bay. Our pitch was right on the beach and stunning it was too.

That's the beauty of going to Spain during the low season, especially on the coast. During the summer months it must be a nightmare trying to find a good campsite with any vacant spaces. This campsite is well laid out and has a fabulous swimming pool complex, which looks more like it came out of a Caribbean Island holiday brochure. The water however, is far too cold for us to contemplate a dip.

This was to be our second visit to Tarragona, as we had stayed for one night several years ago. The great thing about catching the local bus into any city, is that you are able to see the suburbs and all the smaller non-tourist places. We were pleasantly surprised, that most of the surrounding areas we went through were very clean and tidy.

Once in the city, we walk to one end of the main street named 'Ramblas', which dissects the city. There we take in the magnificent views of two stunning beaches and the ruins of a Roman amphitheatre. Walking on, we take time to do some window shopping in the modern part of the city, before heading for the old district. The old district is set above the more modern part of the city and is a very busy area, with plenty to see and atmosphere to absorb. We always take our guide books with us, so we can find the interesting places and read about the history. As we enjoyed a coffee in one of the lovely old squares we reminisce how we once had a very funny incident here, some years back.......

We were eating out late one evening in the lovely Spanish heat, in the very same square. It was then packed with people and abuzz with chatter, as it was the height of the tourist season. I spotted an elderly Spanish shoe cleaner making his way round the tables trying to drum up some business, but there were no takers. By the time he got to our table I was suitably inebriated, enough to take pity and so took my shoes off to let him clean them. He did an excellent job using Kiwi shoe polish, which he took the trouble to show to me before he began the brushing. He held them up for me to inspect his handiwork, as well as everyone else in range. Horror of horrors..... all the thread had come lose from the the soles of my shoes, making them look a fury mess of lose thread...all I could say was "muchas gracias Manuel", whilst under my breath I said to myself "that was very kind of you to hold them up like that for everyone to see" or words very close to that! I paid him quickly and he left with a smile on his face, while mine was slightly crimson.

Our last place to visit in Spain was to be Barcelona. We had also been to Barcelona once before, just for the day, part of an excursion when we were on a Mediterranean cruise. We liked it very much and so were really looking forward to going back and seeing more of the city. That wasn't the only reason though, we had some friends flying in from the UK, to spend the weekend with us. Our visitors were Paul, an old schoolmate of ours, and his friend Jackie. As we drove there, we took the time to pop into a little resort called Sitges, on the coast. My friend Brian Elks used to holiday there and had said how nice it was. It was a maze of small streets, which led onto the sea front, with a cathedral at one end. Sadly, we had to drive straight through, as there was no place to park Belle. It did look nice though.

We chose a campsite about 15km from the centre of Barcelona '3 Estrellas'. It was great. We parked right on the beach front again. We were also very close to the airport, so about every five minutes throughout the day, we watched the planes taking off and flying over the sea. At night, hardly any took off, so that was fine. For some, it would have been a bit noisy, but we loved it. The weather was perfect and so having bought a freshly baked baguette from the shop on the site, we sat looking out to sea eating boiled eggs. Not exactly a gastronomic delight, but as they say "you can't beat an egg"......or can you?

Paul and Jackie were staying in a hotel close to the city centre, so we met them at one end of Las Ramblas. Las Ramblas is the central avenue of the old town and is busy around the clock, a must see place. It has a wide paved central walkway with a road either side. It is alive with throngs of people around the clock. It is a good place to eat, drink and be merry, and take in the essence of Barcelona. However, you need plenty of money in your pocket, as it is not cheap.

We all had a great time together. Barcelona is a vibrant city, full of fabulous buildings, beautiful tree lined streets and lots of good restaurants and bars. The next day we chose to catch one of the bus tours that took us to all the main sights. We thought it was the easiest way to see the city in the time we had. We hopped on and off the bus, along the way to see the sights that interested us the most. It's a really big city and there is a lot to see over a wide area. Highlights of the tour were the 'The Sagrada Familia', Gaudi's famously unfinished cathedral, and his quirky looking wavy house, where there are queues a mile long to get in. Also, futuristic Barcelona, full of wonderful modern architecture, which in places, looked like a cityscape out of a science fiction film.

As you look around taking everything in, you can always spot the obligatory Japanese tour guide, brolly held aloft, followed by their entourage of happy snappers. We believe the Japanese have developed a teleport system, as they seem to appear from out of nowhere. Barcelona really is a beautiful city to visit and has lots to offer for everyone. That evening, we spent an age looking for a restaurant that sold Suckling Pig, as we had told Paul and Jackie how delicious it was. We just had to try this very tasty dish again. Sorry to mention it if it's not to your liking, but for us carnivores, it is sooooo tasty.

The next day Paul and Jackie caught the bus to our campsite to spend their last day with us. It was a lovely sunny day, with quite a cool breeze blowing in from the sea. Paul and Jackie were glad of the breeze, to dry out their coats. When we had left them the previous evening, the heavens had opened and they got absolutely saturated walking back to the hotel. We were lucky to be on the bus for an hour, so by the time we got off, the rain had just about stopped.

A memorable day was spent, with great company, all very relaxed. Next morning, we went back into Barcelona to see them off and have one last drink on Las Ramblas.

In the afternoon we stayed by Belle to relax and plan our journey back into France. We waved to all the Ryanair planes that flew over us, around the time of our friend's flight. The other campers must have thought we had lots of friends or were just 'plane' crazy!

Well that's about it for Spain. Of course we did a hundred and one other things and saw so many wonderful sights, during the six weeks we spent there, it's impossible to include it all. We are so glad we went into the interior, as it has such a lot to offer and reward the traveller. The Spanish people we met were all really friendly, helpful and courteous. We loved every minute of our time there, so I'm sure it won't be too long before we go back.

We are just slightly above budget, as we had spent a bit more than expected, due to one or two purchases in the Spanish sales.

Chapter Five

Southern France

May 1st – May 12th

Céret – Sète – Port Grimaud – St Tropez –Cannes – Monaco – Mandelieu la Napoule

It seemed a long drive that day, but we arrived in France safe and sound. Just over the border, about 30km inland from the coast, we drop into a place called Céret and have no problem finding the 'Municipal' camping on the edge of the town. Our friends from Moëlan, Serge and Nedege, had recommended we pay this mediaeval market town a visit, a favourite of theirs and famous for its summer cherry festival. The town nestles amongst a mountainous valley and has both a French and Spanish influence. This was to be an overnight stop for us, so as soon as we were on our pitch for the night, we took the short walk down the road and into the beautiful centre. The place was deserted except for a few people in one bar, where we stop to have a drink. It was so quiet for early evening, which seemed odd to us. We took in all the history of the place, especially the wonderful sights like the old bridges, charming little squares and the maze of streets, within what remains of the old walls. Suddenly, we came across a large area, where there had obviously been a grand festival of sorts, litter strewn everywhere. No wonder the place was a ghost town, everyone must have been nursing hangovers and therefore a bit subdued by the previous days event.

A new day, we rolled on, skirting Perpignan and Narbonne, through the wine producing regions of the Languedoc. The magnificent cathedral at Beziers dominates our view for a while. We have blue skies again as we drive along many tree lined roads, backed by row upon row of beautiful vines gracing the hillsides. Absolutely gorgeous.

Our next stop, Sète, holds fond memories for us. Our safe haven for the night was to be on an aire situated on a sand bar, between Cap d'Agde and Sète. We had driven along the same road some years back. Then, the main road had been crammed with motorhomes, piled up onto the verges, all along the sea front. Way back then, it had been one of the main inspirational reasons for us to buy a motorhome. We had thought, one day that will be us... and now here we were. All had since changed though. There were now two clinically designated aires for us to park on. Not at all the same as we had been dreaming about for all those years.

We pulled into the central aire and were immediately welcomed by a young English couple, Mark and Liz who were in the next van to ours. We hit it off straight away, which made up for the disappointment of our dream location. They were from Huddersfield and told us they had sold their houses to buy a transit van earlier that year, which they then had professionally custom fitted out. Mark was a singer (and a good one too) and planned to get work in a hotel or bar in Spain for the summer season. His expensive sound equipment was all secreted away in hidden compartments in his van. They planned to do this for five years, or until they had had enough of that lifestyle.

As we chatted outside on our sun loungers, with beers and wine in hand, we were joined by a Frenchman, Michelle and his little black French Bulldog, Fiona. He said he had named her after one of his ex-wives! He was in the luxury motorhome the other side of ours and spoke excellent English. He soon reappeared with a bottle of 'Gentian' to accompany our beers and wine. Michelle owned a wine merchant business, had villas in La

Grande Motte and Cannes, a yacht and a brand new white Ferrari. He said he was on his own as his young wife, who was half his age, did not like slumming it in his motorhome, which he absolutely loved, along with his dog Fiona for company.

As we had just stocked up on food that day, we offered (nothing to do with the drink) to make everyone an evening meal. Michelle insisted we retire to his motorhome to cook it and he would provide the wine. After a rambunctious noodle meal, we were serenaded by both Mark and Michelle, who it turns out, had once been a bass player/singer in a band. "Some more wine" said Michelle, "un petit pois" said Liz, "just a little pea then" he retorts, to yet more hysterical laughter. Time warped and we were soon in the wee hours of the morning. We offered to clean up, but Michelle said to leave it all until morning. He meant every word of it. The next morning he was ready and waiting patiently for us to go and wash the dishes!

Noodle Surprise a la Rigg
Preparation and cooking time, 30 minutes approx

Ingredients:
Chicken Breast (one for each person)
Jar of Wagamama sauce (any flavour, bought in the UK)
Egg Noodles (as much as you can eat)

Method:
Boil some water in a pan and add the thinly sliced chicken strips. Turn down the heat slightly and simmer for 15 minutes.
Drain the chicken and add the jar of sauce and heat very gently in the same pan for 5 minutes stirring occasionally. At the same time boil some more water in another pan and add the noodles and simmer for 5 minutes.

Split the noodles into equal portions on warmed plates and top with the chicken and sauce.
Inexpensive, quick and very tasty.

Just before noon the next day we say our goodbyes. Michelle was staying on for another few days, before moseying along wherever his fancy took him. He did offer for us to stay at either of his villas and borrow his car, now that sounds interesting. He meant the little Smart car he also has and not the Ferrari! Mark and Liz were off to Benidorm and then hoping to get to Portugal, dependant on if Mark found any singing work. Before parting, they gave us the directions to an aire in the centre of Sète, by the railway station, so that was to be our next stop for the night.

Sète has a magnetic attraction for us, we had stayed at the Grand Hotel and had passed a very romantic few days there. We were both looking forward to revisiting the mini Venice, with its city centre bisected by waterways, and of course the Grand Hotel. The aire was actually a bit of a dump, which had an old derelict caravan on it surrounded by old shopping trolleys, not a pretty sight. Still, it had a lovely view of Sète and there were plenty of other motorhomes parked up. It was situated on a long stretch of gravel car park, by the station and next to one of the canals.

After a light lunch, we set off for the short walk over the bridge and into the centre. Our first destination was a trip down memory lane to the Grand Hotel. It is situated on the Grand Canal, at its junction with another canal. The room we had back in 2000, overlooked this juncture. At night, with all the boats clanking and the lights shimmering and reflections in the water, it looked so pretty. The room we had then also had a large balcony facing inside and seating areas surrounded by antiques, all very opulent. This overlooked the interior courtyard, which was old colonial with its chessboard marble tiled floor, palms and fountain. We sat in that courtyard, drinking in that colonial feel and dined on our memories. It had not changed much, but was now a bit more modern in its décor. Over coffee and Amaretto, plus a few complimentary nibbles, we whiled away the time reminiscing.

Sète is a lovely place with its waterways, tightly packed shopping centre on the hillside, and a harbour. The place is a mecca, if you love fresh sea food, with plenty of brightly coloured tabletop restaurants lining the bustling harbour front. There is always something interesting to watch here. During our last visit, we asked the hotel concierge where we should eat, and he recommended the 'Marina', but not the 'La Marina' as he said, "It is a trap". Now what a 'trap' is in French restaurant terms we have no idea, but we got his drift.

Another long drive as we head for Arles in the Camargue region, and then on to Port Grimaud. The Camargue is famous for its marshes and white horses, which we catch glimpses of, as we pass through. Once again, it is a very easy journey and scenic drive. We pass by Avignon, which we would recommend anyone to visit, if in the area. It is a stunning walled city, with a famous bridge…"Sur le Pont d'Avignon", which we sang as we drove past. Because we had been there before, we decided to give it a miss this time round.

We arrive at our Campsite 'Pont de Cru' near Arles, which is very nice, but the toilet facilities are a bit basic and not for Jackie. We are soon set up and off on the bus into Arles. It's a good job we like bus journeys. We had met people who were keen cyclists, who wouldn't dream of taking a bus, but we find most of the cities quite busy with traffic and wouldn't feel safe riding in. Arles is a major town and has a well preserved Roman

Amphitheatre, 'Les Arena'. The two storey grand arched arena and surrounding area, are quite magnificent and very touristy. We explore its photogenic cobbled backstreets with terracotta roofs, pretty window boxes and shutters. We also walk along the banks of the mighty river Rhone at one point. We eventually stop for our usual people watch at one of the many cafés. What a lovely way to spend an afternoon.

Travelling east, we are soon in Provence with its fields of poppies, church spired towns, villages and rocky mountain backdrop. The weather is kind to us yet again, sunny with blue skies. Some of the roads are extremely winding and take us over some rocky hilltops. We could imagine being in a James Bond car chase as we are soon overtaken by three expensive sports cars, with a raspy blip of the throttle, as they roar past with their tops down. We wind our windows down and I blip my throttle for effect. "Not quite the same" says Jackie.

We arrive at the campsite 'Prairies de la Mer' at Port Grimaud. This campsite was the best we would stay on. The location was perfect for us, steps away from a soft white sandy beach, breath taking views of the bay and just a short walk into the pretty little port. The pitches were a good size and were lined by palm trees giving some shade. It is a very upmarket site, with picturesque thatched wooden chalets, restaurants and bar areas. Very 'French Riviera', so we booked in for four days. This was to be our base for visits to St Tropez and St Maxime, both short distances away.

As we arrived, we could see that they were preparing to host a Harley Davidson European 100 year celebration, in the campsites extensive grounds. As you can imagine, the campsite quickly filled up with fabulous bikes and their owners, from all over Europe.

Across the road from the site, was the small picturesque port of Grimaud itself, with its very pretty mixture of pastel coloured buildings. Each has its own character, with arched courtyards, balconies and covered terraces. There are jetties full of boats, of all shapes and sizes. The waterways bisect the port, forming little islands, which are home to some of the rich and famous. It's awash with tourists and stalls, restaurants and shops that cater for all.

We stop at one stall, to buy some very nice looking home-made nougat, it looks delicious. Jackie chooses one flavour and I another. It takes him an age to cut a very thin slice, through the huge block, with a big sharp cutting instrument. The guy wrapped the small slices in special waxed paper and said…".17 euros please". Under my breath, I uttered the Derbyshire War Cry…..'How much?' I nearly pointed out that, we wanted to buy some nougat, and not the stall. We hadn't noticed the small sign, which said it was 52 euros a kilo. As there was a crowd, I nonchalantly handed over the money. Wow, that hurt, still it was very nice and we would enjoy eating it over the next few days, a tiny bit at a time.

The local bus took us to St Tropez. Here there is a large wide harbour, into where the rich and famous sail their magnificent yachts to be admired by the tourists and locals alike. Very kind of them too, as we stroll along the quayside and have a good nosey at each one berthed there. Quite a few are British owned, with their standards blowing about in the breeze.

The harbour front is full of restaurants, catering for most budgets, from the ridiculously expensive to the one we chose to eat at! 'La Jette' was situated on the end of the harbour and had a good view of the boats and passing trade. We had dressed up to the nines, so we could appear to be part of the jet set. We sat outside in the sun, me with my Ray Bans and Jackie with her Burberry's on, so no one would recognise us. We had Moules Mariniere followed by a slice of cake 'St Tropezienne' a cream filled brioche, which was all washed down with a nice chilled bottle of Muscadet. It was one of those feel good moments..... "what what". We then wander into the back streets to window shop at some of the very exclusive shops.

The next day it was off to St Maxime. Very nice, more for families though. It's a typical resort, with its promenade and beach front, backed by streets full of touristy shops and restaurants. After a quick look around, we are soon back at the campsite and have our afternoon meal at one of the beachside restaurants, which is very good and reasonably priced.

Numerous marquees are being erected in which the Harley Davison festival will be hosted. There are already bands playing in the evenings at one of the campsite bars. If you are into Harleys, then it is a treat. The Harley fraternity consist of all age groups and looking at the rigs some have arrived in, some are very wealthy. They are all courteous, some of the guys wearing the trade mark bandanas on their heads, or German helmets. Then there are the girls, wearing mini-skirts and fishnet tights, to the elegantly haute couture biker ladies, some with their own bikes. It's quite a show, just watching them cruise up and down, with that lovely bubbling engine noise. Sadly, we had to leave before the event actually opened, as the whole site was fully booked the following week.

We drove northeast to Cannes and along some truly magnificent coastline. The stretch from Frejus to Cannes is quite stunning, with its rugged reddish hills, beautiful white villas and views over to the bays and little coves. Scenically, it is one of the best drives of the tour.

In stark contrast to Port Grimaud, our next campsite 'La Ferme', was quite small and family run. It had very friendly owners, and was ideally located for the short walk into the lovely Riviera town of Mandelieu la Napoule. The facilities were a bit basic (a bit like the old fashioned outside loo's) but very clean. This campsite was the base for our visits to both Cannes and Monaco.

Now there are buses and then there are buses. This particular one took us into Cannes. We called it 'the happy shopper' because it visited all the outlaying shopping centres on its way, took 40 minutes and cost us the princely sum of one euro each. We caught it right outside our campsite and for one euro it took us right into the centre of Cannes, it was a fantastic bargain.

Cannes is a wonderful place, with its grand harbour and tree lined promenade. The seafront has a special feel all of its own. Cannes, along with Nice, is the heart of the French Riviera and rightly so. As we arrive, they were setting up the marquees along the harbour front for the Film Festival being held the following week. We even managed to walk on some of the red carpet. We walked around the harbour and along the promenade. It's sunny and quite hot and the sandy beach is full of people enjoying themselves, but not many swimming. Perhaps the sea is too cold, as it's still only early May.

We then walked back along the hotel studded sea front and pass the famous 'Carlton Hotel' It is here that many of the film stars stay, if they are not on their yachts in the harbour. We are soon seated at a terraced bar, overlooking the sea front and promenade. We are incognito again, with our 'shades' on and have our cocktails in our hands. Jackie has a Mojito, while I have a Black Russian, our respective favourites. We people watch, as the chic jet set are at play, or perhaps like us they are incognito too. I hail the waiter, "encore sil-vous-plait", except I switch to a White Russian this time. Later we explore the shops and streets of Cannes and both agree, it's somewhere we would definitely like to live.

Another day, another 'Happy Shopper' trip. Again, into Cannes, but this time to the station, to get the train to Monaco and Monte Carlo. The scenery along the coast was so beautiful and as we sped along on the train, we could both take in the views. Fabulous villas were dotted amongst the hills. This is where the very wealthy sun themselves on their elegant terraces. We pass by Nice, which once again, having visited on a holiday years ago, we will sadly have to pass up this time.

A few years ago we had visited Monaco, the Palace and the resting place of Princess Grace. So this time, we were visiting Monte Carlo and the racing circuit. Earlier on at the bus stop, we had met a French couple, Jean Marc and Anita from Normandy, (turned out they were actually staying on the same campsite), who informed us that there was vintage car racing that weekend, a prequel to the F1 Grand Prix being held there three weeks later.

Well, what a surprise for us when we arrived, the full Grand Prix circuit and grandstands are all set up. As it is Friday practice/qualifying day and the vintage cars were already racing round, we really had a win…we were able to sit anywhere on the circuit for free! We made our way up into the seating area and spent a glorious afternoon in the sun watching the superb 50's, 60's and 70's cars roaring around the famous track. We took the opportunity to visit just about every vantage point, as we moved from grandstand to grandstand, interspersed with a few beers along the way. What an experience and so unexpected. It was the next best thing to the actual F1 Grand Prix itself.

So there it was another dream fulfilled, with a slightly different slant of vintage cars. Next year maybe we will come a week later and stop for both the film festival and the F1 Grand Prix.

We really enjoyed staying on this peaceful campsite. It was ideally situated so we could easily walk into Mandelieu la Napoule, which was another great find. It has an old castle and soft sandy beach, along with an extensive harbour area. It obviously has that Riviera feel to it. At the harbour side, we met up with the French couple we had seen at the bus stop, and had told us about the vintage cars in Monaco. We are soon sat in a bar, sipping some beers with them. Anita travels the world with her job in Logistics, while Jean Marc is a Mechanic. His pastime is renovating vintage cars and he would also like to buy a boat. With our broken French and their broken English, we spend a happy hour in conversation. As we leave, Jean Marc and Anita appeared to have talked themselves on board a small boat which is up for sale. We could see Jean Marc thoroughly inspecting the engine. We wish them "adieu", as we pass by on our way for our last French meal in this beautiful town.

Italy beckons to us. Once again we are sad to be leaving France, the Riviera in particular. It proved to be a very interesting and extremely enjoyable part of our tour. We can understand why it is such a magnet for the rich and famous, who want to buy property and live here. We are sure we will be back before too long.

We are still over budget, having had a few more meals out than normal, the odd cocktail or two and of course the 'golden nougat'. Still, we are sure we will pull it back, somewhere along the way.

Chapter Six

Italy

May 13th - May 27th

San Remo – Torriglia – Lake Garda – Verona – Sirmione – Lido de Jesolo – Venice

After France, our other love is Italy. We have been here many times and never tire of the place or the people. In past times we have visited Rome, Sorrento, Florence, Lucca, Venice, Sicily, and many other beautiful places in between. However, the one part of Italy we have never been to is the Riviera, from the French border to Genoa. So this will be new ground for us and we were so looking forward to it. After the Riviera, we plan to cross the top of the leg of Italy, around the Adriatic Sea and to the Dalmatian coast.

We stopped at a resort called 'Menton' to eat our last French baguette for lunch, before making our way to San Remo. We had a beautiful view of the harbour and out to sea. I also managed to watch the Spanish F1 Grand Prix on our satellite system. Further on, and as we imagined, it was a very stunning coastline. It was subtle at first, but somehow we can tell by the changing scenery that we were in Italy. One of the first things we notice is the change in the colour of the buildings on the hillsides. These are now predominantly painted terracotta, instead of the whitewashed villas of France. Around every corner another pretty holiday resort came into view, vibrant flower displays and tree lined promenades.

We drove on across a mountain to Eze, which presented us with magnificent views of the cliffs dropping down into the Mediterranean Sea. Just for a change, we had clouds and rain with us that day.

Our first overnight stop was near San Remo, at 'Camping Villaggio dei Fiori'. This was our first experience of an Italian campsite. The first thing we noticed, was that they pack you in tightly together. Not a lot of space between vehicles, but it was all paved and there was a view out to sea, at the back of the site. The facilities were very clean and reasonably new. We visited the local shops and had a quick walk to stretch our legs, but that was it for the day.

We didn't bother going into San Remo the next day, so continued our journey along the gorgeous Rivera coast. The roads were good, winding in places with a moderate amount of traffic. We tootle along at 60mph en route to Ceriale. There were blue skies above, with a few wispy clouds and the temperature had increased, so it was very warm. We pass through resort after resort, including Diana Marino, a favourite of Jackie's parents. Most are shingle beaches and reasonably crowded for a Monday. After a quick stock up at Lidl, our next stopover is at Ceriale and 'Camping Baciccia'. The campsite is situated off the coast, in a small village, with not much going on and is quite basic, but at least the grassy pitches are bigger than at the last site.

It was at this campsite that we met Ben and Barbara from Surrey. As we were signing at reception, they could hear that we were Brits so waved us over and asked us to go and join them for a drink, which for saying we had never met before, was quite brave of them. As we booked in to stop for only one night, we were assigned a pitch near to the site entrance.

We had just settled in when a Belgian guy and his wife pulled in next to us. Their motorhome and trailer had very impressive artwork painted on them. As I recall, the artwork consisted of wild horses and dramatic waves. We were soon aware that they didn't have much space, so I moved back slightly to give them more room. A few minutes later, the chap came over to thank us and gave me two bottles of Belgian beer. It turned out they were with another couple, in the van behind ours. These people hand painted Murals on lorries, vans, cars and motorbikes for a living and toured all over Europe, exhibiting their work at trade fairs and shows. Hence, their uniquely painted vehicles.

Soon after, I managed to find Ben and Barbara and invited them over to us for nibbles that night. Ben was a very young looking older gentleman that had had cancer, but thankfully had beaten it. Barbara was a very attractive lady and had been Ben's secretary at his business, before they married. What a fun-filled evening we had. Ben had such a positive attitude and Barbara was great, she laughed at all my jokes! The evening passed quickly, as we exchanged good and bad experiences, but mostly it was a laugh a minute. They were on their way north, to Lake Orta and then back through France to the UK. We said our goodbyes the next morning over coffee at Ben and Barbara's. Such lovely people, we just gelled together and hope to keep in touch.

As we travelled towards Genoa, everywhere looked so clean and pretty. Unfortunately, we didn't stop to see this city, but it looked stunning. That's another good excuse for a re-visit then.

Sheila, our Aussi speaking Sat Nav, once again managed to get us into a tight spot in the centre of Genoa, taking us a torturous route over a steep hillside. We had to negotiate parked cars, tight turns and oncoming traffic, up and down some very tight single lane streets. I can just hear her saying "You Poms needed some excitement for your book".

We chose to stay on a Stellplatze (free camping in a parking area) in a mountain village of Torriglia, some thirty miles north of Genoa. It was hairy scary driving for Jackie again, over the tree covered mountains and some narrow winding roads, but oh so beautiful. We arrived only to find that the Stellplatze was disused, the facilities old, run down and completely broken. There were council vehicles of all descriptions parked there, but no other motorhomes. The surrounding views were breath-taking though.

I left Jackie and walked into town, to find out if it was ok to park there, as the signage was not that clear. It was then I bumped into a 'Municipal Polizia'. Thinking it best to use my little knowledge of Italian I enquired, "Mi scusi est parko gratuito Camping Car qui per favore" or words to that effect. The reply came back "yes it's ok to park there". Now, what are the chances of bumping into an Italian English speaking policeman, in a remote village on a hillside in Italy, just when you need one? "Is it safe?" He gave me a wide smile. "Yes, it is. We have no crime in the village." He also said it was probably safer than a council vehicle parking area in Manchester, which is where he told me he had learnt English.

After evening dinner, we explored the old village. It was a one street affair and wasn't really that pretty, although it did have a lovely friendly feel to it. People stared at us as we passed. I don't think they were used to many visitors. Back at Belle, we didn't sleep too well that night, a bit nervous at being on our own. We were also disturbed at 3.30am by workmen, loading up a lorry and leaving the car park, followed by others at hourly intervals, until 7am.

Our next stop was to be Cremona. This was again a Stellplatze/Aire, but we vowed if there were no other vehicles there, we wouldn't stay. When we arrived we discovered it was a huge car park, with lots of graffiti on the walls and barriers. Quite a few motorhomes were parked there, but some were grubby looking gypsy types. After consulting with a French couple, who had just pulled in behind us, we both agreed it was not a safe place to stay. We had hoped to have a good look around the ancient city of Cremona, as it has a wonderful Cathedral and is famous for violin manufacturing. As we were already there, we decided to have a drive round the city instead. We were limited to where we could get with the Belle, but it would have been well worth a proper walkabout. It was at this point, we agreed no more Stellplatze/Aires for us in Italy. We were soon driving out again and north, to Lake Garda, our next planned stop and only another 40 minute drive away.

The drive took us through some really pretty landscapes, with rocky outcrops amongst the tall trees that covered the hills. The views of lakes and villages, dotted here and there, were quite stunning. At various points, you could see for miles, down onto the flat plain below. It was late afternoon when we arrived at Lake Garda, near Peschiera, located on the south eastern tip of the lake. It had been another long drive, so we agreed we would stay here and relax for a while.

It was nineteen years since we were last in Peschiera. We had driven over with our son Howard and his friend Michael, for a camping holiday in a Eurosite tent. We loved Lake Garda so much, we knew that we would be back one day, and here we were. We tried to find our old campsite, but managed to pick one on the other side of town by mistake. Still, it was so nice to be back. Our Campsite was 'Bella Llakia' and there were only three slots left on this absolutely huge site. We managed to get a pitch with a view of the lake, by squeezing ourselves into a slot meant for a tent. All around were amazed at my sixty point manoeuvre, to get in there and have room to deploy our overhead awning, seats and table as well.

Wow, the campsite was huge, very well managed and spotlessly clean. We were told that when it was full, it had the same capacity as the town of Peschiera. There were many fixed tents and chalet bungalows on the site for hire and about a dozen or more tour operators running them. The facilities were excellent, with several bars, good restaurants and a swimming pool complex.

In the caravan in front of us, we met Ueli and Ruth, who hailed from Lake Lucerne in Switzerland. We would spend two very pleasant evenings with them, during our six night stay. They had been to Costa Rica and Nicaragua amongst many other places and had some interesting stories to tell. They gave Jackie a gel patch, (medication for joint pain, only available in Switzerland), to help her knee, which had been acting up again. It worked well, so did the trick for a while. They also introduced us to a nice Swiss white wine, we didn't even realise the Swiss made wine. They of course spoke perfect English.

We spent a relaxing day in the sunshine around Belle, with our view through the pencil ferns and flower border, to the lake. It was backed by blue-grey shaded mountains and clear blue skies, stunning. Later that day we wandered into Peschiera, a short walk along the lakeside from the campsite. The old town is situated in and around a walled fortress. It is full of brightly coloured bars, restaurants and shops buzzing with people. We stop at one of the moat side bars and have an 'Aperol Spritzer'. This is the must have drink, as recommended by our good friends Alyson and Freddie, who had holidayed by the lake the year before.

Our next visit is to Verona, an hour's bus ride away. Verona has many ancient Roman ruins, being second only to Rome itself. It's massive focal point is the 1st century AD Arena, which dominates the Piazza Bra central square. It is mid-day when we arrive and the sun is out again. We have decided to eat early today and are soon seated at a table, underneath the canopy covered terrace, looking out over the Piazza and the Arena. We are at the restaurant 'Ippopotamo' and have a delightful three course meal. For a starter we share an anti pasti dish of sliced meats with cheese, tomato and bread. To follow, I chose a pasta dish and Jackie had Caesar salad. Finally, lemon cake for Jackie and Rum Baba for me. We shared a bottle of Pinot Grigio, followed by coffees and Grappa, to help it all digest. It was a delicious meal and we had a magnificent view, all for 65 euros.

We had so wanted to go and see an opera at the arena, but they did not open till later in the year. Apparently, it is one of those must see events. Perhaps next time, we will remember to look at the performance schedules, before we go. Well-fed and watered, we strolled through the pedestrianized shopping areas and gazed at the many wonderful sights. The Piazza Erba was one such, with its flowing fountain surrounded by colourful market stalls selling craftwork and various foods. We came across Romeo and Juliet's balcony, at the Casa di Giuletta. As you enter the courtyard, the archway is covered in graffiti of the 'Adrian loves Jackie' kind, and for once it's not tacky. We squeeze our way in (holding onto our valuables) and kiss under the balcony. Who said romance is dead?

As ever, the next day we caught the bus, to another pretty little lakeside town, called Sirmione. It's situated on an island, with a fortified bridge for an entrance. Once again, the views over the lake are breath-taking, it is picture book Italy. We had a couple of hours wandering around and another obligatory Aperol spritzer break, at a street side bar. As usual, we got chatting to a couple of Brits who were there, before catching the bus back to the campsite.

That night, we went over to the big TV screen that had been erected pool side, and by one of the many on site bars. It was put up for the European Champions League football final, between Chelsea and Bayern Munich. The bar was full of Germans and a few Italians, all supporting Munich. There was just one true Chelsea fan, and Jackie and I, supporting Chelsea. Munich outplayed Chelsea and were ahead, right up until the final minute of proper time, when Chelsea scored an equalizer. From ear piercing cheering, hoots and beer drinking, it all went to silence, except for the lone Chelsea fan and us two. The game went into extra time, then penalties. Chelsea missed first, to raucous cheers from the Germans, then Bayern missed the next two kicks and amazingly Chelsea hailed victorious.

I have never seen a crowd clear so quickly, leaving just Jackie, myself and the solitary Chelsea fan with one other English speaking chap. Now, if that had been a British crowd, most would have stayed at least to see the opposition pick up the trophy. Not the Germans. We all said as much to our English speaking friend, who agreed with us. We all cheered when the Chelsea team lifted the cup. I turned to the English speaking chap and asked where he was from? His reply was "Munich". Ah well, at least he had the decency to stay and applaud the winners. Our lone Chelsea fan was ecstatic, jumping around like a lunatic. He told us he was actually working at the campsite and was there for the season.

We spent the whole of the next day catching up on things in and around Belle and to top it off, it rained heavily all day. We could hardly see the lake, the clouds were so low they totally obscured the beautiful mountains which surrounded it.

We awoke to another lovely warm day. Our next short stop will be Vincenza, then on to Lido di Jesolo, for a boat ride into Venice. Our drive was very scenic, as we passed emerald green fields, some filled with poppies. We stopped at the Palladian city of Vicenza, for a quick look and were well rewarded for doing so. We parked on a busy street, so felt reasonably safe leaving Belle on her own for a while. The city was full of interesting buildings, statues and of course the obligatory Roman ruins. We were pleased we made the effort to see them all.

We had chosen a campsite at Lido di Jesolo, which is a very popular seaside resort, east of Venice. The beautiful clean sandy beaches go on for miles and miles, as does the resort, although it is made only one or two roads deep. The campsite 'Parco Camprero' is very well-kept and organised. We were shown to our pitch by a nice lady on a bike, who looked just like the actress Lucile Ball. Here we met a couple from Birmingham, Jim and Sue. They were travelling in what looked like a converted red postal van and like us were on their way to Croatia. As ever, they were friendly, fun people to be with. Maybe we will see them again along the way, who knows?

We would spend a pleasant five days at this campsite, watching the Monaco GP on my satellite system, visiting Lido Di Jesolo and just relaxing. There was also a walk through woods to the beach, with its own little bar and free wifi, all very nice. Not all the campsites have or offer free wifi, this one didn't. So we took our lap top with us to the beach one day and caught up with our e-mails, family and friends via Skype, while looking out to sea.

The main event here was to be a trip to Venice. We had to catch two buses and a boat to get there. It took us two and a half hours all told. Venice is one of those must see unique places in the world. It is for us, a very romantic place. It is also somewhere you can spend a lot of money, or a little, if you so desire. If you are prepared to explore, there are some hidden gems at very reasonable prices, to suit all. As the boat draws closer, we get our first view of the domes and spires of the city. It's an amazing sight. We are soon at a jetty and moored close to Piazza San Marco.

Once again, we decided to have our main meal at mid-day, so chose another good looking restaurant. Here we had a great view over to San Giorgio Maggiore. With its magnificent domed church of Santa Maria della Salute and cloudless blue skies for a backdrop. It really is one of those 'feel good' factors in life, to sit, eat and drink with the one you love. With beautiful Venice for our venue, it's so good to be alive and doing what we are doing. Occasionally, in life you have those moments that you want to last forever. This is one of them.

After the meal, we moved along to the Piazza San Marco, with the Doges Palace and the glorious Basilica San Marco. On top of this buildings entrance are statues of four horses, the originals are in the museum below. They were looted by Venetians from the Hippodrome in Constantinople. The sack of this capital city of Byzantine Christendom by fellow Christians, due to jealousy and the lure of treasure, would ensure its fall to the Turks 100 years later. The Christian army had been tricked by its leaders, into believing they were going on a Holy Crusade against the Infidel. The greedy and envious had other plans though. I had just finished reading these interesting facts from one of the books on my kindle.

As we walk the covered arched ways to three sides of the square, we do a bit of window shopping. Suddenly, we spy some Murano Glass (famous Venetian glass) cherries on a lovely glass tray, in a shop window. They are exquisite and are priced at the princely sum of 400 euros. We both admire the handiwork and so I said to Jackie, I would go in to make a silly bid for them. For no other reason than having a bit of fun and no intention of buying, we enter the shop. Besides that, we have no house to put them in at the moment, only Belle. The thought of travelling along bumpy roads, with fragile glass ornaments, would be a crazy thing to do? Now being slightly inebriated from our little tipple at lunchtime and the fact there was no one else in the shop, I offer the young lady 150 euros for the whole ensemble. I was expecting a firm rebuff and to be shown the door. Surprise! Knock us down with a feather. The young lady gets on the phone to the boss and comes back with a counter offer, "200 euros?" "Errr… what do you think Jackie?" "Well umm err yes, it's a bargain". "Is it?" "Must be at that price eh?" Needless to say the sale was done and we arrange to pick them up later. We did ask for them to be packed very well, due to the journey ahead. Later, we marvel at our bargaining skills, obviously sales are slow!

Having bought a day ticket, we catch a water bus and hop on and off around the city, taking in its sights and sounds, it really is a fabulous place. We floated along on the stupendous Grand Canal, lined with its historical buildings that litter the way, each with its own story to tell. We marvel as the many gondolas, that nip and tuck their way around and down the many little arteries that feed the canal. It has a magical feel to it all. Each view is thought evoking and rewarding in its own way. We linger on the Rialto Bridge for a while, take a few photos. Then wander the back ways of San Polo and Dorsoduro. To top the whole wonderful day off, we are refused drinks at Harry's bar. Apparently, there is a different dress after 6pm, shorts are not allowed. So, as I am in my knee length shorts, I cannot be served. I ask again tongue in cheek, "no shorts after six then?" "Yes said the bar man". "Strange for a bar not to serve shorts", I retort as we make our way to the door.

Our lasting impression of Venice, is of a truly picture book, stunning place to visit. Our fondness for the rest of Italy is also still intact. However, our feelings on camping in Italy are mixed. We certainly would not recommend staying anywhere, other than on official camp sites. The aires we attempted to stay on, or saw as we passed by, all looked unsafe.

Next stop Croatia.

As a foot note, if you include the Murano glass, our budget is truly blown. We decide not to include items like this in the future, as they will distort what we planned to spend. Having discounted the glass, it still leaves us over budget, due to our extravagant spending on food and drink yet again. You see, the sun and feel good factor, are definitely having an effect.

Chapter Seven

Croatia

May 28th - June 18th

Novigrad – Rovinj – Pula – Zadar – Split – Dubrovnik

We discussed maps as we skirted around the coast towards Trieste and into Croatia. Up until now, we have felt comfortable with where we are going, as we had visited the countries before and had taken detailed maps for reference. Croatia would be new to us and we are not sure what the roads or the signage will be like. We have a map of Europe, but it's not as detailed as we would like. On this occasion, we are relying heavily on Sheila to get us to our first destination, Novigrad, situated on the coast. We will pass through a small strip of Slovenia to get there.

The countryside from Lido di Jesolo to Trieste, is a pretty wine growing area with vineyards dominating the scenery once again. We admire the beautiful houses, pencil pines and picturesque villages as we roll along. We also take the time to stock up at a Lidl again, the wine is exceptionally good value at two euro's for a bottle of Tempranillo, which has to be a bargain. We pass through the harbour front at Trieste, which looks like another nice city, but one we had to give a miss. We press on to the border and the narrow strip of Slovenia, that separates Italy from Croatia. We are both a little nervous as we are unsure what to expect. The first thing we notice is how very green everywhere is and how mountainous it has become.

We are soon at the border and waiting in the queue to enter Slovenia. We were immediately put at our ease. The guards are very pleasant and spoke good

English. Our passage through Slovenia was swift, as the roads are good and before we knew it, we were passing another border control, into Croatia. Here, the border guards tell us we should stop longer in Slovenia, as it is a very safe country to visit. The villages we passed through looked well-kept and modern and we would have liked to stop and have a proper look at some of them. Once again, we have to tell ourselves, we can't do everything. Plus, that morning, while preparing our documents, I had discovered that our insurance did not mention Slovenia. That was an oversight that could have caused a real problem. Thankfully, we passed through without incident.

Novigrad is on the Istria Peninsula, nestling on the northern end of the Adriatic Sea and just a few miles from the border. The signage and roads are good and we are soon at our first Croatian campsite 'Sirena'. They speak English at reception and we are made to feel very welcome. There are two parts to the campsite. The first is well set out pitches in a wood and the other is a cheaper, 'park where you like' area on a grass covered hillside. The campsite is almost full and we decide to park on the hillside, with a view of the sea.

As it is late afternoon by now, we decide to reconnoitre the site and then spend the evening in. The campsite facilities are brand new and are still being extended, we are impressed. On our hillside, there are all nationalities, in all sorts of vehicles. Our closest neighbours are an elderly couple from Austria holidaying with their son in a small caravan. The majority of motorhomes are from Germany and Italy, with only a few Brits about. The sky is blue and it is pleasantly warm well into the evening.

After setting up, we take a stroll along the waterfront, into Novigrad. We are now feeling quite relaxed, as everyone we pass seems friendly. What were we worried about? In this area, the earth is terracotta red, which adds to the vibrant colours of the flowerbeds and lush green lawns that front the houses. Huge rocks had been placed along the coastline for protection against the sea, which at the time was a shimmering sapphire blue and very calm. There were brightly coloured boats and pedalos in the bay. From what we had gleaned from our guide book, this was just as we imagined it would be.

As we approach the centre of Novigrad, the houses that line the seafront are built from sandstone and have terracotta roofs. We observe how each house has an abundance of potted plants and flowers in the garden. There are some unusual trees, with feathery pink and cream fronds on, which we had never seen before. All this beauty was to be just the beginning of a unique Croatian experience.

In Novigrad, the sea front terrace, promenade and fortress wall, have all been recently renovated. It all looks so clean and well set out. We walk around the sea front of the town, with its far reaching views and sandy grey walls. The odd boat chugs along the coastline going about its business. We actually feel like we are on holiday now. There are very few tourists about and we have the walk to ourselves, for most of the time anyway. We visited a red stone church, which had a high square tower, very different architecture. A short distance past the church, we came across some café bars on a terrace, looking out to sea. A little weary and thirsty, we park ourselves under one of the cream canvas sun parasols and it's not long before we are sipping our Mojito's and Black Russian's. Yes, as you have already guessed, the prices are relatively cheap, so that's good news for the budget.

It is here we started talking to a German couple, Josef and Angelica, who were sitting on the next table. They had asked me to take a picture of them, with their camera, not with mine because that would have been silly. We are soon chatting away like long lost friends and they, it turns out, are staying on our campsite. After arranging to meet later, we wander back into the town centre. It is all very picturesque, with its harbour and many boats bobbing up and down in the glassy water, with each boat casting its own mirror-image. Adding to the ambience, we could smell the sea and the occasional waft of fresh fish, as we pass the fishing boats. Novigrad is indeed a little gem.

That evening we had a light meal outside Belle, then it was off out to visit the lovely German couple we met earlier in the day. Josef and Angelika have a large pitch in the woods, close to the sea, so we had all agreed theirs is a better venue for an evening's entertainment. We arrive armed with bottles of white and red wine and some traditional Croatian cherry pasties, we had bought in the town. Their English is very good, so conversation was soon underway, with nibbles and drinks flowing freely. We all agree the cherry pasties are too nice, we could have easily eaten more. We are so lucky that most Europeans want to, and do speak our language. It would be much more restrictive for us on the tour if we couldn't communicate with people.

Josef and Angelika come from Munich where we plan to visit later during our tour, so they gave us lots of information on where to go and what to see. Josef works for the council statistician's office, while Angelika helps at a school. They say Croatia is a popular destination now for Germans, taking over from Spain in recent years. They are on holiday for two weeks and will stay at this campsite for one week, before heading back to Munich. Very much later, we say 'auf wiedersein' and make our way back to Belle for some well-earned rest, after another full and memorable day.

Next stop Rovinj via Porec along the coast. The roads we travel along remain of a good standard and the surrounding fields are full of neat rows of crops. All is very pleasant. The sun is shining, our music is playing and we feel very happy, having made the break to do the tour at this time of our life. Some will say that we are lucky, but we've always worked hard, so this is 'pay back' time and we would sooner be doing this than anything else.

Porec is a very busy seaside harbour resort and so we struggle to find somewhere to park Belle. We eventually spy another motorhome in a car park at the back of the town and decide to park next to it. We hesitate at first, but then I went over to ask a guy who was selling snacks from a kiosk, if he thought it was ok for us to park up. He replied in Croatian of course. Having consulted my travel guide, I'm sure he said "yes, you can", although I did have a slight itch at the back of my neck.

The town itself is very quaint and full of very interesting Romanesque buildings and narrow cobbled streets. There is a nice café culture, with people sitting reading papers or chatting. The harbour front is also very picturesque, with its lights, palm trees, potted plants and benches. There are also the obligatory churches dotted here and there. We are glad we have taken the time to have a look around, but it's now time to travel on.

We cross the car park on our return, only to find that Belle has been wheel-clamped and there's a notice on the windscreen. We are mortified. How 'very dare they' touch our beautiful Belle while we are away? The man in the kiosk shrugs his shoulders and I can see by his expression "I told you so", that what he had said earlier was obviously not "yes" in Croatian. Living in the UK, we are used to clamping and the horror stories we hear about the penalties that are applied by some rogue traders. The prospect of a £200 - £350 fine looms high in our minds. We didn't waste any time going back into town to find the wardens office and to pay the fine. We enquired at a few shops in the town to ask directions to the council office. Within minutes we were in the traffic warden department and explain to the assistants what has happened. They are all very sorry and upset over our plight and the officer who carried out the deed is called back into the office.

On his return, by means of a scooter and with many apologies to us, he explains the situation to his superior. Then he mentioned the word 'campervan' and the mood changed. Apparently, they have had a lot of trouble with people camping overnight in the car park. "Did we not see the sign saying no campervans or lorries?" Well, obviously not. We are then directed to the adjoining office for fine payment, We are quite annoyed about it all, but realise we will have to pay. We hand over the fine notice and wait with dread to find out how much we will have to pay. The lovely young lady behind the counter smiles very politely and says, "100 Kuna please". Has there been some mistranslation? I hear myself uttering yet again the 'Derbyshire War Cry'. "How much?"…".100 Kunas please". "So, how much is that then Jackie?" "12 euros". I stare. "Yes Adrian, 12 euros". The relief must have been written on our faces. I think the young lady mistook our reaction for horror and began apologising to us. What a let off that turned out to be.

Back at Belle, the clamp man arrived to take off the clamp and still apologising said "It's my job". He looked quite upset. It was then a young lady, who had just parked her car, came across to us and spoke to the guy, as he was removing the clamp. She then turned to us and in perfect English told us that she works at the tourist office and was appalled that the council treated tourists in this way. She then began to apologise as well.

We point out to her that the sign, which apparently says 'no parking', is just beyond our vision. On inspection, it has a picture of a lorry and a campervan on it and has a blue letter 'P'. We did not recognise this as 'NO PARKING', until consulting our table of international road signs. It was also located on a temporary road, marked out by concrete blocks and not that obvious because of where it has been situated. The lady was in agreement and said she would take it up with the warden's office. As we drive off, to the waves of the clamp man and the lady, we laugh with relief...12 euros? In Derby it could have been anything up to £250. Still, another lesson learnt, we will be more vigilant in future.

The drive to Rovinj took us through some very different countryside, with low lying hills, interspersed with an occasional glimpse of the sea. Some of the fields are starting to look quite parched here. From time to time, along the road we see people selling freshly picked cherries. They range from young children to old folk, some have just a table and chair to display the cherries, whilst others have elaborate kiosks. We just had to buy some. You get a big bag for a few Kuna. The cherries are huge and absolutely divine, being soft, juicy and so full of flavour. We both agree they are the best we had ever tasted.

Our campsite 'Amarin' is 3.5km outside Rovinj and has a water taxi into the old town, which is just across the bay. It is a big campsite, which can house six thousand people when full. We had a magnificent spot right on the beach, shaded by trees and with a wonderful view over to Rovinj. All this for sixteen euros a night, including electricity. The trees that shade us look like those we had seen in Spain, we now call them the 'Broccoli' trees. The facilities are very good and the toilets and showers very clean. The weather is now hot and sunny and will remain so for the next two months.

We are soon set up with our awning out and sun loungers and table, strategically placed to take in the stunning view. After the angst of the morning, it's nice to just sit and relax. We watch, as in front of us on the beach, there are children at play. It's amazing how tired one can get just watching these energetic young ones run around. Our sound track for the day is a buzz of leatherbacks or perhaps crickets, accompanied by waves lapping on the beach and kids playing. The sea must be nice and warm too, we could see lots of people enjoying themselves out there, playing games and swimming. Not for us today though, it's chill out time as we sip our G&T's.

During the course of the next morning, we have a nice chat with our neighbours, George and Rosie from Austria. They leave their caravan on site and come for a month at a time. Also, a young German guy called Franc popped his head in and asked if he could have a look at our van. He was interested in our rear layout and was very impressed. He had two very small children and as he and his wife travelled with their work, thought the layout would be ideal for them.

The boat trip over to Rovinj made for a pleasant change from our usual method of using local buses or trains. Rovinj is set out on a promontory of land, crowned with a church spire sitting on top of the hill. The spire is surrounded by terracotta roofed houses, five and six storey. All were brightly painted, lemon, red, salmon to a golden sand colour. The houses are interspersed with pencil pines, as they descend down to the sea and are built right onto the rocky seafront. It's all surrounded with that mirror finish sapphire blue sea. It was a very hot day, with a clear blue sky for a backdrop. It is a photographers dream and we and the other tourists were 'snap happy too'.

On arrival, the boat dispenses us on the harbour front at the foot of the town. We are greeted by street stalls, selling all sorts of bric-a-brac and objet-d'art, or to Jackie, hand-made jewellery and hand crafted items. We ascend to the church, along narrow cobbled streets and through arched alleyways. There are the usual shops, selling all sorts of touristy things. As it was so hot, Jackie was looking to buy something cooler to wear. She eventually managed to pick up three lovely linen dresses and decided to wear one straight away.

Still climbing the streets, we came across a rather unique café bar set outside on a narrow walkway, with very steep steps. There are cushions to sit on, on the steps as well as very low dark wood tables. It looks really inviting with overflowing pots of beautiful flowers. It's rather Turkish in effect and more importantly, shaded from the sun. The background music is 1930's blues/jazz, which adds to the ambiance. From where we sit, there is a nice view of a little courtyard at the bottom of the steps. We are soon served with our perfectly chilled pint of beer and an Aperol Spritzer... for guess who? Well, it is thirsty work, all this climbing.

At the top, by the church, the views over the bay to the small islands are quite something. We rest for a while taking it all in, before making our way back down. There are photo shoots around every corner as we descend. It all has a very laid back, lazy feel to it.

The harbour in contrast, is all hustle and bustle. After a brief walk round, we decide we are ready to eat. We spend some time perusing up and down, trying to decide which restaurant and what sort of prices we are prepared to pay. Then we spy one of my favourite dishes, 'Chateaubriand' (the best end fillet of steak for two people). The restaurant was right on the harbour front and had views of the boats and passing tourists. Oddly, we chose to have a bottle of Muscat white wine with our meal. We normally have a red when eating steak, but it was such a hot day, we thought that something cool and refreshing was required.

As everyone knows, when ordering steak you have the choice of how it is cooked to your liking. The four choices are usually; rare, medium-rare, medium and well-done, or five if you fall asleep at the BBQ like I have, then blackened and crispy comes to mind. Fortunately, both Jackie and I like our steak cooked rare to medium-rare. The problem arises when in the company of others, and having chosen the same cut of steak but cooked differently, there is always the risk that the chef gets it wrong, or the waiter switches the order round. In the past we have endured eating the tough well-done steaks of others, whilst we watch our companions tuck into ours and declare, "isn't this steak lovely and tender?" This can also apply to curries too, but at least when that happens you know about it. Hands up those who got the hot one by mistake! On this occasion our steaks were perfect.

During the meal we chatted to our waiter. He said the tourist trade was very important, as there was not a lot of other work by the coast. He lived inland and came to the coast for the tourist season. He was happy with life in Croatia as things were on the up, after all the turmoil of the wars. He also said that he hoped, as more countries joined the European Union, it would bring some stability to the region. I told him that he should invent a Croatian cocktail for tourists, as we were still drinking Aperol spritzers, which we associate with Italy.

As we waited at the harbour for our boat for the return trip to the campsite, we watched two sailing boats moor up. I muse to Jackie, "What a way to see the coast? "No" says Jackie, "it would have to be something far bigger, like a cruise liner".

I don't know if we were slightly merry by the time we caught the water taxi back to our campsite, but we got off at the wrong jetty. Thankfully, it was only a fifteen minute walk along the coast to the campsite and our pitch.

The next day, after a short drive along the coast, we were soon at Pula and at 'Camping Stoja'. We chose a good pitch, with views through the trees of the Adriatic Sea. The campsite was pleasant enough and the facilities were clean. I tried in vain to get satellite reception so we could watch TV, but it was a case of the swirling satellite dish again. We had managed to get reception in Italy. Little did we know, but we would not get satellite reception again until we reached Austria, much later on the tour.

It was at the same time we spotted another British motorhome close by, and a chap trying to put up his satellite dish. His was a manual set up that came out of a case, whereas mine was fixed on top of the van and had an auto search facility. I wandered over and advised him that I hadn't been able to get reception. He said it was the first time he had tried to use it and carried on with his set up. He was determined to get it working and would spend the next few days trying. He even left the campsite and set up on a hillside a few kilometres away, but to no avail. We both had the same satellite map, with a footprint of where we should get reception which included the northern part of Croatia. Anyway, it was not to be.

Michael and his wife Rita came from the Isle of Man. We invited them for drinks that evening but Michael was off to a concert, so we didn't get together until two days later, on the occasion of the Queens Diamond Jubilee. We decided that we would hold our own street party. Jackie made egg mayonnaise and cheese and onion sandwiches, crusts cut off, of course. She also made some scones and we had strawberry jam and cream to go with them. Soon Michael and Rita arrived with cucumber sandwiches, no crusts, cakes and biscuits. What a great British tea party it looked, all set out on our little tables under the awning. As we had no bunting to hang, Michael bought his Isle of Man flag to add a little decoration.

So there we were, sitting outside Belle enjoying our afternoon tea party, accompanied by Michael's cd of 'Music from the Proms'.   There were several toasts to the queen, throughout the day. For our grand finale, we stood for the Royal Anthem and a rousing Land of Hope and Glory. We created quite a spectacle for the passing onlookers, as we celebrated, as only the Brits do, and on this very special occasion, in Croatia. Michael and Rita are both retired and are touring Europe, but unlike us, they had no plans to stop and may still be out there now. The afternoon whiled away into evening and soon it was the end of another very memorable day.

Our visit into Pula, was made by a short bus ride into the centre. The town is situated on the coast. Its main claim to fame is its magnificent monuments from the Roman era, including an amphitheatre. We wandered around the streets for a while, finally arriving at the amphitheatre, which almost rivals the Coliseum in Rome for its grandeur. We take the time to visit the museum and walk around the interior structure. It always amazes us, how people built such impressive buildings, all those thousands of years ago. This one stands four tiers high, but sadly today the interior is almost hollow. You can however, still feel the haunting echoes of its past glory.

Back into the town, we pass through Roman arches, columns, and an intact Temple of Romae and Augustus. It's all very impressive and you can easily conjure up images of what it must have been like when it was home to the Byzantine fleet. Suddenly, we appear to have the streets almost to ourselves, obviously it's siesta time. We make our way up to the fortress on the hill and back down again, before having a rest and a beer in the main square.

We enjoyed our day in Pula and back on the bus we looked forward to an evening's entertainment with Rita and Michael. They would be staying at the campsite until their discount card from ACSI turned up, in the post. This was an essential item, as it is needed to get discount at most campsites. It was being sent from the Isle of Man, as they had forgotten to bring it with them. Unfortunately, they had already been waiting ten days for it to arrive. We said our fond farewells the following day, before setting off around the bay and south towards the Dalmatian coast.

The drive was to present us with some quite stunning views, as we pass through valleys with mountains either side. With creamy grey church spire villages perched on hillsides and roads that wind their way through. The countryside is green with forests and is also very rocky in places. The roads are very good and we have no problems with Belle negotiating them. Then we are out on the coast again, with magnificent vistas out to sea. We are by now quite high up on the coastal road, with views which go on for miles. The colours of the distant mountains are subtle shades of green blue, as they dip their feet in the sea.

After a few hour's drive, we are at our next stop for the night 'Medvej' camping, which is situated in a valley leading out to a bay. It was very picturesque, with its dramatic backdrop of tree covered sheer faced mountains. The following morning they would be capped with mist. The bay itself is set out to cater for tourists, having a small promenade, a few bars and sun loungers on the beach. The following day, we spend a pleasant morning exploring the bay, before setting off again.

We have a long drive ahead, as we make our journey to Senj, further down the coast. For the most part, the views out to sea will be blocked by the island of Krk and Rab. They look very barren islands and not that inviting to us. The roads are surprisingly good as we drive along the steep mountainsides. They offer some stunning views down to the towns, villages and coves along the way. We passed a few campsites situated right by the sea, so made our minds up to stay at one when we tire of the drive.

At Senj we found the campsite 'Skver' situated by the sea. It was not that big, similar to most of the aires. It consisted of a wine bar and several parking spaces along a quayside. In the next space to ours, was another Autotrail motorhome and as usual, we were soon talking to Colin and Sheila from Lancashire. They had had a puncture and were waiting for a guy from a nearby garage to arrive and repair it. Luckily, it had happened just as they arrived at the campsite.

After visiting Senj, which was a bit of a one street affair, we were soon back at Belle. We sat in our recliners, taking in the view out to sea and chatted to Colin and Sheila. They had by now had their tyre replaced, as it could not be repaired, but said the cost was comparable to the UK, so were happy. We spent a very entertaining evening with them and they gave us lots of tips, as they were on their way back from Dubrovnik, which was on our agenda. They advised us to go to Nin on the way, as it was Sheila's (not our sat nav lady) favourite place.

We are up and off the next day and on our way to Nin, near Zadar. The coastal road winds its way around stunning bays, up hills and down, around houses and harbours. It really is beautiful scenery, but we still have the view out to sea of the very barren islands, which after a while become a bit boring to look at. However, some of the little villages by the sea, with boats tied up alongside the houses, are picture book Adriatic. Soon our coast road becomes barren and edges closer to the sea. Eventually, we turn inland for a while and then over to our next chosen campsite.

As we approached the campsite, we spent a frustrating half hour trying to find the entrance to 'Zaton Camping', This was because the original road entrance is now closed. We have several attempts at finding the right road in, before finally succeeding. Zaton campsite is absolutely huge so we couldn't understand how we missed the main entrance. At reception, we are given several choices of camping pitch, by the sea, close to the sea or in the woods. After a quick inspection, we choose a space in the woods, as it is very quiet and well shaded. The pitches by the sea look cramped and there were lots of children, so lots of noise.

The facilities are very good, with both water and electric 'hook ups' to hand. We settle down for a relaxing afternoon and evening, before turning in. It's so tranquil; all you can hear is the rustle of the trees. About 3am, some young Swedish people arrive back at their van, which is parked a few metres off to our rear. They have obviously imbibed of the alcohol, if not more, because they proceed to laugh, debate and play music for the next three hours until sunrise. Not surprisingly, they did not appear for the whole of the next day. So much for the peace and quiet in the woods!

We of course are late to rise and it is past mid-day before we explore the camp and head for the beach. Camp Zaton is a holiday resort in itself, which also attracts visitors for the day. It really is a big complex, with water slides in the bay, pedalos and swimming pools. The beach is packed with people enjoying themselves, stretched out on sun loungers under parasols and the bucket and spade brigade. The sea is warm and shallow for quite a way out, ideal for kids. We walk the promenade and eventually stop at a bar under some trees, providing shade from the hot sun. We sit for an hour or so at the busy café bar that overlooked the beach and watched the children enjoying themselves on the waterslides.

That evening we walk into the small town of Nin. It is situated on a small island, joined to the mainland by a sandy coloured stone built causeway. The houses are all low lying and made from the same sandy coloured stone, with terracotta roof tiles. Trees and a church spire break up the landscape. There is a beautiful reflection in the almost mirror glass surface of the surrounding sea. The centre obviously caters for tourists and there are all manner of craft shops, cafés and restaurants. Some of the restaurants look like they are in residential gardens, with tables on the lawns and patios. All are family friendly.

It is not a very big island and takes only half an hour to explore just about everywhere. We are lucky enough to encounter a religious procession, which leads from a chapel to the tiny cathedral in the centre of the island. Small children walk ahead of the procession, sprinkling red and pink flower petals along the pathways. At the head of the procession and under a canopy, is the priest and his attendants, adorned in all their finery, along with various icons and relics. Finally, they reach the church, and hold a service in the street, amid much incantation and singing. We immerse ourselves in the moment, as all around us people are singing. There is definitely a raising of the spirit that even we feel part of.

After a while, we make our way to a restaurant, in one of the gardens. We are soon seated and drinking some of the local Plavac Mali red wine to accompany our steak, salad and chips. We chat away and also comment that we hadn't seen any Brits there. Well, knock us down with a feather, just then a couple with two young children arrive at the next table, chatting to each other in broad 'Derbyshire'. Tim and Kate, were from Netherheage, which is a village in the Derbyshire Peak District, just a short drive from where we used to live. Their children, Flora aged 7 and Eban aged 5, were so well behaved and very polite.

They were staying at the same campsite in one of the fixed tents, so after the meal, we all walked back together. It really was a lovely warm barmy evening and nice to stroll along chatting and laughing. They were interested to see Belle, as they thought they might like to have a motorhome in the future. So it was back to our place for a night cap. It's interesting to talk to children and typically Flora was more talkative than Eban, who was a bit shy. Flora told us what she was doing at school, about her new dress and the tattoo (a false one) of a dolphin, she had on her arm. They were leaving the next day, so we had to say goodbye that evening. What a coincidence and how nice it was to meet them, they were such a lovely family. That night in bed we reminisce about our family life and holidays with our two young children. You don't miss it until it's gone, because life is so full-on at the time. At the end silence reigns, no noise from the Swiss tonight!

What is amazing, and it's not a complaint at all, is that although we are having a great time and socialising now and again, it really does get exhausting. We are either travelling or sightseeing, which is exactly what we want to do, so when we rest up for a few days it seems like a real treat for us.

We had to walk for a good few minutes to get into the nearest village for the bus stop. It was early morning and the sun was already hot. The bus journey was fine and we arrived in the modern city of Zadar, where the large old town is situated on a partly walled peninsula.

Thankfully, the bus dropped us off close by the walls and so we only needed to walk across one of the many bridges into the old town. There are many different sized boats, dotted around the harbour, which runs along the land side of the peninsula. The first thing we notice is that the streets are paved with large polished stone tiles. The tightly packed three storey buildings are mostly light coloured sandstone, with different shades of yellow and pinks in between. Around every corner is a Romanesque building or church, with a history to tell. Also there are areas left in ruin, because of their historical interest. It's all interlaced with picturesque squares and extremely narrow side streets.

There is a hustle and bustle about the place, as tourists and locals go about their business. There are plenty of shops for us to peruse, as well as the historical sights. Down by the sea, at the tip of the peninsula, there is some type of underwater instrument, which is activated by the motion of the sea, pushing wind through pipes beneath the quay. The sound is both haunting and magical. There are sailing boats in the bay, breezing up and down, with their multi coloured sails. We take time to sit on one of the white painted wrought iron benches under the leaf laden trees and watch the world go by. It's all very relaxing, admiring the magnificent flower displays whilst listening to the melodic sea.

We went to find a nice shaded restaurant, as by this time it was very hot. Our fish meal was delicious and all was quaffed down with a crisp Muscadet, followed by coffee and Maraska liqueur, which is locally produced from maraschino cherries. Yes, life is hard work at times. We enjoyed the Maraska that much we had to stop and buy a bottle on the way back to the bus. Whilst in the shop, the young lady that served us gave Jackie a small trinket. A tiny turtle made from shells from the local beaches. It was given to us to bring good fortune. Zadar is definitely our sort of town and another of Croatia's gems.

Split is next on the itinerary. Split lies midway along the Dalmatian coast. Once again, the drive takes us along the twisting coast road, but this time, the views out to sea are of smaller scenic islands. Some look uninhabited, while others are crammed with houses from sea to summit, and look like they have come straight out of glossy holiday magazine photos. The Dalmatian coast is definitely the most scenic part of Croatia we will travel. It is at times like this, it reinforces our decision to take time out to travel on 'Our Big Adventure', it really is that good. We do the usual weekly shop at the ever famous Lidl along the way, as our provisions were running dangerously low.

The next campsite is 'Stobrec', which will prove to be one of our favourites, for many reasons. We have decided to relax for a few days, from our hectic pace. The campsite runs to the sea, but the pitches by the beach are all taken, so we take one which offers some much needed shade. That evening, we talk to a lovely Dutch couple, Hilda and Ed who are in their caravan on the next pitch. They kindly invite me watch their telly, as the European Championships have just started. That night, the campsite is alive with the sound of football from the many German motorhomes, as their team is first to play.

As we awake next morning and look out through the window, I spy a motorhome leaving a pitch on the beach front. Even before Jackie is decently dressed, I have moved us to the seaside pitch. We now look straight out across the beach and out to sea. Ok, the sparse sandy beach is a bit gritty and has grass growing out of it, but we have a view of the bay, with a harbour and the town to one side. Perfect.

As we were finishing off our breakfast, out on the 'patio' (we have plastic matting down, loungers, table and fully extended awning), a very nice Brit couple stop for a chat, Louise and Graham. After an hours banter, we arranged to meet up that night at theirs. In the meantime, another Brit motorhome pulled in at the back of us. Pauline and Colin came from Beverly in Hull. No sooner were they parked up, than we spent another pleasant few hours chatting to them. We also exchanged pleasantries with the French couple, Francois and Bridget who were next to us. They, like us, had sold their house and were out travelling around until they grow tired of it. It was their second year out. They had found an aire in France which is open all year and wintered there for free of charge. It was ideal for them as it was in close proximity to their families.

As planned, the day was finished off with drinks and nibbles around at Louise and Graham's. Graham is a keen amateur photographer and had just bought a Fuji X100 which is a retro replica of a camera dating back to the 1960's. It reminded me of my old Zenith E SLR, from the same time period. In those days, you manually focused and had a dial you turned to get the lighting and shutter speed correct. You had to pay for each roll of film and for the development and prints. Great care was taken in using this expensive medium and 12, 24, or 36 shots was usually your lot for a two week holiday, perhaps 72 if you were well off. Then there was the disappointment with the results. "Who's thumb is that?" "Try to focus next time". "Where has the image gone?" and "Where did he come from?" Thank goodness for digital, snap to your heart's content and delete the rubbish.

The following morning, our French neighbours, Francois and Bridget, left their pitch. Before leaving they gave us the remaining 8 hours of 24 hours internet access they had purchased at the camp shop. How nice was that? Colin and Pauline immediately pulled in next to us, so they had a prime position looking out to sea as well.

The area that surrounded the campsite wasn't really that nice, but everyone seemed happy and courteous. We had to walk down a rough, litter strewn pathway to the main road and bus stop, but it all felt very safe.

Split is another fine Croatian city, littered with Roman relics and ruins. Some have been incorporated into other buildings, but the echoes of the past are still there. The harbour is quite large and active, industrial in parts. In the old town, we walk around the splendour of Diocletian's Palace. There are many Renaissance buildings and squares to visit, in one of which, we take shelter from the sun and have a beer or two. Later Jackie eyed up a shop selling Pandora jewellery and we were soon inside. Here she bought a couple of charms for her bracelet, one had amethyst stones in it, which apparently are very popular gemstone in Croatia. We wander the narrow cobbled streets back to the bus stop and home early as England were playing that night. We had seen that there was a wide screen TV in the site restaurant/bar, which is where I thought I would go to watch the match.

Later, as I walked to the campsite bar to watch the match, I noticed a chap in front of me in shorts, t-shirt, sandals and socks, now that had to be a Brit. I quickened my pace and overtook him, as I knew seating places with a view of the telly were few, and that Jackie intended to join me later. Sure enough, I grabbed the last double seat facing the telly. The chap I passed came in just after and sat opposite me, craning his neck to watch the match. After a few minutes and feeling a bit of a rotter, I asked if he would like to sit next to me (not what you think!). That was it, Danny came over and we began to chat. What a great guy.

By the end of the evening we had been joined by Jackie and also Danny's wife, Jackie. They came from Macclesfield and had both retired early. Danny was getting over his younger brother's sudden death from a heart attack. Tragically, Danny was out playing golf with him at the time. If ever we needed reassurance that we are doing the right thing by doing it NOW, there it was. This was what had prompted Danny and Jackie to retire early and to live their lives to the 'MAX'. They were such good fun and we had such a good laugh with them, which made up for the boring England match on the telly. To finish off, we went back to their place, which was also an Autotrail like ours, but a Cheyanne, which is a different model with a different layout. We were also joined by Colin and Pauline, who just happened to be wandering by.

We relaxed around Belle the next day, while Danny and Jackie went for a bike ride and Colin and Pauline went into Split. That evening we entertained Danny and Jackie and we had another evening of fun and laughter. They enlightened us on how they had toured India on a train with rats running around their feet. Their favourite all time place was Turkey.

It was during the nights frivolities, Danny and Jackie introduced us to the electronic mosquito zapper bat. We were experiencing our first few mossies here, so it had come up as a topic. The bat looks just like a plastic toy tennis racket, but has an electrified net, which when wafted about, will burn any mosquito in its path. They lent it to us to try that evening, amid much laughter, they pointed out that it was to be used for mosquitoes and not Jackie's bottom! It worked a treat in the pitch black, I heard one of the little blighters and began to wave the bat franticly to and fro, immediately there was a blue flame and a tsss. How satisfyingly good is that? The human bites back!

Next day, Danny and Jackie came over and said farewell as they were off to Dubrovnik for a few days. We gave them the bat back, in the hope that we could buy one somewhere on our travels. They also gave us several DVD's to watch, which was good, as we couldn't get anyth ng else on our little screen. Not that we are telly addicts, but it is sometimes just nice to tuck ourselves away and watch a good movie.

Pauline and Colin came over to apologise for nct making it to our revelries the night before. Pauline was a retired hairdresser, who had had a string of salons, earlier on in life. In conversation, she offered to put a colour on Jackie's hair. So, that afternoon, they went off looking fcr hair colourings and then got busy hairdressing on the patio. I tried to help get Colin's ipad and pc internet working again after it had died on him. We entered a time warp and before we knew it, it was evening again. Wow, Pauline had made such a good job of Jackie's hair. She looked a new woman.

After a relaxing walk around the bay, it was off next door for an evening meal, with Colin and Pauline. They invited us to join them for 'Tapas'. A gourmet delight greeted us. Parma ham sat on melon fans fcr starters, followed by marinated chicken, vegetable skewers, roast potatoes and finished off with chocolate marble cake, cheese and biscuits. It's amazing what you can rustle up in a motorhome.

During the course of the evening, they told us the story of how they became an item. It remains one of our most endearing experiences of the entire tour, a moving love story. All set against a barmy warm starry night overlooking the bay, with the moon casting a twinkling beam across the sea. Here goes.......

Colin was a widower, who had one son. Colin had tenderly cared for his wife during her 5 year illness, before she passed away. Pauline's wealthy husband had left her and their two daughters. Pauline immersed herself into her business life, running the chain of ladies hairdressing salons. By then they were both in their mid-50s and this is when they met. After a while, and because they were in love, Colin proposed to Pauline on one knee. Pauline was delighted, but needed time to think about it. Pauline was not known for making rash decisions and this, along with her past experience, was causing her to hesitate. So it dragged on, until Colin gave her an ultimatum, "Yes or no?" but still no answer. Colin decided it obviously wasn't meant to be and told Pauline that he wouldn't wait forever, as he knew only too well, that life is too short.

Of course, when he had gone out of her life, Pauline realised what the answer should have been. So she made enquiries via his son, as to where he had gone. He was in his apartment in Spain, so Pauline booked herself a flight and went out there to find him. Her heart pounding, she knocked on the door, only to be confronted by another attractive lady. She rushed away from the door with Colin shouting after her. He knew where she would be, as she had been there before with Colin. After a short search, he found her in tears, looking out to sea with a drink in hand.

He explained that he still loved her and that the lady meant nothing to him and was just filling the void left by Pauline. She flew home alone and thought hard and long about life and where it was going for her. Then, a few weeks later, she received a call from Colin and he sang these words to her over the phone "Put your sweet lips a little closer to the phone. Let's pretend that we're together all alone." Pauline's heart melted there and then and she said "Yes."

At this point Colin sang for us the rest of the Jim Reeves song 'He'll have to go' as he played his acoustic guitar. They held hands across the table. To say there was not a dry eye around the table is putting it mildly.

They had been married for twelve years and are still very much in love. Pauline said it was the best thing she had ever done as Colin was so kind and considerate, and had kept his promise to make her life a dream. So, they lived happily ever after (until they met us, that is). The stars were out that night over the bay and the magic woven by good company with a wonderful story to tell, eventually came to end, but we will never forget it.

After giving Belle a wash and a spring clean, we were on the road to Dubrovnik. Once again, the scenery along the winding coastal road is stunningly beautiful. With mountains, pretty red roof villages, church spires, tiny coves and harbours. There were numerous fishing boats, pleasure boats and even more tiny islands. The blue sky and turquoise sea, all make up the rich tapestry for us to feast our eyes on. From straight, to hairpin bends, the road is sometimes so close to the water's edge and then a few miles on, high up above. This offers magnificent vistas as far as the eye can see. All is well maintained and we agree there is an Italian feel to the coastline.

As we approach Dubrovnik we pass high above the city. Our first campsite choice is called 'Kate', where we hope to meet up with Danny and Jackie again. Unfortunately, it is full. A convoy of French motorhomes had just arrived and there was no sight of Danny's. So we headed back to another campsite called 'Solitudo', which is closer to Dubrovnik and had thankfully, had plenty of parking places.

That night, I went to the local bar to watch Croatia play Ireland in the European Championships, while Jackie prepared our evening meal. I have quite an affinity with the Croatian national team, as two latter day Derby County star players came from here, Štimac and

Asanović. Back at Belle for the evening meal, we were joined by a rather scrawny looking female cat, who we fed some milk and pieces of pork steak. She stayed with us for the next day, as we relaxed around Belle, but kept disappearing with pieces of food we gave her. At one point, we were also joined by a black squirrel with tufty ears, in the tree above.

Rested and ready to see the sights of Dubrovnik, we made our way (by bus) into the city. We alight from the bus just outside the fortress walls. Dubrovnik is indeed the jewel of the Dalmatian coast. It has a wonderful old town centre, situated on a headland, that juts out into the sea. Its old fortification walls dominate the exterior and around by the harbour. Although there are signs of the recent war, it has all been rebuilt, to match exactly as before. The only give away, is that some of the stone looks new.

We enter through the Pile Gate, via a path which winds down from Brsalje. We pass over the beautifully gardened moat, with its flowering shrubs and cropped privet lined walkways, interspersed with trees. The main street is paved with large slab stones and made into patterns in places. You are greeted by the church of St Saviour and the fountain of Onofrio. Once again it's all made out of large sand coloured stone, some polished while others pieces are rough-hewn, all topped off with red/orange terracotta tiled roofs.

The place is alive with tourists and just as I am about to take a picture of the fountain, the Japanese teleport in again. Their guide appears with brolly aloft leading her entourage. The way they appear from nowhere is almost frightening. They proceed to block any chance of taking a picture, so we give up and decide to go back later. There is a loud babble of voices from the people perusing the shops, restaurants and bars. The main street is quite wide, but has narrow cobbled streets leading off, like arteries radiating in all directions. We take the time to explore these back streets, which are very rewarding in views and atmosphere. On one side, they lead upwards via shaded steps and the mountainside greenery can be glimpsed, through the gaps in the streets.

We pass by the Rectors Palace and the Church of St Blaise, situated around the main square. Finally, we arrive at the old port with its two piers, dominated by the huge fortress walls. It's a busy port, boats and yachts sailing in and out and a fabulous cruise liner anchored out in the bay. The sea is turquoise green. With the mountainous backdrop, it is breathtakingly beautiful.

We are soon seated at a table in the restaurant, which was amusingly named 'Arsenal'. It is situated within cloisters, with three huge open arches to one side, with views to the port and coast. Our table overlooked the bustling harbour. After aperitifs we opted for our main course, consisting of a seafood platter. The plate was piled high with mussels, large Adriatic prawns, langoustine, sea bass and swordfish, all on a bed of Swiss chard and potatoes. This represents just about every bit of sea food we both like. As we sat there drinking the wine and taking in the atmosphere, we feel very lucky to be doing this. What more could you want, good company, good food, wine and an eye candy view to die for.

We spent the next two days relaxing around Belle and exploring the area around the campsite. As I wanted to watch England one night, we found a bar in a complex, just a short walk from Belle. We had a good evenings banter with the locals over some beers and the match. We also discovered our pussycat friend had four kittens, which were living just across the road from us, in a utility building. That explained what she had been doing with the food. At one stage, they all ran over and went under our van. We gave them some milk and a few tit bits we had left over.

On our final night in Croatia, we went back into Dubrovnik for an evening meal. It's amazing how different a place looks at night, when it's all lit up by lights. It took on a whole different ambience in the warmth of the beautiful Adriatic and had that typical holiday feel. It was party time in town, as Croatia were playing their final match in the group stages of the European Championship. They would be knocked out if they did not win. Everybody was out and the bars and restaurants were crowded with people. We had a meal in the old town square. Every now and again we could hear loud ear-piercing cheers followed by low pitched groans, as the match progressed. Sadly, the party never got going, as Croatia lost the game. It was so sad to see the children, in their red and white shirts and painted faces, all looking unhappy. The adults were consoling themselves with a few more drinks and conversation over missed chances.

So, that was Croatia. This was the first country on our tour that we had never been to before. Some of the places we saw were akin to those in holiday magazines, and did not disappoint. In fact, some of the photographs of Croatia we had seen, did not do true justice the places we visited. The people were friendly and in the tourist areas, most spoke very good English. Our high expectations from the tour guides had been vindicated. Some of the coastal drives had been the best we had experienced, for both scenery and excitement, especially for Jackie. The Dalmatian coast is definitely near the top of our list of favourites. Also, as prices in Croatia are relatively cheap, including all the meals, we are back within budget.

Chapter Eight

Montenegro

June 19th - June 25th

Herceg-Novi – Budva -Ulcinj

We have to pass through Bosnia & Herzegovina to get to Montenegro. The check point on the coast road consists of some rudimentary porta cabins, but we are through in minutes. We pulled over on the roadside for lunch and took in the views over some tiny islands, lying just off the coast.

It's not long before we are waiting at the border post to enter Montenegro. We are asked to provide proof that we have motor insurance, which initially catches us off guard. It takes some time for us to produce the proof, by which time we have been taken out of the queue and off to the side, while we find the right documents. There is a bit of fun and games, as the guards only speak a little pigeon English and it takes time for us to understand which document they are after. It turned out that they wanted to see our green card.

Montenegro is a small country, nestling on the coast between Croatia and Albania. Our initial drive into Montenegro took us inland for a while and through a lush green valley, with mountain ranges either side. As we continue through we are once again a little apprehensive, as we are not sure what to expect, this being more new territory for us. The excitement level is raised in the cab, as we are also not sure how we will be received by the locals. We need not have worried though, although it is a bit raw in places, especially towards the Albanian border, the people prove to be extremely friendly.

To begin with, things look very much like Croatia and the first town we pass through has a beautifully landscaped roundabout and well built houses dotted up the hillside. Soon however, the roads became a bit uneven and things look a little more basic in appearance and less well-kept. We were heading for a campsite, which Jackie had found on-line, at a place called Zelinka, just outside Herceg-Novi. The countryside we pass through is undulating and very green, as we wind our way along the coastal road. We passed the campsite entrance, before realising it. We knew before we had gone too far, that we had missed it, so we quickly turned Belle around and glued our eyes to the roadside, looking for anything that looked remotely like a campsite entrance. It wasn't in your face, glaring at us, but we could see a small sign and a pathway, off to the right and presumed this to be it.

We pulled in and up the narrow path, to a small wooden hut. The shutters were closed and as there was no one about, we wondered what to do. Suddenly, an old chap appeared from a house further up the hill. With a big smile, he welcomed us, in what sounded like a German/English accent. He directed us up the hill to where we should park and then gave us a tour of the facilities, which were only just acceptable. It's a small campsite, very basic and only enough spaces for perhaps ten vehicles. The open air kitchen area didn't look at all hygienic, so we didn't venture anywhere near it. We are the only ones there and so are able to park in the prime spot, in the shade under an old oak tree. There were some hand painted plastic chairs and tables, which looked very 1960's, along with some open sided huts with facilities for backpackers to use, all a bit ramshackle. Undaunted and having our lovely motorhome to sit in, we quickly sort ourselves out and make our way down into the town, to reconnoitre and check out the surrounding area.

A couple of hundred yards down the road, we came to the beach area, with its grey concrete promenade. It is tree lined and provides shelter from the hot sunshine. There are a few families sunbathing and children playing in the sea. It all looks rather uninviting to us. On the opposite side of the road, there is a café and a few shops. I spot a bar with a fair sized flat screen TV. England were due to play the Ukraine that night, so that was the evening's entertainment sorted out.

When we arrived back at the campsite, there is a tent pitched close to Belle, an old bike rested against a tree and a young chap was sitting on the grass. We are soon chatting away to Sacha. He was tall, very tanned and with his curly black hair, he was indeed a very handsome lad. He was Swiss and spoke excellent English, with a French accent. He is only twenty years old and I can tell right from the start, that Jackie wanted to mother him, as he looks very like our own son, Howard. He is travelling alone and has cycled all the way from Switzerland. He hoped to get as far as Greece, where he would then take a boat to Italy and then a train back home to Geneva. His bike was old and well used, but this is a deliberate choice so no one will want to take it. We are well impressed with his endeavour, already having cycled over the Dolomites. He loved to ride up the winding mountain roads and enjoyed the peace and tranquillity of the surroundings. He said the flat roads were boring for him. He was very thin and looked as if he could do with a good meal, so we invited him to join us for evening dinner, to which he eagerly accepted. We enjoyed his company and although we only had a stir fry meal, it was tasty and hot and filled our hungry tummies. Unfortunately, during the meal, we were all well and truly assaulted by mosquitoes. The site was alive with them.

We all made sure that we put on plenty of repellent before venturing out for the evening.

Later, Sacha joined us at the bar with the locals, who thankfully were also watching the England match. We had a lovely evening, hearing more of Sasha's adventures and escapades. He had camped in woods and had been served wild mushrooms, by the locals in the Croatian mountains. Naturally, as he lived in Switzerland with his family, he had an affinity with mountains. We could only marvel at his bravery, as we would have been petrified at some of the things he had done, and all on his own too. We enquired if his mother was worried that he was out here alone. He said not at all, as the whole family are very adventurous and they had all been brought up that way. He admitted to being a bit of a loner, but liked Jackie's motherly attention all the same. It was a good night with a few beers and England won the match.

The first thing we did when we got back to Belle was to carry out a thorough inspection for mossies, before we could even consider going to sleep. We thought we had done a good job at zapping a few, but they still managed to get us. We felt safe enough security wise, to have the windows ajar and our mosquito blinds down that night. It was incredibly hot at night as well as in the day, so we really needed the fresh air.

After breakfast under the oak tree with Sacha, we said our goodbyes and off he went on his bike. His bike was laden with his belongings and camping gear to the front and rear. We hoped to meet him further along the way, as our routes, in theory, should pass. Despite the mosquitos, we decided to stay another day and catch the bus into Herceg-Novi. As we travelled along the roads on the bus, we noticed there are no pavements and quite a bit of rubbish here and there. Most of the cars are old and some of the houses are in a poor state and very run down. Herceg-Novi was pleasant enough seaside town, with some up market areas. We walked through the old town and down a hill to the promenade, which looked newly laid out with paving stones. There were lots of people in the sea and sunbathers lying on grey concrete bathing platforms.

Before heading back, we had a beer on a sun terrace outside a relatively posh hotel, with a view of the clear blue sea. It was here, a rather drunk Swedish man, plonked himself down beside us with a "Do you mind if I join you?" He introduced himself as Ulf. At first we thought he wanted a free drink and were not sure what to make of him, as he was obviously well on his way. "You are English?" He promptly called over the waiter and ordered a drink and offered to buy us one. He rambled on in good English, regardless of whether we wanted to listen or not. He told us he used to be a sailor, but now owned his own taxi business in Sweden. He said he was retired and had just recovered from cancer. Apparently, we could have a free taxi any time we liked, provided we were in his home town in Sweden "hic!" He said he was holidaying with his second wife, but that she had gone up to their hotel room for a rest. More like worse for wear we assumed. "She's a lot younger than me", he slurred. They had both been drinking since their arrival that morning. I daren't ask what time that was. At one point he asked for my hand, as he said he was a medium. I told him that Jackie was too, as it said so in her undies. Not sure if he got the joke. He proceeded to read my palm. "You have a short life line" (that cheered me up no end), so to get my own back, I told him that my mum had a life line just the same and that she is eighty seven. After another round of drinks, we managed to politely excuse ourselves. Ulf declared he was off to bed, after "just one more waiter please… hic!"

We decided to walk back to the campsite along the coastal path, which the campsite owner had explained we could do. It was so hot, we couldn't resist the temptation to dip our feet in the sea. We passed some lovely beachside houses, apartments, hotels and coves, but all were shingle beaches. Hundreds of people were out soaking up the sun and swimming in the sea. The seaside cacophony of noise and the background of lapping waves was delightful. It was a very pleasant and relaxing walk back along the coast, with plenty of interesting things to see.

Back at the campsite, we had been joined by three groups of people, in varying modes of transport, from all over the globe. One couple in a small camper, were from Munich, another couple on a motorbike were from Canada and another young couple with two small children, who were in a camper and hailed from Melbourne, Australia. All these interesting people travelling around, taking time out to explore Europe, it's just amazing.

Our next port of call was 'Avala Campsite', in Budva, further along the coast. Some of the scenery we passed was absolutely beautiful and parts of the drive were a real surprise. Trees laden with pink and white blossom lined the roadside. In places we were right by the inland sea, as the road wound its way round the hillsides and mountains. We passed little islands with monasteries and pleasure boats plying their trade, sailing to and fro and loaded with tourists.

By midday, the heat was creating a heat shimmer, as we stopped at the historic town of Kotor. Two huge cruise ships had just docked in the magnificent bay, as we arrived. The old town is surrounded by a mediaeval wall in grey stone, while the interior buildings are sand coloured, which is so typical of the region. Inside the wall, there are many shops, restaurants and picturesque squares. A twin towered church dates from 809AD and once again the Roman influence is everywhere. It is heaving with cosmopolitan hustle and bustle, as people of all nationalities disembark from the cruise ships.

As we journeyed on, we crossed over a range of mountains and then descended to some very flat countryside in a valley below, before nearing Budva, our final destination for the day. Our campsite was just on the outskirts of Budva and looked a bit intimidating at first, being made up of mainly old caravans, that frankly had seen better days. Quite a few looked as though they were permanent residents. We were put on an area of hard standing, close to the entrance and toilet facilities. Again, the standard was appalling and so only just useable. We had intended to stay on this site for two nights, but feeling a little uneasy, decided to stay for only one. The campsite staff were friendly and helpful and did speak some English. They gave us advice and directions for getting the bus into Budva.

Without wasting any time setting up, we were soon on the bus to the resort town and beach. After a short ride on a very old bus, which still had its original curtains and carpet, we alighted at the main bus station. The building looked old and tired, but functional and reminded us of Derby bus station, when we were children. Everything was very rudimentary and basic. Still, we were lucky, there was a tourist information desk. In fact it was a trestle table and was occupied by two very young girls. We asked one of them if she spoke English. Well, I felt like I had caught a rabbit in my headlights, her eyes nearly popped out and she froze. The other girl gave her a prod and said "Yes", "No", "Little". I asked for the directions to the beach and main town area. They talked among themselves, which gave the first girl time to gather her thoughts. She then produced a map and pointed out the way to go. I asked what time the last bus was. They both looked blankly at one another and gestured 'sorry don't understand'. They were lovely and it was all so genuinely innocent. They obviously don't get many English tourists at the bus station and we felt sorry for them, they were so taken aback. It was one of those instances we will remember forever. We gave our thanks and appreciation for trying. As we walked away they shouted "Have a nice day".

Prior to this, we had already decided that we needed a map of Montenegro, so as soon as we got to the first shop that sold maps, we were in and had bought one. Much to our amazement, the lady behind the counter spoke good English and told us the last bus was at ten. We then walked to the beach area, which was absolutely packed with sunbathers. It was a shingle beach again, with a promenade full of bars, restaurants and typical seaside amusements. The beach was covered with sun loungers and yellow and orange parasols up to the sea. We walked along the prom and into the old town first. The old town of Budva is another interesting historical place, based around a fortress situated on one side of a bay. Part of the harbour by the fortress was filled with a plethora of fabulous yachts, obviously owned by very wealthy people. Their expensive sports cars parked alongside each one. This was obviously the upmarket part of town, with people who like to flaunt it.

Further round the harbour, we came across the other place to be. It was full of bright lights, had music blaring and all types of fast food on offer. It reminded us of a tacky seaside resort, with all types of stalls selling balloons, windmills, buckets, spades and 'Kiss Me Quick' regalia. The stalls were festooned with the usual different coloured flashing light bulbs. Everyone was enjoying themselves, as were we, the atmosphere was a bit like that of a funfair. We found a nice beach side restaurant/bar, for the obligatory pint of beer and glass of wine. We tucked into a bowl of chips and sat for a while, with a view of the bay, as the pretty lights slowly illuminated the night sky. Children were still playing in huge sealed plastic bubbles, which allowed them to look as if they could walk on the water. By the time we had made our way around the bay it had gone eleven, yet things were still going strong, with adults and children enjoying their holiday. As we had missed the last bus, we walked back up to the main road and hailed a taxi back to the campsite.

Our final destination in Montenegro was Ulcinj, close to the Albanian border. Sheila, our navigating assistant, was still doing a good job of keeping track of where we were going, but we also started to follow the map we bought. As we drove along the coast, the views were just as breathtakingly beautiful as before. We now could see small mosques in the villages along the way, as well as churhes. As we arrived in Ulcinj, we were surprised to see a Tourist Information Centre. The guy inside spoke English and gave us directions to a few campsites on the beach. We had at this point, only a vague idea that there were campsites on the beach road. This information had been given to us by fellow campers we met.

We chose camping Safari Beach, as it had free wifi and a restaurant/bar facility, all fairly new. We were met at the gate by a chap on a scooter, who turned out to be the owner. He spoke perfect English and gave us a guided tour of the campsite. He was very keen that we gave his site a good review, as he hoped more tourists would come to Montenegro and see it as a friendly camping destination. It got our vote immediately. The toilet facilities were spotlessly clean, having an attendant in full-time residence on the site. We were soon parked up under the trees, close to the wifi at reception, with a nice view of the beach and sea. This was to be our base for the next three days.

Our immediate neighbour was a German lady named Sonja, from Stuttgart. She was in her early forties and touring on her own, in a very small converted estate car. She was a Social Worker and was just coming back from her second trip to Albania, a country which she loved. Also close by, in a VW camper, were a young couple, Simon a Web Designer from London and Cynthia, a Project Manager from Keighley, in Yorkshire. They were keen sport climbers, who scaled high mountains, pre-plugged with brackets for climbing.

We all met up that evening for drinks at ours, as usual, chatting until the small hours of the morning. Sonja said she had found Albania very safe and friendly and gave us directions to two campsites, along our planned route. This bit of information and her positive description of Albania, gave us confidence for the next stage of our journey.

Simon and Cynthia had also travelled through Albania, on their way back from Greece. They advised that we must go to a place called Meteora in Greece, where monasteries have been built on cliff tops, a rare sight to be seen. They also recommended a beach paradise, on Sythonia, in Greece. Both would prove to be excellent recommendations. Simon and Cynthia were out touring until August, then off to tour South America for a few months, before going back to work. They had previously lived in Geneva for a while, where Simon worked in IT and Cynthia cleaned chalets, to support their snowboarding activities. They emailed a pdf of a brochure, with details of campsites in the Balkans, which was to prove very useful to us. (See appendix i) They were great company, as was Sonja, so another entertaining evening was had by all. As ever, we are transfixed by people's stories and just how adventurous and brave some folk are.

While we were on this site, we were lucky enough to witness a traditional Montenegrin wedding. We awoke one day, to find the extensive bar/restaurant facility, being decked out in full dinner service. From glassware that held pink napkins and white linen tablecloths, to white linen covered chairs that had pink ribbon tied in huge bows across the back of each one. It looked totally different to when we had been in there the day before.

We had by now befriended the young lady at reception, Monika, a local girl who spoke many languages. She gave us all the gen on what was about to happen. The bride and her attendants would arrive early in the morning and would be quickly ushered into a wooden chalet. The chalet was across from our pitch and just a few metres from the beautifully decorated restaurant.

Apparently, the bride's family, who were from Ulcinj, would arrive first and while she was getting ready in the chalet, gifts would be brought over one by one, by the guests. Then later, the groom, who came from the city of Podgorica, would arrive with his best man and they would join the bride's family for a meal, dancing and festivities. Post party and at whatever time he was ready, usually some point in the afternoon, he would make his way over to the chalet to his awaiting bride. He would then escort her to a waiting limousine, which would take them both back to his home town, where they would meet with his family. The marriage service would then take place in the church, followed by a meal and festivities for his friends and relatives only. It all sounded so different to a marriage in the UK, so we were really looking forward to seeing it.

Around 11am, friends and family began to arrive. This was all taking place right in front of us. We set up a row of chairs in front of Belle. Jackie, Monika, the campsite cleaning lady and her daughter (such lovely people, very poor though), were all enjoying having a prime view of this very special occasion. Over in the restaurant, the party was soon in full swing, with around a hundred wedding guests. The men wore trousers or jeans and smart shirts, no ties or jackets (it was too hot). In total contrast, the ladies were all in the latest fashion, very elegant dresses and four inch heels. The music had an eastern sound to it and people were dancing in pairs, or in a circle, with their hands joined in the air. There was a steady procession of guests walking over to the chalet, with gifts to give to the bride.

During a lull in visitors to the chalet, Jackie asked Monika to enquire if she could see the bride. Jackie was allowed a quick peek and reported back that she looked absolutely stunning, lying on a bed, in her white wedding gown and crystal jewellery. However, she did not know how the bride could survive the heat, it was devilishly hot in the chalet and she was in there a very long time. She was attended by several other ladies, who were probably her close family. Then eventually, around 3.00pm, the groom and best man, who were both wearing a suit and tie, came to collect the bride. She was whisked away by her husband and into a big black limousine. Within a couple of hours, all the guests had left too. I have to comment, that nearly all of the young ladies we saw, looked absolutely stunning. Their outfits were very chic. With their dark skin, long dark hair, long legs and high heeled shoes, they would have made good models for any catwalk.

Jackie had learned from Monika, that the cleaning lady had eight children. Her husband worked away, while she had come to the site to work full-time, along with her youngest teenage daughter, Benjalrister. They lived on the site in a caravan and were fed all meals as part of their wages. The lady saw her husband and family twice a year at the most. The young girl had never been to school. She was only 17 and was proud to tell Jackie that she had a boyfriend. Jackie had to keep it a secret though, as her mother didn't know anything about it (nothing new here then!). He was one of the young waiters at the bar and she told Jackie that they had already kissed. Jackie said she was so young, sweet and innocent and very excited with her secret romance.

That evening we reflected on the lovely occasion we had the pleasure of witnessing. In celebration we made a meal of bangers, mash and peas, served 'al fresco'. We know how to live it up!

Most of the time at Safari Beach, we just relaxed reading books, swam in the warm sea and sunbathed. The beach was dark gritty sand, rather than the fine golden sand we prefer. It was also used by the locals, who parked their cars under the trees at the back of our campsite. They made their way across the site, with their children excitedly running by, clutching their buckets and spades. There was a pleasant breeze most days, which helped take away some of the intense heat.

We also had a new visitor one afternoon. A very active tortoise passed by our door. When I looked more closely in the woods behind us, there were several others pottering around. It was quite a little tortoise community. This particular tortoise was about 250mm long and looked almost exactly the same as the one I had as a pet, when I was a young boy. I was reminded of our school boy humour, with a story my friend Fred had told me.

A guy was sitting watching telly one night, when there was a knock at the door. He went to the door, but there was no one there, except a tortoise. He shut the door, sat back down, when suddenly there was another knock at the door. He opened the door; again there was only the tortoise. He was so angry, he kicked the tortoise as far as he could. Three months later there was another knock at the door. The same tortoise was looking up at him and said "What did you do that for?"

Well that was Montenegro, it had proved very interesting and in places just as pretty as Croatia. We could tell it was not as prosperous and living standards were quite basic. However, we had once again found the locals very friendly and eager for our custom. We had also felt very safe as we travelled along and didn't have any unnerving situations. The cost of living here had proved very good for the budget with a beer about £1.50 and food about 50% of the cost in the UK.

THE GENTLE GIANT

(Caring for the Newfoundland Dog)

by

Margaret Brazear

TABLE OF CONTENTS

Chapter Nine

Albania

June 25th - June 27th

Durrës – Karpen – Himare

Albania. We were both excited and also very apprehensive about our trip into the unknown. Quite a lot of our fellow campers had advised us not to come here. When asked why, most could not give a rational answer, other than it was a very poor country. Without exception, those voicing concern, had never been here. Sonja, our German friend from the last campsite, had given it a glowing report and she was a single lady, travelling on her own.

So, it was with a mixed bag of emotions that we neared the border. Luckily, the map we bought in Montenegro also had a map of Albania on the reverse. This now came into good use. Sheila was still keeping track of where we were, but quite a lot of detail was missing from her maps.

Albania had been under a strict Communist regime until 1990 and its recent history was one of economic collapse and political unrest. Of late, Albania had become part of Nato in 2009 and was currently applying to become part of the European Union. This gave us some comfort, that things were not that bad at the moment. Another concern was that we had been unable to get any Albanian currency. It was impossible for us to get the Lek in Derby, or along the way, which said quite a lot about the value of their money. Our last stop in Montenegro, had been to stock up with food and diesel, just in case we could not buy any in Albania.

As with Croatia and Montenegro, we would be following the coastal route, heading directly south and across the border into Greece.

Once across the border into Albania, our first impression of the villages we passed were reassuring. Some of the houses were quite lovely and there were quite a few people wandering about who all looked well dressed. The countryside was very green, with broken scrubland to the hill tops. We were a few miles inland at this point and the roads were quite well maintained.

At the first village we drove through, there was a funeral in progress, which blocked the main street. From the attire of those attending and the deceased's photograph displayed at the church, we got the impression he was quite a high ranking soldier. All the men had some part of their uniforms on and were wearing berets on their heads. Some of the older gentlemen looked in their sixties or seventies and many wore medals on their chests. They all saluted the photograph of the soldier as they passed by. At first we couldn't see any women, but a bit further down the road, we passed a group of elderly ladies, who had also obviously been in attendance. After about a fifteen minute wait, we were able to drive slowly through and both the men and the women nodded politely, as we passed.

We were pleasantly surprised at how well kept their little villages were, with tidy gardens full of flowers and neatly painted render to the two storey houses. Some of course were a bit run down, but on the whole, things were a lot better than we expected. We soon joined the main highway towards Tirana, the capital. The main highway was really busy, with all sorts of vehicles, from modern to clapped-out old heaps, making their way along.

We were passing through what appeared to be a flat central plain, with neat fields of crops and farm buildings dotted here and there. In the distance, we could see grey mountain ranges that ran either side of the highway. There was also a smattering of mosques, with their tall slender minarets, situated close to the villages. It added to the uniqueness of it all. One thing we did notice was that there was a petrol station every few miles. They all looked newly built and had perfectly landscaped entrance areas. In contrast, accompanying them here and there was what I can only describe as meat vending kiosks, or to you and me, the butchers shop. These kiosks were small one room constructions. Some had glass windows, while others had none, so offered no protection from the fumes and dirt to the exposed hanging meat. There were kebabs on sale too. The cooking areas were interspersed along the roadside and the produce sold from makeshift huts and tables, again all open to the elements. At one point, a young man appeared in the middle of the carriageway, waving a dead rabbit, in the hope that someone would stop and buy it from him. All these different sights were amazing, but didn't faze us. But then, just as we started to relax and settle back, we were suddenly confronted by a horse and cart coming towards us, on our side of the road. We, like everyone else, just skirted around them. The family riding up front on the cart didn't seem at all concerned. We decided from then on to expect anything and everything here.

We turned off the highway, to our first port of call, Albania's second city and seaside resort of Durrës. We hoped that here, we would be able find somewhere to get some money. Amazingly, when we looked, Sheila had directions to the banks in this city.

Getting into Durrës was a bit nerve racking to say the least. We entered via an eight lane (four either side) concrete surfaced highway, which, as we neared the city, was bumper to bumper with traffic. The city itself seemed very hectic, full of hustle and bustle, many high rise blocks of flats and office buildings. The outer ring road of the city was a contrast of two halves. The city side was framed with elegant buildings, some upmarket car washes and garages. While the outer side, was a shanty town. It appeared the outer two lanes of the highway were for parking, or having your vehicle repaired. I had the feeling that if we stopped for any mechanical reason, it would be fixed in seconds, with the parts made there and then. It also reminded us of the streets in the industrial shanty towns of India, with swarms of people going about their business.

As we drove down the wide three lane boulevards into the main shopping area, we could see that random parking was also the norm here, both sides of the road were two vehicles deep in parts. The high rise blocks either side looked fairly new and well maintained. The wide pavements were full of shops that swelled with people. To one side and in between the buildings, we had a view of the seaside resort in full swing, packed with holidaymakers. You could actually hear people having fun over the noise of the traffic. Sheila soon had us double parked outside a bank. There was an ATM outside, so Jackie jumped out and soon returned with a bundle of Lek, no problem whatever.

We made our way out of the city and to our first campsite, just off the main highway. Boy, what a difference once you are off the main highway. It was a humpety, bumpety track, with a maximum speed for Belle of ten miles per hour. We were following the signs for Kavaje on the coast. Amazingly, some of the houses we passed on our way to the campsite were stunning, and would have dressed any wealthy country. We bumped our way down side roads and side streets, through the villages, following hand painted signposts to the campsite. At one point we began to ascend a mountainous hillside and pass through a ravine. We wondered where were we going and if there would actually be a campsite when we got there. We were getting rather worried by now. Then, just over the next rise, there was a stunning view of the coast and there was our campsite.

It looked idyllic. 'Camping Pa Emer' was only 15 euros per night, including electricity. The owner's house was on the hillside overlooking the campsite, and there were parking places all the way down to the beach. From the beach there was a wooden jetty, that lead out to a small island. The straw covered parking places on the beach were each framed by four white painted bamboo posts, supporting the roof. All had water and electric hook ups. It really did look tropical. However, the sand was still that earthy dense type we had seen elsewhere along this coast. We reversed in, so we had unrestricted views of the island and out to sea and more importantly, under cover from the intense heat.

The owner of the site was a young man from Tirana. He spoke perfect English and told us that he also owned a garden centre in Milan, Italy. His father lived full time in the house on the hillside and managed the campsite, while he worked away for most of the year. He was investing all the money he earned in Italy into the campsite and its facilities. He had built the jetty out to the island, which he was also constructing himself. The jetty was made out of huge rocks with a boardwalk to the island, which was in the shape of a horseshoe to harbour small boats. The small island had a bar, bamboo sunshades and a terraced seating area. He hoped to have it completed and fully operational for the next season.

The large chalet style house up on the hillside had been custom built on three levels from huge logs and had a wide veranda surrounding the top level. It looked Tyrolean. It would not have looked out of place if a cuckoo had popped its head out the door, or even a weather man and woman appeared on the veranda. There were rooms and apartments for holiday lets and it served as a fish restaurant in the evening. You could also buy fresh bread, 1€, each morning from the house. When we booked in we enquired what fish was on the menu. The elderly gentleman replied in French, as he spoke little English. It translated as, "Whatever I catch on the day!" There were roses and rhododendrons in full bloom all around the house. The shower facilities, which were also modern and clean, were a little further down the hill.

As we didn't fancy fish that evening, we decided to eat at the hotel on the hillside, next door to the campsite. The modern hotel had a long wooden terrace which overlooked the beach. The white wicker chairs and pristine linen covered tables looked the perfect place to eat. We had great views looking out to the island. When the waiter appeared with the menu, we just looked at each other, they only served fish. My main course was sea bass. Jackie chose the king prawns, which were on ice when they arrived. It was a delicious meal and we accompanied it with a bottle of Prosecco. We had to leave the veranda and our fabulous sunset, as by then, we were the main course for the mosquitos. We continued the meal at a table in the main restaurant, chatting to the owner of the hotel, who was also from Tirana. He told us that he had recently had the hotel built and that it was frequented by high ranking government officials. It certainly looked palatial with its marble floors, high ceiling and crystal chandeliers. We finished off with coffees and a shot of his homemade Grappa, which is one of my brother Keith's, favourite after dinner drinks. I asked if I could buy some to take back to Keith, as it tasted so good. As we were leaving he gave me a small bottleful as a parting gesture, refusing to accept any money for it.

The next morning about ten o'clock, there was a knock at the door and we were greeted by a young boy, pointing over to his mother. She was standing on the track holding onto a wheelbarrow which contained three boxes full of their own grown produce. He looked about eight or nine, was cleanly dressed in shorts and t-shirt and his mother looked in her late twenties. She was well dressed and had make up on to enhance her pretty face. She was still very attractive, but a hard life was taking its toll. Even though we didn't really need any fruit and veg, we bought some to show willing. The young mother charged us a few Lek, which worked out about sixty pence, for a bag full of vegetables. Then came one of those moments. As they were walking away, she sent the boy back with another bag full of plums, free of charge. We were absolutely floored by such kindness, from those who obviously had so little. After they had gone, we both sat down in silence for a while and felt very humbled.

We spent the next few days relaxing and exploring the surrounding beach and countryside. During the course of our stay, we had neighbours from Finland, Germany and Spain. There were also people staying in the chalets and rooms, back at the house. All were very friendly and spoke to us in passing. We watched farmers that still used horse and carts to collect crops. Sadly, a daunting sight to see, were the concrete bunkers, that blot the landscape, left as a reminder of the forty year reign of Communist leader Enver Hoxha. We will remember this campsite fondly, for its tropical views. Each night, we watched a spectacular sunset over the beautiful little island and couldn't believe this was actually in Albania.

We said our farewells and made our way down the rutted track and back out on to the highway. It was a while before we joined the concrete surfaced motorway. We heard a big scrape and a crunch as we mounted a big step up to the motorway. We stopped and checked it out, but nothing looked out of place. However, I had managed to damage the cables connecting the bike rack brake lights. This would not become apparent until we arrived in Athens, when someone pointed out that the lights were not working.

We were now heading for Vlore which is closer to the Greek border. Our last campsite was at a place called Himare, again situated on the coast. After a while, we left the motorway and were soon climbing up to a coastal mountain range. Cattle sat in the middle of the road and only ambled along when we tooted the horn. Hold onto your seat Jackie!

The drive to Hamare, was to prove one of the most spectacular and exciting. We passed through mountain gorges, James Bond style winding roads without barriers and sheer drops to the side. The road snaked down, then up, then down again, and on we went. The rockface was now more of a pale grey, and the mountainside dotted with parched shrubs. It was extremely barren in places, especially on some of the highest peaks. We thought we were very brave driving through such a mountainous area in a motorhome. Astonishingly, we weren't the only ones and we saw a holiday coach attempting to reach one of the summits. Jackie was more than relieved to see the ground starting to level out and Himare in the near distance. As we dropped into Himare, we could see it was situated in a wide bay with a sandy beach, wide promenade, restaurants and a hotel. It all looked very cosmopolitan at a distance.

We were scanning the roadside looking for the campsite. At the opposite end of the bay there it was, or was it? We parked on the seafront and walked over to the campsite sign, which said in big letters, 'Tents - Caravans – Camping Cars'. Well, there was definitely a campsite sign and tucked around the back of a house, were some tents. There was a small track, to one side of a makeshift bar area, which led to an olive grove and a few houses. Where could we park Belle then? We asked the guy behind the bar if he spoke English, which thankfully he did. He told us he was the manager and said there was parking for motorhomes, at the side. He then proceeded to show us the area under the trees, where we could stay for the night. The power supply was hanging from one of the trees and there was a tap by the road for water. What more could we want? "Is it safe here in the field," we asked? "Yes," he said with a chuckle, "not like London, here no one will bother you, here we are all friendly".

We miraculously manoeuvred Belle down the track into the uneven field and under the tree with the power supply. The guy told us he hoped to expand the area, as there was currently only room for two vehicles. We asked about the mosquitos, which we knew would be around in their thousands. He said they were about and we should take care He then went off, only to come back and spray the whole area for us. We quickly leapt inside Belle, as the spray smelt very toxic. He, of cause was oblivious and was wearing only a pair of shorts and flip flops!

That night we had pizza in a local beachfront restaurant and watched Spain play Portugal on a flat screen telly. It was all very civilised and just like being in any other southern European restaurant. We arrived around six o'clock, the place was empty. Suddenly, we had that 'scared chicken' feeling all over again, as none of the waiters could speak English. They were all young and we could tell they were reluctant to serve us, they giggled and teased each other over who would come to the table. Eventually, an older guy who looked like the manager came over and took our order. Initially, we asked for the 'Cow Steak' but that was apparently not available, as were several other of the more exotic choices on the menu. In the end it was pizza, pizza or pizza. So pizza it was! By about eight o'clock the place was full. Families piled in, having arrived in very smart off-road 4X4's and filled the place. We are not sure if this was because of the football, or just par for the course.

Later in the evening we relaxed in Belle and were soon fast asleep, until about two o'clock, when we awoke to hear voices outside. On investigation, it was some young people making their noisy way down the track, to the houses further along. After that slightly concerning incident, all went quiet, so we went back off to sleep for the rest of the night. Our morning showers were taken in the open air, in crudely built cubicles, in view of anyone else in the vicinity.

Sheila now decided there were no roads in the bottom corner of Albania, so we were totally reliant on our map. We were travelling towards Sarande and on to the Greek border. It looked like you could either travel around a river, which seemed would take us on a massive detour, or catch a ferry? We stopped at a petrol station and asked if there was indeed a ferry. We managed to make ourselves understood and were told there certainly was. So, onward to the ferry. Sure enough, there was the river, and there was the ferry. The ferry turned out to be a raft! There were large oil cans lashed together with wooden decking on top. This contraption was being pulled by a winch rope that crossed the river, using a motor either side. Oh dear, what should we do?

The raft was coming back from the other side with two big dumper lorries on, which gave me some confidence in the ability of the ferry (raft) to carry weight. But on the other hand, there was a German in his motorhome, who had pulled up next to us and said "I'm not going on that" and then left. "Oh err, Jackie what do you think? "Well, there's only us now and it's just carried those big lorries". So, we pulled on with a squeak and a fair bit of plank movement. Before setting off, I was asked to move over to one side because another van had pulled up to cross. Scary!

Suffice to say we crossed safely and it wasn't that wide a river anyway. The track that now presented itself was the worst we had to travel on in the whole of the second part of our tour. It was a very rutted track indeed, in places very wide and in others very narrow. We went wrong at a cross roads at one stage, having deliberated for ten minutes on which way we should go. No sooner had we started to go wrong, than an Albanian guy in painting and decorating overalls waved us down. He had been watching us from the garden of a house he was painting. "You're going the wrong way mate" he said. Now, I'm not very quick at times, but I could tell straight away it was not Albanian he was speaking. "Where are you from then?" I asked. "I worked in London for ten years." He replied. "Now I'm back home." We thanked him profusely, as we reversed and went off in the right direction. How bizarre. What are the chances of that?

So how did we find Albania? I can only say that we found the people very friendly. At times and in some of the more remote places, we notice that they stared at us. It is quite understandable, as we don't imagine they get that many British people in motorhomes travelling through. There was also a stark contrast, between the very poor and the wealthy. Crime wasn't visible and there was no graffiti. It surprised us how well kept the main roads were, compared to what we had been led to expect. Having said that, once you were off the main road, it was another matter altogether. There were some architecturally stunning buildings and the one major city we passed through, Durrës, looked to be thriving.

Jackie took one of my favourite pictures of the tour while we were in Durrës. It was of a car wash, which was totally empty of cars and people, except for two workers sitting outside on chairs watching the world go by. The sign above the entrance and above them was in English and read 'Non Stop Car Wash'!

Chapter Ten

Greece

June 28th - July 23rd

Igoumenitsa – Méteora – Delphi – Athens – Kavala – Alexandroupolis

At the time we pass through this beautiful country, it is in turmoil, due to overspending as part of the European Union. As with Spain, the national debt meant that public services are being cut back, causing unemployment and civil unrest. In particular, there was some resentment being aimed at Germany, where the terms of the tight Greek monetary policy, appeared to be originating from. We had heard of mass soup kitchens being deployed in Athens, to feed the unemployed, along with riots and demonstration's. But you have to keep these things in context, as the media goes on a 'news frenzy'. If you look hard enough, you will find there are food hand outs for the needy in most cities in the UK. As we crossed into Greece, the only immediate sign of the unrest was fresh graffiti advising "Germans go home" aside a swastika.

We cross the border with no problems and are soon making our way along the coast to our first stop, a port called Igoumenitsa and to 'Kalami Beach Camping'. The campsite was perched on a hillside, directly on the beach. The staff were, as always, very friendly and welcoming and they gave us a nice spot in the shade, overlooking the sea. We also have another win, as our young cycling friend Sacha whom we met in Montenegro, is staying here. We are soon all together again and listening to his cycling adventures through Albania and into Greece. He too loved Albania. He said people would offer him drinks and food as he stopped to take a rest along the roads. We are still overawed by the physical feat of pedalling over the mountainous roads, with his bike and camping gear. We spend a couple of nights relaxing here, before heading off again. Sacha was riding back into the port, to board the ferry back to Italy and then the train home to Switzerland.

The weather was extremely hot, as we wind our way through mountainous and somewhat barren countryside. We are driving inland for our next port of call, a place called Méteora. The roads are superb, and as with Spain, we can see where some of the Euro cash has been spent. Cynthia and Simon, the young couple we met in Montenegro, recommended a campsite called 'Vrachos Camping', at Kastraki. Several other of the motorhome fraternity, had also recommended the visit to Méteora, as a 'must see' for its monasteries that are perched on top of staggeringly high finger-like rocks. We leave the motorway (which cost 10 euros to traverse) and arrive in the village of Kastraki, and to the centrally located Campsite. The family run campsite was all very neatly laid out and the staff very helpful.

It took us no time to settle in and we were soon making our way to the camp shop where we bought a carton of Tzatziki, (creamy Greek yogurt, cucumber, garlic and mint) Greek bread, and a couple of ice cool Mythos beers. We sat out at one of the tables next to the shop and ate our improvised meal, under heavily laden vines, providing much needed cover from the sun. It's amazing how some of the simplest of meals, offer the most satisfaction at times. We chat to one of the bearded proprietors, who fill's us in on the bus times for the trip up to the monasteries and information on the local village.

That evening, we wandered into the village for a look around. The pretty village is surrounded by grey green mountains reaching to the skyline. It is basically a small two street affair. It is all subtly different and somehow very Greek, with an Orthodox box tower church and very typical white washed houses.

The next day finds us up and off early, to catch the bus for the ride up to the highest monastery, Mégalo. We decided we would walk back down, to take in the sites at our leisure, as there is supposed to be a 5km way marked track. We opted to do it early, before the midday sun is up. The little bus climbed higher and higher, seeming almost vertical in places. Well, to say the views that greet us are stunning is an understatement. To my mind, these monasteries perched in huge finger point rocks, should be classed as one of the wonders of the world. The rock formations themselves are quite unique. We marvel once again at man's engineering ingenuity, in constructing these magnificent buildings on top of such inaccessible pinnacles.

The panoramic view, from the 'Mégálo Méteorc' monastery on its sandstone towers, is a photographers dream. It dates from 1382 and at 623m, is the highest of several monasteries that sit on the surrounding tops. They can be visited and most people on our bus were doing so. As we walk back down the winding road to the village, the views just keep on coming, thank goodness for digital photography. Sadly, the way marked track did not exist for us 'none climbers'. On the other hand, if you are a goat, you would be absolutely fine. Having to walk the road, does not detract from the natural and manmade beauty that surrounds us. On some of the high rocks, we spot tiny dots, which turn out to be people, ascending the vertical rock faces.

The sun is well up as we slowly descend back into Méteora. By this time, we are both ready for a well-earned ice cool beer. We mull over what we have just seen and both agree, it is perhaps one of the most unique and stunning sights we have ever had the privilege of experiencing. It's worth repeating, that the rock formations in themselves, are something well worth seeing on their own. Then, with the added incredible sights of the monasteries on the tops, you truly have something that should have a place amongst the best sights in the world.

That evening we eat out at a roadside taverna. First we had deep fried feta cheese with spinach parcels, then for our main we had meat from an open spit roast. We marvelled at the chef, cooking the meat on the open flames, it was red hot from where we were sitting a few metres away. To this day we don't know how he coped with the heat. Thankfully, we were being cooled by a slight breeze. It was so nice for us to immerse ourselves in that unique Greek atmosphere, and while away another evening under the stars.

Our next destination was Delphi. Due to the distance, we would make one stop off at Stylida near Lamia. The road surfaces were smooth and the drive through the mountains and out onto the plain was pleasant enough. The plain reminded us of those in Spain, with mountains far in the distance. The land was being well tilled and there were fields full of different crops, including sunflowers. The roads on the plain were again very good to travel, and here and there they were lined with what looked like, an array of coloured rhododendrons. Our stay at 'Camping Interstation' at Stylida, was nothing special. The only thing of note was our unexpected evening's entertainment. This consisted of some young girls from the campsite, sitting around a CD player, singing and dancing their little hearts out. Typically, the young boys just ran amok, kicking a ball around.

The next day we were off to Delphi. We decided that on our way we would take a detour to visit the site of the battle of Thermopylae. A short drive from Lamía, and on the Athens road, stands a magnificent bronze statue of Leonidas. It is dedicated to the 300 Spartans, who fought here against the mighty Persian army, in 480BC. Situated around the monument, are plaques explaining what took place here. The only surprise is, that it is now somewhat inland, due to the silting of the Gulf of Corinth. The battle site was originally on the coast.

Onwards, our drive took us up into the mountains again, which gave some magnificent views along the way. The campsite 'Apollon' at Delphi was top notch, with clean modern toilets and showers, as well as a swimming pool and sun loungers. Our pitch gave us magnificent views, out over the Gulf of Corinth. However, Jackie did ask that I make sure the hand break was on and the wheels were chocked, as it was a steep drop from our terrace-top view. We were soon talking to and having drinks with the lovely lady next door, whose name was Pat. She had travelled from Athens alone, as her husband had had to fly back to the UK on business, returning a few days later. Pat was a retired policewoman from Truro. During her working life she had travelled the world, lecturing on safety and security. As you can imagine, Pat told us many interesting stories, without mentioning any names of course.

After spending the morning sunning ourselves around Belle and the pool, we set off for the Delphi site and museum, a short 3km and five euro taxi ride from the campsite. We had elected to go there later in the day, to avoid the 40° midday heat. We had been told by the campsite owner, that the historical site was open until 8pm. Unfortunately, he did not tell us the museum closed at 4pm, so we had to return the following day.

We passed through the new town of Dephi, which didn't look much of a place to visit, so we continued out to the ruin of the old city. It sits in a natural amphitheatre, high in the mountains and commands magnificent views of the access routes for miles. Delphi was not only the place where the Oracle could be consulted, to hear the words of the god Apollo, but also a centre of culture in its own right.

Slowly over the years in ancient Greece, Delphi became the mecca for people to visit and worship the gods. Each of the city states built their own temples on site, to out-do the others, and to ensure the good will of the gods for their town/city. These now form the ruins as a tribute to its former glory, with the Temple of Apollo as its centrepiece. This is backed by a stone amphitheatre and a stadium, hewn out of rock further up the mountainside. As one walks the paths and steps and ruined temples, it's easy to visualise the pomp and ceremony that must have accompanied the rites of worship to the gods. It's one of those places that leave you in awe of the sumptuousness, that must have represented extreme wealth to the mere mortals who visited.

The place still echoes in the mind, to the roar of the crowd, at the ancient games and through to the sacrifices and processions, as they progressed up the Sacred Way, with its 3,000 statues lining the road to Apollo's temple. One can easily imagine the giants of history stepping out from the pages, such as Agamemnon, Leonidas and Pericles, who must have all visited as part of the 'must see' place of its age. It truly is an incredible place, suffice to say, we were very impressed.

As we sat close by Apollo's temple, marvelling at one of the sights of ancient Greece, sipping our water, we were bought back to reality with a 'trump'. I was asking Jackie, did she think the water sluice running down the side of the steps was for water, sewerage, or perhaps even blood? Before she could answer, there was a loud and crisp retort, a fart echoed out through the air, one that even I would have been proud of! We both looked around, to see who and where it had come from. There were two angelic looking children sitting close by (our only immediate company), a little girl reading and a little boy listening intently. Both carried on regardless, as if nothing had happened. Jackie was quick off the mark and said, "obviously sewerage". The alternative, if you truly believe, perhaps Apollo himself was having a laugh at our expense!

The museum, which we visited the next day, is a treasure trove of ancient artefacts and another 'must' visit. We would recommend you visit after you have walked the site, as it tends to put some things you see in context to the site. Some of the intricate jewellery and ornaments defy modern day production, as do the bronze statues. You are left wondering, how they achieved such attention to detail, way back then.

And so on to Athens and a stop at 'Central' campsite, close to the heart of the city. Athens is like every other capital city, in that the traffic is extremely heavy. The trick, when you are new to somewhere, with either a car or motorhome, is to take it slow. This gives you time to take in the road signs and not approach junctions too quickly. If you get honked a few times, ignore them, you are more important. Good old Sheila took us straight to the site. We pitched Belle in the shade and the lady at reception gave us plenty of information about getting to the centre and seeing the sights. We relaxed for the rest of the day, as once again, we knew we would have to visit the Acropolis before the sun was at its most intense.

The bus into the centre was packed with people on their way to work, and we had to stand for the whole 25 minute ride. People looked quite affluent and relaxed, unlike the sensationalised media we had seen recently. We then caught the metro to the Acropolis and somehow managed to get off one stop too early. It was now 10am and already swelteringly hot and busy. Those pesky tourists must all be on the same page. The Acropolis represents the centre of culture and politics of Ancient Greece, and is perched on a hilltop that offers absolutely no shade whatsoever. It houses the Parthenon, a grand pillared temple to the goddess Athena. We slowly wind our way up to the top, fanning ourselves with our information brochures. Eventually, the spectacular panorama of the outlaying city with all its temples and theatres came into view. Even in a state of ruin, the temple of Athena is imposing, with its classical lines of pillars. It's easy to see where the rest of the world got its architectural influence from. Even the Romans copied and took the designs, wherever they went.

We try to make the most of our visit, but after half an hour the heat and sun are getting to us, as it is very exposed up there. So, we carefully made our way back down and across to the Acropolis museum, to see the treasures it holds and to make the most of its air conditioning! Walking around the museum does make one ponder, what it must have been like back then. Life for some must have been hard in the extreme. We are astounded at the craftwork and skill of the ancient designers, workmen and the labours it took to create such beauty and magnificence, in an age gone by. This is another place not to be missed, as it contributes to our understanding of the culture at that time.

Back out to reality, we amble into downtown Athens for a nice cool beer, while trying to stay in the shade. We are soon seated and partaking of our favourite pastime, people watching. Contrary to all the reports of civil unrest, we see none. The waiter tells us however, that tourism is down 60% for this time of year.

Once again, the pictures on our TV screens and the sensationalizing in the newspapers of civil unrest, have taken its toll. The tourist trade and people that support it are suffering accordingly. At times I think the media has a lot to answer for, in taking images and blowing them out of all proportion, for the sole reason of improving their ratings or revenue.

We spent the rest of the day window shopping and taking in the sites of Athens. While it is all very nice and littered with both the old and the new, we are a bit underwhelmed. Perhaps it was the heat that was making us lethargic. We had a meal at a taverna in the city. Jackie chose Moussaka and I chose Lamb stew. Both dishes were average and did not taste homemade, as described on the menu. We mosey on a bit more, but our batteries are almost flat, so later that afternoon we went back to Belle.

For us both, the Acropolis and Museum were well worth the effort, but the rest was disappointing. We had planned to stay another day in Athens and visit the National Museum, but we were both 'citied out'. We had had enough of headless/armless statues for one day (is there a museum of heads and arms somewhere?) and as said, the city held nothing special for us. We had also covered some miles, with little rest over the past few days, so we decided to make for the coast and some well-earned R&R. Athens would be as far south in Greece as we would go. Sadly, the Peloponnese would have to wait for another time.

Our journey now took us northeast past Lámia again and into Macedonia to Halkidiki. We planned to stay on the middle of Halkidiki's three fingers, Sithonia. Macedonia was the area where Alexander the Great came from and it fed my memory banks with images, as we passed through. Due to the distance we had to travel and the heat, we decided to use the motorways. It was to take three days, with two stops en route, as we wound our way along the coast, heading in the direction of Turkey. The scenery was as ever, green and mountainous, all very pleasing to the eye. The roads were fairly empty, which made for a very relaxing drive, with cruise control on and our music playing.

'Camping Venezuela' is just past Lámia and on the coast. It was a very nice area and we would have stayed longer, but we had to get on. The elderly lady, who looked after us, spoke very good English, having relayed to us that she had been on a student exchange to the UK when she was much younger. She said she had enjoyed herself immensely and would have loved to return, but felt too old to undertake the journey now. She was very sweet and softly spoken. We were both moved by how lovely this lady was.

The next part of our drive would see us pass Mount Olympus, the seat of the Gods. This is a chain of mountains 12km wide that imposes itself along the coastal road. The beautiful views were continuous and they reassert our reasons for being here. Our next campsite was situated close by, and called 'Agianis'. It was absolutely packed with caravans but we were lucky enough to get the last pitch. It had some nice facilities, a swimming pool and beach, but still remained quite basic.

The following day we passed through Thessaloniki and parked up to buy ourselves a second free-standing fan. We desperately needed one each, it was that hot. We also shopped at a local supermarket and a Lidl, to stock up for our stay on Sithonia. Thessaloniki is a big city and from what we could see, looked very nice, but we had had our fill of cities for a while, so did not stop. We rode along, music blaring as usual, as we made our way across Chalkidiki to the Sithonian peninsula. 'Camping Amenistis', is just past a place called Sarti. It had been recommended to us by a lovely young couple called Richard and Gemma, who we met along with their gorgeous little puppy Maisie, at the campsite in Igoumenitsa. They had been touring Greece for a few weeks and said it was the nicest beach they had been to. They were not wrong, as it turned out to be just what we were looking for.

We found the campsite, which was very large, jam packed with tents and vehicles and located in a smal very picturesque bay. We were lucky enough to catch someone just leaving a perfect well shaded pitch, with a view of the sea. How lucky are we? Our pitch was also on the quieter side of the site, in some woods and beneath palms. The younger generation were situated in the middle of the site, in 'tent city'. The other side of the site was very exposed, having no shade at all.

On our shaded side of the site, each pitch was surrounded by flowering shrubs with large fern and palm trees that provided cover and looked very tropical. Our pitch was just big enough to house Belle, with her awning out. The wonderful soft white sandy beach and warm turquoise blue sea nestled in a rugged bay, which al provided an idyllic panorama. The facilities were of a good standard and extensive, with several beach bars and shops. This was to be our home for the next seven days, to wind down and relax.

Our routine would be to get up late and have a relaxed breakfast, visit the shower block, then perhaps mosey over to the bar or taverna for a beer about mid-day. After this, we could do no more than relax by Belle till five, by which time the sun was past its hottest. We then took our chairs and parasol, the few yards to the beach, to swim/snorkel and sunbathe, till around seven. After that, back to Belle for our evening meal and drinks. Ahh....life can be hard work at times.....did I mention it was very very hot?

The resort itself was a mixture of both families and the young generation, all enjoying themselves with beach and bar activities. From volley ball to football, sand castles, buckets and spades. The sand sloped very gradually into the sea, so was safe for children. The bay formed a beautiful setting, with rocks either side. The beach was packed by day and the bars were packed by night. However, when we hit the beach at five, it was relatively quiet. One night, there was a rock group playing at the bar and the music and revelry went on until four in the morning. I had my first taste of fresh octopus at one of the on-site tavernas, it was delicious and not fishy at all.

One day, we were having intermittent problems with the electricity supply, as our fridge kept cutting out. This was to prove to be another caravan, using up several power points, to power its multitude of appliances and air conditioning unit. In the end, we had to switch to a power source a bit further away. It was at this time, there was a knock at our door and there stood a very attractive lady. In a distinctive Australian accent, she enquired if we had problems with the electricity. "Now funny you should ask that" I said, then went on to explain to her what had been happening. They switched source as well.

The lovely lady was Heather and her husband's name was Mili (Milavoy) and they lived in Sydney, Australia. We were soon chatting away and invited them round for an evening meal. They were both Serbian, but had lived and worked in Australia for 27 years. Mili was a very gentle person, who spoke no English at all, but could understand what we were saying, most of the time. Apparently, there is a big Serbian community in Sydney, which is why Mili had never fully learned English. He was seventy and must have been very handsome and dapper in his prime, not that he wasn't now of course. He was a traditional Serbian dance choreographer. Heather was quite a bit younger than Mili, slim and very attractive, with a very bubbly personality and translated for Mili all the time. Heather had her own mobile creperie business, back in Sydney.

Over the next few days and nights we were to get to know them quite well and had a lovely time together. They taught us some traditional Serbian eating and drinking customs and of course we tasted some lovely crepes and pancakes. I taught them how to say "Aye up me duck" and "Ooh eck", our Derbyshire slang. They had flown over from Sydney, to tour Europe and visit their families, who lived near Belgrade, Serbia. They had bought a motorhome in Germany, on a sale and return basis. This meant they could return the motorhome for a given price, subject to mileage, wear and tear. Their principal reason for visiting, was that Mili had retired and had a property in Belgrade, which they were renovating. They had to decide, whether they wanted to stay in Australia, or move back to Serbia. Heather left the decision to Mili, as she was happy to do either.

After seven days of relaxing we were ready to move on towards the Turkish border. Our first stop will be near Kavala. The scenery we pass through is once again rugged, with tracts of unkempt bush land interspersed with well-kept farm land. Occasional glimpses of the sea, with mountains for our landside backdrop. Well-kept roads wind their way through some beautiful countryside, with the occasional village nestling in the mountain valleys. Water sprayers are hard at work in the fields, keeping the crops green and irrigated. We pass the occasional whitewashed chapel, standing all on its own in the remotest of places. One minute we are snaking around the side of a huge lake and the next a tortoise is trundling crossing the road in front of us. Good job the roads are relatively traffic free. All this splendour adds to the rich tapestry of views, sounds and smells we take in, whilst we travel along with our windows down and the warm breeze airing out Belle.

We arrived at our next campsite near Kavala, called 'Batis Multiplex'. We would be staying for three days, as it was my birthday on the 19th. The reception staff spoke English and we were able to choose a nice shady pitch, one road back from the beach. The site was a mini resort in itself, having facilities that cater for all. They were quite modern and the site had shops, a beach-side bar and restaurant, disco, swimming pool and a lovely sandy beach, with parasols and sunbeds. The place was thronging with holiday makers, in their beach wear of tight trunks and skimpy bikinis. Oh how the young look so beautiful, if only they knew it.

We had just parked up and were doing the usual milling around the pitch, setting out our viewing platform, when a young couple with two children passed by and said hello. We chatted for a while, before inviting them round to ours for drinks that evening. Haval, Sazan and their small children, daughter Bravia, aged 7, and Valo, their son aged 4. The family lived in Sweden, having moved there from Kurdistan several years ago. They all had that healthy looking lightly tanned skin, very dark hair, and were very smiley people. They arrived later that evening, armed with plates of food, Turkish sausage, Haloumi cheese and Kurdish cucumber, something different for us to taste. Haval was a master diver and had his own successful business. He was also a hunter and had hunted bears in Lapland. Sazan was a lawyer, but had not worked since having their children. They were touring in a motorhome and had driven from Sweden to Kurdistan to visit family. They were now on their way back, taking the route we had just come through Albania and Croatia.

We gave the children some fake tattoos we had acquired from somewhere, I think a cereal packet springs to mind. They thought they were great, we are not sure if the parents did! Their children were very polite and so well behaved, it was a pleasure to chat with them, once they got over their initial shyness. We were having a great time, when about 11pm, an elderly lady came to the dividing hedge between the pitches and told us to "Shush". She was our neighbour from the tent next door. We were not making a lot of noise at all, only chatting and had no music playing, so continued on. However at 11.30pm, we had another more forceful "Shut up" which sounded quite rude, from the same lady. Haval said she looked very nasty and more to the point ugly. We all laughed at this and called it a day. People sitting chatting and laughing is the norm on a campsite and most have the rule of quiet after midnight, which we think is quite acceptable. Not to bother our neighbours again, we agree to meet at Haval and Sazan's motorhome the following night, which was just a few pitches away from ours.

Once again we had a great night feasting with this lovely family. Haval barbequed some very succulent beef and chicken on skewers, which they had bought from a butchers in Kavala that day. We took some potato wedges, spinach and feta parcels and fresh melon and orange segments. Sazan showed us photographs on her laptop, that they had taken from all over the world, of places they had been when they had travelled with Haval's work. Haval proudly showed us a photograph of him, with a huge bear he had shot.

They said they had chosen to live in Sweden, because it had one of the highest ratings for people who were satisfied with their lives and also it was one of the safest places to live. That evening we had no one telling us to shut up. In fact, there were others on the site making a right racket and then the site disco kicked in at midnight so the background music went on well into the night. We wondered if the lady from the tent went and told them all to be quiet as well. Haval, Sazan and the children left the next day, driving north east through Macedonia.

There are such interesting people out there, with such interesting lives. You need to get out on the road to experience it, it's just amazing. Mind you, you have to be the type that likes to chat to anyone and everyone. The knack is spotting the opportunity when it arrives. In talking to all types of people, you soon learn, you cannot judge a book by its cover. Also, we never really make the running and would never invade anyone's space. It all just happens casually, when people are passing or visa-versa. You can usually tell if people want to chat, many don't, they prefer their own company.

On the day of my birthday we visited Kavala, which is a town situated on the coast, and has a fortress that sits on a hillside overlooking the harbour. It is the place where St Paul first set foot in Europe. Latterly, it was occupied by the Turks from 1371 to 1912 and their influence can still be seen everywhere. There is also a statue to Mehmet Ali (1769-1849) who was born here and went on to become the Pasha of Egypt.

We caught the bus into the town and picked up a town map from the tourist information, before setting off to climb the streets to the fortress. The streets are narrow and winding, with closely packed terraced houses snuggling up to one another in whitewashed or pastel shades. Windows and balconies complete the hotchpotch and variety of build, heights and quality. We visit Mehmet's house and statue, then at the top of the hill, the walls of the fortress and the church. We finally take refuge from the hot sun, in a café bar. Sitting on the covered terrace, we are rewarded with a beautiful view of the town and harbour below.

Then like the Grand Old Duke of York, we wind our way back down again, for my birthday lunch in the harbour. The harbour has its own pleasing views of the town and fortress, along with the obligatory mixture of pleasure and fishing boats, of all shapes and sizes. Here we watch the ferry ply its trade to the Aegean islands, situated over the horizon out to sea.

My birthday meal was to be at a little harbour side taverna, which looked as though it was just about to close as we arrived. However, at the sign of customers, the owners were soon out and making a fuss of us. We eat out on the quayside, all on our own, as it was now 2.30pm and the place is deserted. The food was delicious, freshly prepared and home cooked. I had octopus, which this time was a hefty portion and still had all its suckers on. Jackie had one of the best moussaka's she had ever tasted. This was washed down with a couple of carafe's of nice crisp dry house white and followed with traditional honey balls for dessert, and ending with coffee and ouzo. A superb meal, and all for forty six euros. Whilst we were there I took calls from my mum and the family, all singing "Happy Birthday" down the phone. Another perfect day, apart from the fact, that I am another year older.

Up and off east, through Thrace to our last Greek campsite at Alexandroupolis. Here we will spend three days. It's another sweltering day with clear blue skies, which we are beginning to take for granted. Our journey takes us through lots of wheat, sunflower and vegetable fields, all very lush and green, stretching out across the landscape. Our final stopover will be Municipal Camping, which as the name suggests, is run by the municipal authorities, and so only ten euros a night. It is conveniently located, being just a twenty minute walk from the centre of Alexandroupolis. Unfortunately, our very large pitch has no shade at all, but this is made up for by the sea views.

Alexandroupolis was a poor fishing village, until it was built up by the Turks and named by them as, Dageadec (tree of life). It is really a two street town, with the main shopping street running parallel to the seafront shops, restaurants, promenade and beach. In the centre of the tiled promenade, there is a light house and water feature. Under the shady trees lining the walkway, you will find old men playing chess, draughts and other such games. Although this town is described as being 'a bit featureless' in the guide books, we quite liked the place and would go back. It's all a little laid back, with a slight ambience of hustle and bustle, in a funny sort of Greek way.

We while away a really enjoyable few days at 'Batis Municipal Camping', doing a bit of retail therapy, as the sales are definitely on here. We both treated ourselves to some designer sunglasses and I had my hair cut for seven euros. The first haircut I had had since before we left the UK. I told the lovely young lady not to take too much off, which must have translated into 'short back and sides'. Still, armed with my new shades, who cares? One evening, we strolled along the promenade and back along the long sandy beach. We just had to have kebabs twice (not on the same day) as they were so tasty. One was at a basic little back street café, which was always busy and a contrast to the surrounding large department stores. The other was at a very nice restaurant, overlooking the sea.

At the back street café, they cannot speak English and we have some fun with the ordering. My kebab arrives in a pitta, lukewarm with chunks of un-spiced meat (they are spiced in the UK). Jackie pointed to the spit roast, with traditional kebab meat on and asked for that one and also to include the spices. The old guy serving nodded and smiled, only to give Jackie exactly the same as the one I have. We never did manage to have the sliced kebab meat, perhaps it was just for show, rotating on its upright spit for effect. Still, at these prices, ten euros for two kebabs and four beers, who's complaining? The local thirst quenching beer is called 'Fix Hellas' and is quite nice too.

Our very final stop in Greece and not surprisingly, was to be at Lidl, to stock up with food and wine. Then we had to find a petrol station to fill up with diesel, as the prices of petrol in Turkey are reportedly very high.

So that was Greece. It had been a long time since we had last visited and had quite forgotten just how beautiful Greece and its people are. We had never been to the mainland before, and like many tourists with children, had only visited the island resorts. The country has such a wealth of history and we had to pinch ourselves at times. We were finally visiting some of the places we had only read about in books, where the legends of ancient history must have walked and lived. To top this off, the visits to Méteora and Delphi, are up there at the top of our tour highlights. Both these places took our breath away, for very different reasons. We saw none of the recently reported unrest and were always made more than welcome, wherever we went. Still, for us, Turkey beckons........

Chapter Eleven

Turkey

July 24th - July 29th

Selimpasa – Istanbul – Edirne

Turkey, another country we were yet to experience. We were so excited and really had no idea what to expect. As we came close to the river crossing and border, and despite the blazing sun beating down on us, the countryside is very lush and green. Before long, we could see large red Turkish flags flying from the top of very high flagpoles across the river, announcing our crossing from Greece into Turkey. We cross a long bridge over the river Turca, to get to the Turkish border control. There are armed guards present at the checkpoint, as we are now stepping outside of the European Union. This is much more akin to the old days of official border crossings. We had to purchase visa's to enable us to enter. They cost fifteen euro's each and we were efficiently dealt with by the border guards. We were quite taken aback, good English was politely spoken and they were very welcoming.

We will be following the E84 dual carriageway to Kesan and then the coast road at Terkirdag, to our first campsite near Silivri. Sheila is still doing a fine job, as we program in short distances at a time. We are heading towards two campsites shown on our ACSI program, on our lap top. Our journey this day will be quite a long one, there are very few campsites in Turkey, so this fact determines our travel time. The first thing we notice, is that the roads are less well maintained in places and a bit rough at times, with filled in pot holes. (just like the UK then).

The countryside we pass through is however, very pleasant, with well-tended fields. Sunflower fields abound, intermingled with other crops and farms. Every now and again, at the side of the road, we see small kiosks or trailers, with local farmers selling their fruit and veg. One we pass consists of two tractors, with pallets on the back, stacked with vegetables for sale. We can see terracotta roofed villages, dotted about the landscape, as we drive through the rolling hillsides. Beautiful Mosques, with their tall minarets and domes, all colours and sizes, appear along the way. The roads are quiet, very straight and stretch for miles into the distance, so cruise control is set at the usual 60mph and the miles seem to just whizz by, as we take in the different sights and sounds. Sometime later the sky clouded over and the weather turned pleasantly warm, rather than roasting hot.

As we near the coastal area, both buildings and traffic start to pick up. We then hit our first town, complete with ten, twelve and fifteen storey apartment blocks, each coloured in creams and whites, topped with terracotta. It all looks reasonably new and well maintained and quite wealthy. The little shopping centre is like any other you would encounter in Europe. As we head out of the area, the houses look quite 'European housing estate' in places, except most have balconies. The main difference here is the presence of Mosques instead of churches, some completely dominating the residential area. This will set the tone for the rest of the towns and cities we will pass through in Turkey.

As we travel along the coast, the traffic becomes heavier around the built up towns, villages and villas fronting the sea. Along an empty stretch of coast, we come across a sign for our first campsite, close to the town of Silivri. We had been traveling for quite some time and having decided not to stop en-route, we were both by now ready for a rest. We left the motorway, drove down a side road and then down a sign-posted track. Well, what a hovel greeted us, it was a cross between ramshackle and pigsty, with an array of small wooden buildings. There were a group of campervans off to one side, which was the only promising sight. We stopped at what appeared to be the office, a wooden affair with windows, built by men with no eye for asymmetric design. It could have been called a lean-to as it was leaning everywhere! The chap spoke no English, but soon found a man who did. He said they were full, but did have one space left which he showed me to. With one look, I said I would think about it. I pulled Belle into a parking spot by the entrance while we had a cup of tea and discussed our situation. What he had shown me was disgusting, as it was close to derelict buildings and wasteland. I decided that I would go and have a chat with the other campers. There were about ten vans parked up together in a cramped area and obviously no room for us. They were a mixture of Italian and French. I was greeted by an Italian gent, who told me in his broken English, they were all part of a group. While they were not happy with their surroundings, they were making the best of it, as they did not know of any other campsite close by, and of course, there is safety in numbers. He said that they had hired a bus to take them into Istanbul the following day and very kindly asked if we wished to join them.

Back at Belle, I explained all to Jackie, who said she had found another campsite on the map, not too far away from here. It was a bit closer to Istanbul, near a place called Selimpasa. "That's it then, we should go", I said. It was all a bit off putting at this place, to say the least. I went back out and told them all we were leaving, and with that, we were on our way.

We did have a bit of a jaunt, along small roads into the countryside, but thank goodness for ACSI, the next campsite was a gem. It restored our faith in Turkish campsites. It had a high wrought iron entrance gate, with two hexagonal buildings either side. The facilities were custom built and relatively new. We were greeted by an attractive lady, in her early thirties who spoke no English, but directed us to a book on a desk in her office. The book contained instructions in several different languages, including English, for everything we needed to know. Fresh bread was available to buy each morning.

The perimeter of the campsite was fenced and hedged, which gave a high screen to the site. There were newly planted trees, to give much needed shade in years to come. We were the only campervan on the site, which could house about a hundred. Our only company was a solitary tent, with a motorbike parked outside, with UK number plates. We chose our perfect pitch and parked up. With the awning out and relaxing with a cuppa, life was wonderful. As I looked around, I was strangely reminded of England, and felt quite at peace with the place. To one corner of the site, was a ploughed field, with a hedge and on the hill behind, a row of poplar trees. The colour of the greenery and soil looked very familiar as well. The site obviously was also a working farm.

Our fellow camper was John, from York, who was touring the world, having recently come out of the army. He was very tall and thin, with a slightly haunted look about him, and a gentle stillness of character. We chatted with him for some time over coffee, but had the feeling, he was happy in his own company. I had the feeling he had seen action in the army and was saddened by something, and was now looking for answers. His bike was a small Honda 125cc, that had an extra complete spare wheel attached, as apparently in India, he had had to abandon and sell another bike, for want of a spare tyre. He said he had been on tour for two years and was now making his way to eastern Turkey, and beyond. He had already visited Istanbul and gave us lots of tips and information. My lasting memory of John was of a tall chap on a small motorbike, heading off the next day, laden with all his gear. It all looked almost Vietnamese, except for his height.

Having had a good night's rest, the weather continued to be very pleasant and ideal for a bike ride. We took the bikes off the back of Belle, only to discover a flat tyre on Jackie's bike. After attempting to repair it for an hour, it turned out to be a faulty valve. So I elected to ride into Selempasa to get some money and a new valve. I pedalled away from our campsite and then free wheeled downhill, all very pleasant and easy going. The farmland still looked reasonably well kept and was obviously a very wealthy area. I passed several gated and walled villas, and one very large guarded estate.

Selempasa is a pleasant little town, with a mixture of five storey apartment blocks, a thriving shopping area, along with a mosque or two. There are a few cafés, all sporting elderly Turks with moustaches, drinking apple tea. No stereotypes here then! I first try and find a bike shop (armed with my Turkish traveller's guide). A security guard, outside a bank, directs me down a side street. The bike shop comprises a single window, with a door and a bell on a small street, along with several other shops. Across the road is a barber's shop, with a single chair occupied by a man having a shave. The other customers are all watching me as I arrive. It's obvious from my attire, height and colouring, that I am not one of the locals.

The bike shop is a cross between a workshop and second hand bike sales. There are all sorts of bike parts hanging off nails, randomly banged into the plaster walls, along with boxes and boxes full of used parts covering the floor. There are also a few well-used bikes stacked against a wall. It is open, but there is no one there. After waiting about for ten minutes, a guy in a wheelchair appeared and asked me what I am doing, he spoke a little English. It turns out he is a friend of the owner and has been phoned by the barber, to say there is someone acting suspiciously in the bike shop. Who me? We wait another twenty minutes, but no one turns up, so I decide to go back to the bank, to get some Turkish Lira. I return to the shop once more, before I go back to the campsite. There is still no-one in sight and the shop is still open!

The return journey, up and down the hilly roads, proves much more of a slog than on the way down. The sun is high up in the sky and although there is a breeze, it's extremely hot. I have to stop half way up one long hill, as I am wet through with sweat and out of puff, even with full electric assist. Back at Belle, I recount my story to Jackie and we marvel at how honest some places still are, where you can leave a shop unattended, with no fear of theft. I have also reconnoitred where the buses leave from and the times, as we have decided to travel into Istanbul by bus, the next day. Once in Istanbul, we plan on staying overnight in a hotel, as we know that the journey will take a good few hours, and there is a lot we want to see.

We are up very early the next day, to get our pre-arranged taxi, into Selimpasa. (15 minutes/13Turkish Lira) We then had to catch the bus to Yeni Bonar (2 hours/10TL each) then the metro (20 minutes/2TL each) into Askeray, one of the many suburbs of Istanbul, and then for our final leg of the journey, a fifteen minute tram ride into Sultanahmet, the main tourist centre of Istanbul. Amazingly, this all went like clockwork, with only a few minutes between each connection. This all sounds very clinical, but was fraught with excitement, as we cross from one means of transport to another. It is also very busy at the metro and the tram station, with people in a hurry to go about their business. In between the metro and tram, we called at a tourist information kiosk. Here we were given a map and information on where best to get a hotel and how much to pay.

Our first view of the absolutely huge metropolis of Istanbul, from our rickety old bus, is of many high rise apartment blocks, littering the undulating landscape. The bus is by now packed with people, like sardines in a tin, as it winds its way through very heavy traffic. It's all a bit rough around the edges, in a Turkish sort of way. For most, our fellow travellers look reasonably well dressed, attired for a hot day, although a few should have definitely washed under their armpits, before leaving home. The place looks incredibly busy, with hundreds of people in the streets and lots of cars, lorries and heavy vehicles on the roads. We have only one incident of Turkish 'man power' when a portly middle age man, pushed in front of Jackie to get on the tram.

Alighting from the tram at Sultanahmet, we are greeted by wide pavements, heaving with people of all nationalities, it really is over-crowded. Jackie did not use a handbag whilst we were travelling. For safety, I took my 'man bag' instead, which contained our passports and the DK tour guide. So, armed with our map, we proceeded to find a hotel for the night. After several hotel enquiries, we found the 'Arden Court Hotel' to our taste and price range and perfectly located, within walking distance of the sights we wanted to see. Our room was very nice, had air conditioning, boy did we need it. On the roof of the hotel, there was restaurant and bar, with far reaching views of the city. Out across Istanbul's rooftops, we could see the Bosphorus and the magnificent Haghia Sophia and Blue Mosque. After a quick catnap back in our room to recuperate from the journey, and a couple of ice cool beers on the roof terrace, we made our way down into the maze of streets below. We now drank in the sights and sounds of the city, in a more relaxed fashion. Our first impressions were good and we were not to be disillusioned as time went on. The atmosphere was all very eastern, captivating and seductive. It was just a short walk to the Haghia Sophia, Topkapi Palace, Hippodrome (well what's left of it) and the Blue Mosque.

Our first port of call was to be the alluring Topkapi Palace, which was home to the Sultans, from 1465 until 1853. With its four courtyards and various pavilions, it is truly a magnificent sight. It houses treasures and gifts from the past, as well as outfits worn by the royal family throughout the ages. From gold encrusted daggers, to shields and guns. Diamonds, rubies and emeralds, made up the most stunning of jewellery. One diamond was eighty six carat and shaped like a huge teardrop. The buildings abound with history. Some of the interior walls are covered with wonderful blue and white mosaic's and externally with gold. These sumptuous rooms were where the Sultan held court, war council's and met his ministers. There is a terrace overlooking the Golden Horn, where in mediaeval times, the fleet would set sail into the Bosphorus each year, to conquer and raid the Mediterranean. It also was home to his Harem, not just a place for keeping his many wives, but a place where he could be in private with his family. It reminded us in many ways of the Alhambra Palace in Spain. The Topkapi Palace is indeed a place to see, absolutely stunning with a mystical feel all of its own.

Next up was the Haghia Sophia, built in 537AD. Anybody who has been to St Peter's in Rome, will appreciate the similarities to the architecture of the magnificent dome, except this church now has four minarets, one on each corner and is now a Mosque. The dome is truly awe inspiring and a marvel to the ancient world. The galleries and mosaics reveal some of its Christian past glory. While the calligraphic roundels and applications to the walls and adornments, add Eastern promise. One cannot but help feel the mix of 'East meets West' in styles of worship.

Across from the Haghia Sophia, past a large feature fountain, that separates these fabulous structures, is the Blue Mosque. We pause by the fountain and draw breath, to review what we have just seen. We could hear the wailing of the call to prayer, and see throngs of people hurrying towards their place of worship. When you walk these historic places it always rakes up mixed feeling for the past. The blood soaked turmoil of war and lost sons and daughters, on which empires are built. The toil of the common man and woman, some in slavery, in raising these magnificent buildings and artefacts is unbelievable. To have lived in an age of hardship, where medical treatment could border on barbaric and sanitation was almost none existent. Finally, for the chosen few, living the life of opulence and luxury, built on the misery of others, which we mere mortals of today, can now walk and marvel at.

The Blue Mosque was built in 1609, another masterpiece of architectural design, but totally Eastern. It has six minarets which rival Mecca, most have four or less. We are greeted by the sight of men cleaning their feet at taps and basins along one of its walls, before entering. The whole of the building has a blue grey hue to it and the arabesque semi domes flow together, with their original stained glass windows. We arrive in the cloistered courtyard, just at the point of main prayer. Shoes litter the steps and men on prayer mats fill the courtyard, all facing one way. For westerners, this is a sight to behold and sadly for us, means we cannot enter the main part of the Mosque due to the service. The prankster in me thinks about moving a few pairs of shoes around, instead I chuckle to myself, at the thought of the mayhem.

To the side of the Blue Mosque and the Haghia Sophia, is the Byzantine Hippodrome. It is now just a couple of obelisks that used to adorn the centre of the chariot race arena. It was from here, that four horse statues were looted by fellow Christians and taken to Venice, where they are now on show in St Mark's museum. Today, the bronze replicas adorn the façade of the Basilica in St Mark's Square. It was this treacherous looting of the city of Constantinople (now Istanbul), a hundred years before the Turks arrived, that ensured it's downfall to the Ottomans. Its downfall was also due to the jealousy of the Pope in Rome, who refused to send any help during the siege in 1453, unless they renounced their Orthodox Christian way of prayer and adopt the Catholic way.

As we walk through the gardens where once the thundering races took place, you can still imagine the roar of expectant crowds, echoing through time. It is this sort of haunting magic of the past that Istanbul shares with Rome. This city held centre stage of the world, as Byzantine Constantinople took over from Rome, as the centre of the Roman Empire. Istanbul, so renamed by the Ottomans, turned it into the centre of their Empire and began their conquests west from here. These campaigns were to take them to the very walls of Vienna, before eventual defeat in the eighteenth century.

It is now late on, as we meander back into the ever busy streets. We passed the entrance to the Basilica Cisterns, which sadly, we had to miss visiting. These vast water caverns beneath the ground, looked truly amazing and were built to water the city, in times of siege. We just ran out of time and will have to visit another time. We wearily walk back to the hotel, for a well-earned rest, before going up to the rooftop restaurant for our evening meal. It was now 8.30pm and we were never told it was the feast of Ramadan. Muslim's fast from sunrise to sunset. As the sun had now set across the Bosphorus, the restaurant was now Ramadan full of hungry Muslims. The waiter politely told us we could come back at 10pm, but we decided to venture out and find another restaurant.

After wandering the streets, debating the value of this menu or that venue, we finally decide to go for one that provided us with a view. We chose to eat at another hotel that had a rooftop restaurant, from where, we had the most fabulous illuminated views of the Blue Mosque and Haghia Sophia. Unfortunately, the meal was very disappointing and probably explains the lack of other Muslim diners. The food looked good and was served by the maître d'hôtel, but lacked in both flavour and content. Wine was forty pounds a bottle for nothing special, so we gave it a miss. Still, the views and the atmospheric calling to prayer, made up for the meal.

We were up early again the next day, as we wanted to visit the bazaar quarter. Jackie hoped to buy a handmade Persian silk rug, something she has wanted for many years. We had to vacate our room at 12 noon, so that gave us a three hour window. Our map reading proved good again and we were soon in the Bazaar. Contrary to expectations and advice, we were not hassled over sales at all. The brightly coloured tiles covering the arched alley ways, along with the exquisite lighting, was a great surprise. We spent a very pleasant few hours, perusing the goods on sale and enjoying another highlight of our visit. We bought a lovely black and gold embroidered throw, depicting all sorts of eastern scenes, as well as two small hand painted dishes. No magic carpet though.

Just as we were about to leave the bazaar, we spotted another carpet shop. We had been in several by then, but all had proved too pricey for what we wanted. So, in we went and were soon sitting drinking apple tea and perusing the wares. The shop was festooned with carpets and we even sat on benches covered in them. The little tea table is covered in a richly coloured mosaic pattern and the tea cups and saucers are made of glass, decorated with gold foil. The young man was very keen to sell and Jackie finally spotted one she wanted. The haggling started.... £1200, £750, second apple tea, £500, (the guy calculated into pounds for us), another apple tea and my final offer £350. It looked exactly the same make and quality of silk, as those we had previously bartered for £550 elsewhere. "Ok then, that's a sale". "I'll just give it one more look over", says Jackie. Luckily she did, as there is a white mark amidst one of the patterns, not that easy to spot at first, but is definitely there. We asked if he had another one. He and his assistant then proceeded to turn the shop upside down, looking for that 'Magic Carpet'. Sadly, it's not to be found and much to the chagrin of the young man, we depart without our 'Magic Carpet' and have to walk back to the hotel instead.

One last thing to do on our agenda was to cross the Bosphorus into the true East and into Asia. We caught a tram and went across to the end of the line on the other side of the estuary, just to say we have been there. We alight for a photo shoot at the bridge, before a short ride and walk back to the hotel. Then its one last beer on the terrace before we depart for our journey back to Belle. So that was Istanbul. Seriously full of eastern promise, we loved it, and we will go back again one day. We both felt it was a very romantic place, which we only skimmed the surface of. We did manage to make two other purchases while we were there. One, a memento for me, a blue velvet flat fez type hat, with gold braid, no tassel though. The other a cd by Omar Faruk Teilbilek, entitled 'Sounds of Istanbul', traditional Turkish instrumental music. We are sipping apple tea, listening to the enchanting music and I am wearing my fez as we write this chapter. Ah, the memories.

Back at Belle, we spend a quiet day relaxing and reminiscing and catching up on a bit of housekeeping. Whilst strolling around the campsite, we watch as the lady owner and her little children sit in the sun on a big cream hessian sheet, sorting some type of large grain from the husks. Their lifestyle was fascinating. Despite being surrounded by modern day living, here was a young family carrying on traditions, put in place by their ancestors all those years ago. We were joined on the campsite by a few other caravans and camper vans but they were dotted about the site, their owners absent most of the time, no doubt visiting Istanbul.

On our departure the following day, we are bid farewell by the whole family who run the site, who assembled by the gates to see us off. They were unable to speak English, but had made us very welcome indeed, so we would highly recommend this site to anyone visiting Turkey. It must be popular at times, as there were pictures on the office wall, showing the site absolutely full.

For us, it was now time to do an about turn and in some ways, this marked the return leg of our journey. We were now headed northwest to the city of Edirne, on the river Tunca, close to the Greek and Bulgarian borders. We travelled along a modern three lane motorway, passing by some affluent looking towns and villages, and the obligatory mosques. Once again the countryside is surprisingly green with neatly tended fields.

Our final campsite in Turkey for one night is the 'Grand Amir', just a short bus ride into Edirne. It's all a bit basic, reasonably clean and is run by a German lady, who speaks good English. We did manage to use the facilities, but they were a bit dark and dingy, with rusty fittings. The bus into the town, is a small cream and blue vehicle, similar to a Sherpa van, seating about ten people. It is a bit rickety, basic and old. Still, it serves its purpose and soon drops us off outside the main mosque, in the University City centre. Edirne was once the capital of the Ottoman Empire, before the conquest of Constantinople and was also previously called Adrianople, after the Roman Emperor Hadrian. I'm sure you know this chap, besides having a jolly good name, he also built a wall somewhere in Britain.

The town is dominated by the Selimye mosque, which is situated atop a hilly street in the centre. This mosque was designed by Sinan, a famous Ottoman designer. Four minarets corner the large courtyard and the large dome is a work of art in itself. We enter through landscaped gardens and are soon in the courtyard. The cloisters in the courtyard are lined with grey concrete pillars, topped with red and cream arches, all decorated with ornate blue and gold circles and intricate patterns. At the entrance steps, we have to leave our shoes and Jackie has to cover her head and arms with a shawl.

The first thing you notice on entering is the low hanging central chandelier, about fifty feet in circumference and festooned with lights. The main floor is covered by a plush red and blue deep piled carpet. Looking up we admire the magnificent dome, with its circle of windows highlighting the blue/red patterns that surround the centre. All is supported by tiered arches, edged with an alternate red and cream brick-like design. We marvel at its Eastern influence, and yet in places, there is a similarity to our western architecture. The entrance to the Sultan's lodge inside the mosque, is supported by marble columns and bedecked with floral Iznik tiles. It's all very different from what we are used to and at times, we almost feel like intruders, viewing someone else's sacred belongings. Yet, at the same time we feel at ease, as other Turkish visitors go about their business and seem uninterested by our presence.

From there we wander around the exterior of the mosque and back through the gardens, to the Old Mosque, at the foot of the hill. By contrast, this has less ornate trappings, with its massive Arabic inscriptions, bedecking the walls. The dome is hexagonal on the inside and even more elaborately patterned than the Selimye mosque. The place has a raw Islamic feel to it. Outside its main entrance, we rest on a bench with shade provided by decorated cloisters. We sit in silence for a while and contemplate the world and its many religions. We reflect "If only we could all live in peace". At times, you would think Satan had given us all these different religions in the world, to divide us all. But in the end, it's only man and his intolerant, divisive ways that lead to problems.

Next up is a trip to the shops. We enter a single aisle type bazaar and purchase some apple tea from one of the vendors. Some of the women shoppers are dressed in various western styles, while others wear the hijab. It all feels very relaxed and there is a busy feel about the place. We stopped for a kebab at one of the street cafés, with its plastic tables and chairs and enjoy a pitta filled with well-cooked spicy meat. I have a glass of coke and Jackie has iced lemonade, no alcohol here. We sit and people watch for a while. We in turn are stared at. I think we are a bit of a novelty, in this neck of the woods.

That night at the campsite, we were accompanied by a group of scouts from Slovenia, who all seemed to be having a good time. The next morning we are off to Bulgaria. We make one final stop at a 'MMM Migros' supermarket before crossing the border. We are intrigued to see what a typical Turkish supermarket has to offer. Surprisingly, there is a good selection of food in the supermarket and we load the trolley up with fresh meat, fruit and vegetables. It is set out like any other Western supermarket with aisles of produce, some of which we weren't too sure was for consumption, as we couldn't read the labels. Even more typical these days, are the fast food chains, like 'Burger King' that sat alongside this supermarket.

Turkey has been a very pleasant experience. At all times we have felt safe and welcomed, in the land where East meets West. It deserves our support, as the country genuinely feels both religiously, and ethnically tolerant. It also appeared to have a thriving economy. We judge this by the standard of dress of the people, the condition of the property, and the age and condition of the cars. Also, some of the housing looks very British 'housing estate' in places, which was a surprise.

Our brief Turkish experience has really been another highlight of our tour so far. Istanbul is a gem. We promise ourselves we will come back, we liked it that much.

Chapter Twelve

Bulgaria

July 30th - August 1st

Plovdiv - Sofia

We crossed the border from Turkey into Bulgaria, with no problems, except that we have to buy a 'Vignette' (sticker) costing nine euros, so we can use the roads. These are obtained from little roadside establishments just past the border. We planned to make one stop at Plovdiv, then Sofia, following the main road all the way through to the Serbian border. The road started off as a dual carriageway, but soon became single lane, with quite heavy traffic in parts. The countryside changed and now consisted of low rolling hills, with trees forming hedgerows and a copse of woods here and there. The surrounding fields and countryside looked parched from the sun.

The first village we passed through looked very run down, with weeds on the kerbside and gravel covered pavements. The houses were a bit of a mismatch of sizes, types and building materials, many just made of grey breeze blocks. The side streets comprised either broken concrete or dirt track. The intervening farmland looked less well tended and rough and ragged at the edges. This would set the tone for most of the villages and countryside we passed through. Our first impressions were of a very poor country.

After about sixty miles we approached the outskirts of Plovdiv. The buildings change from predominantly two storey houses to five storey apartments and high rise accommodation.

We had searched the web for campsites, but could not find one listed until Sofia, the Bulgarian capital, which was another days' drive away. We had been given one address by John, the guy at our campsite in Turkey, but we managed to totally miss the signage on our way to Plovdiv. This left us with only one option, a hotel. So we drove around the centre seeking accommodation. We finally came upon the 'Park Hotel' which also had secure parking. We pulled into the secure parking and made our way to reception.

The lady at reception spoke perfect English and greeted us with a nice smile. We asked how much a room was. She advised that it was 110 euros, which was more than we had anticipated paying. We then explained we had a motorhome and asked if it would be safe in their secure car park. She obviously mis-understood us and said it would be ok for one night, if we wanted to stay in it. We had meant just to park it there. Well, what a bargain, 17 Bulgarian Lev (£9) and we had our secure accommodation for the night. She also gave us a map of the centre and told us where to visit.

We were able to walk into the old town centre, which is situated on and around three rocky hilltops. Some of the views are impressive, with the hills forming a nice back-drop to the buildings. The architecture is a mixture of Romanesque, Ottoman and modern day. We walk around the cobbled streets and pass the diamond patterned Dzhumaya mosque, churches and a well preserved Roman marble amphitheatre. Out on the main paved pedestrian street, in a galleried aperture, are the remains of a once huge Roman stadium. In its day it must have been an impressive sight to see.

This part of Plovdiv looks newly renovated and very pleasant, so we decide to find somewhere to eat. We are soon seated at the outside terrace of the 'Arena' restaurant. The two young ladies who serve on are very welcoming and speak a little English. The menu looks very interesting, so we ask what the traditional Bulgarian dish is. We are told chicken liver and heart with onions, accompanied by fried potatoes garlic and cheese. Jackie thought we should also order the spare ribs, just in case we don't like the traditional dish.

Next it's onto the drink. I spot champagne for 5 euros, so I ask, "Is that per glass?" No, it's for the bottle! So we order one. Yes, you've guessed, it's not champagne, but Bulgarian sparkling wine. It's called 'Iskra' and is very nice. The chicken heart and liver casserole is served in a hot skillet. We both agree it's very tasty and would choose the dish again. We are soon joined by lots of little kittens, all with different coloured fur. They knew they would get a feast from us, we love cats. Not wanting to feed them from the table we took some scraps over to a tree at the back of the restaurant. They are soon fed and licking their paws with gratitude.

To walk off the meal, we make our way to the main square which has a large fountain edged with lights that change colour. To cap the night off, we sat outside at one of the many street café bars and had a few cocktails. It was a lovely warm evening and there were a lot of people out enjoying themselves. Sadly, we ended our lovely evening with a difference of opinion, which was over nothing really. We put it down to the fact that I had too many black and white Russian cocktails and Jackie had too many mojito's. It was one of our full blown fall outs. We certainly wouldn't be repeating that again in a hurry. It soon blew over and we quietly put that one to bed.

The next day we are up and off to Sofia. We are all patched up from the night before, as we have a rule never to carry arguments over to the next day. We are taking the motorway, as the alternative routes look winding and we are not that impressed with the state of the minor roads, to say the least. The countryside between is fairly flat farmland, interspersed with villages and low mountain ranges in the distance. At times we pass through densely wooded areas, then out into the plain again, with the mountain range creeping ever closer. We drive for a few hours like this, with the cruise control on. Over the brow of a rolling hill we are presented with the panoramic view of Sofia, sprawling out across the horizon.

As we entered the environs of Sofia we began to scan the roadside for signs of the campsite 'Camping BPAHA'. Sheila would not accept the address, so we were on our own. We knew that it should be located just off the main road, so were hoping to see a sign of some kind. At one point we approached a cross roads, so had to slow down, and by the purist fluke, I caught site of a red sign down an embankment. We doubled back and down a slip road and there we were. To say we were somewhat relieved is an understatement.

The lady at reception was very friendly and welcoming and spoke a little English. She gave us lots of information on buses, taxis and a map of Sofia. This campsite was situated in a wood and had the aforementioned large sign over the entrance. We parked in the woods alongside a few other motorhomes from Germany and one Belgium. The main path/road through the camp had lamps, so would be well lit at night. So far, so good. However, the facilities were housed in dingy old chalets and were beyond dilapidated. Quite frankly, they needed demolishing. We decided to use our own facilities whilst we were here.

The lady at reception booked a taxi for us (5 euros), which dropped us off at the tourist information in the historic heart of Sofia. First impressions were that it had a lot of grand buildings. There is a mixture of influences from Roman, Ottoman and Russian. Orthodox churches, mosques and art nouveau synagogues of all shapes and sizes are dotted around. All of which were dominated by the central Alexander Nevski Memorial Church, a very remarkable building, both inside and out. Four tiers of green (tarnished copper) semi-domes surround the striking gold plated central dome.

We follow our guide book tour of Sofia and wind our way through its many interesting sights. Some of the roads are very wide and on a grand scale, like the buildings that line them. There is quite an array of greenery, with tree lined walk ways and the odd fountain fronting the buildings. We watch the changing of the guard at the Presidential building, which is not far from the wonderfully imposing column, topped by a statue of Sofia herself.

There is the usual smattering of people going about their business. All look well dressed in a European style, from t-shirts and shorts, to pretty dresses and smart suits. In certain quarters there are street vendors and bars. We even managed to find a curry house, so chose to have an Indian meal to finish our day off. We concluded that Sofia is a very nice relaxed city and well worth a visit. It certainly appeared more affluent than the countryside that surrounded it.

On returning to the campsite we notice that some of the chalets are occupied. We can only hope they are in a better condition than the ones being used as the communal toilet and shower facilities.

Well that was it for our short foray into Bulgaria. We had been quite wary on entering Bulgaria, not knowing what to expect, which caused some apprehension. We need not have worried, as once again we found the people one of the friendliest and very welcoming. I found it quite an interesting journey, but Jackie was not that keen. She did not care for the run down nature of the place. Lack of campsites in the areas we went through, ensured we did indeed just drive through, instead of deviating to take in other sights. We are however, still on budget and roughly in line with our tour schedule.

After another good night's sleep we are up early the following day, for our drive into Serbia. At the border we are greeted by a very long queue, it was extremely busy and so took us two hours to pass through. It's strange having all these border crossings again, after the non-existence within the European Union.

Chapter Thirteen

Serbia

August 1st - August 5th

Belgrade – Novi Sad

Serbia is another new country for us and we were eager to explore. We were also looking forward to seeing our Australian friends, Mili and Heather, who we met in Greece. They were meeting us in Belgrade, as they were renovating Mili's house there. Our route will take us along the E80 through Pirot, joining the E75 at Nis, onto Belgrade and then eventually on to Hungary.

What a change in the countryside, it looked so green. Initially we drove through a tree covered mountain pass, along roads that were well maintained and then out into the plain. We had planned to stop just before Pirot, but never saw the sign to the campsite, or more likely it did not exist. As we had no tour books (we could not obtain any), or idea where there might be another campsite nearby, we elected to drive all the way to Belgrade. The only two campsites we had some idea of were given to us by Heather, and we had just missed one of them, which is easy to do.

The five hour drive along the toll motorway (£7) was pleasant enough. The farmland and villages looked clean, neat and tidy. Cruise control was on (60mph) as was the music, so the drive was not too tedious. Traffic was reasonably light, with quite a few articulated lorries to keep my concentration up. The road surface was good, with only a few lorry tyre ruts to make us wobble a bit at times. Our front 'wheel to wheel' width is narrower than the rear and sometimes the rear wheels fit into the grooves left by lorries, causing the back to snake ever so slightly. Once you are accustomed to this phenomena, it's not a problem, as you know nothing serious is about to happen.

Heather had given us really precise directions for the campsite, 'Camping Dunav' just outside Belgrade. After briefly entering the suburbs of Belgrade, we were out and at the campsite. It was situated next to the river Danube, of which we had views, if you walked to the perimeter fence. We had a nice pitch in the shade, a necessity, as the weather is still sunny and very hot, most of the time. On the site were many German and French motorhomes, and a couple from Doncaster in a tent. There was also a Belgian couple, in a very nice motorhome, that we recalled parking next to on the campsite in Sofia. The guy looked a bit strange to us, with bright coloured clothing and long red hair, plaited into dread locks. Once again appearances can be deceptive, as he turned out to be a really nice chap, as we chatted over a beer, later in the week.

The guy at reception was very interesting too. He had only just started working at the site and was very smiley and liked to laugh. He kept apologising for his English, which actually was good. You could tell he was a bit nervous, especially when the boss was around. He would give us lots of information and go out of his way to make us feel at home during our stay. There was a shop on site, from where you could buy food and drink and then consume it at the tables outside under parasols. There were also some holiday chalets and of course the toilet and shower block, which was basic but very clean.

We spent the next day around camp, catching up on things and just relaxing in the sun. In the afternoon, while having a drink at one of the tables at the on-site shop, we noticed a car drive in. A middle aged gent got out and went to reception. Shortly afterwards he went back to the car and he and a very attractive young lady went over to one of the chalets. After about half an hour, the door opened and out came the chap smoking a cigarette (just like in the old films). He had left the door ajar. Inside we could see the young lady putting her make up on and adjusting her dress. A few minutes later they were back in the car and driving away. "What was that about then?" I teased our young friend from reception, as he passed by our table. "Don't ask" he said, "is very old trade!"

It's around this time that the London Olympics are taking place, which up to now we have managed to miss completely. The only reason we realise the games were in full swing, is that our son Howard text to say he was at the games with his girlfriend Amy. We caught glimpses of some of the events, on the TV screens in bars, as we passed by. That will be it for us though, as we have no TV reception on our motorhome satellite at the moment. We will have to wait until we get to Austria, to pick up TV again. Not that we needed it at all, we had quite enough to keep us occupied.

During our first full day on site we saw a young couple check in. The poor things looked totally exhausted as they arrived and endeavoured to erect their small two-man tent. They arrived on foot and their back packs were nearly as big as them. On top of that they were towing what looked like a two wheel sack trolley, with a large object on it. This young couple were Raphael and Isabel from Switzerland. Both were music students. The item in the pack was a canvas kayak, with a wooden skeleton that screwed together.

We introduced ourselves when they were trying to hang some washing on an old piece of rope. I offered them use of our plastic washing line, which was gratefully accepted, in perfect English. During conversation over drinks and nibbles that night, it turned out they had never been kayaking before. They were planning to catch the tide and row along the Danube as far as they could get in the days they had. They had a beautifully illustrated book of the Danube to navigate by. Each double page spread had a map of a section accompanied by a picture.

They had borrowed the Kayak from a friend, had never erected it, or even thought about if they would get all their kit in it. What a laugh watching them try to construct it, over the next few days. Still, it was completed before we left and in the water, with no leaks and ready to go. Only young free spirits would have the confidence and naivety, to embark on such adventure with so little preparation.

We had e-mailed Heather to say we were at the campsite, but had no response, so decide to go into Belgrade the next day. We walked down the long country lane from the campsite to catch the bus. It was a cloudless clear blue sky and the birds were singing away, another hot day in prospect. We were soon in the centre of Belgrade and located the tourist information, to buy tickets for the guided bus tour, which started out from the town hall at eleven.

We had good views from our seats on the top deck of the open top bus. The tour itself lasted just over an hour. It was very informative and interesting. However, we felt a bit embarrassed as we passed a few blackened military/security buildings that had been bombed by NATO during the recent Balkans unrest. Our guide just passed it off as matter of fact and made no comments.

Belgrade is a sprawling city, with a mixture of old and new, wide boulevards, parks and an old fortress on the river. The official buildings range from grand Romanesque state buildings, to colourful new mirror finished high rise. There is an unassuming Palace and a large domed church on a hill. A tram system runs through the centre and to the outskirts. Most residential buildings are six to eight storeys high, with landscaped public courtyards here and there. There are hints of the Ottomans, but not as strong here as in Bulgaria. To one side run's the Danube and its river bridges. It is all very pleasing to the eye, but nothing in particular grabs us.

Back in the city centre, we do some window shopping before finding a place to water and eat. We are now in the upmarket area, around the grand hotel 'Moskow'. The hotel used to be the main residence of the Turks and Russians when visiting. Latterly, it has been the haunt of the rich and famous, when they visit the city. We are dining outside at the 'Petit Piaf' and order some traditional food. The meal consisted of strips of meat and cheese as a starter, then spiced meat balls, shredded belly pork and goulash for main. When the meal was served, it didn't look anything liked we envisaged, but it tasted good. Don't think we are eating and drinking all the time, we are not. Trying local dishes in different countries is all part of the tour. One can have salad anywhere.

So that was Belgrade, a nice clean city, but nothing spectacular in our opinion.

The following morning Heather and Mili arrive in their motorhome. After catching up on things, we planned for a lazy afternoon of food and entertainment. We would be supplying the starter and main, Heather some of her tasty crepes for afters. With this in mind, I set off on my bike to get some food from the mini supermarket, which was on the main road, at the bottom of lane from the site. When I arrived, I found that the store was actually only a small corner shop with two aisles, so more like a corner shop than a supermarket.

Browsing around thinking of what I should buy, I spotted what looked like cooked ham on a long roll on the deli counter. When I say deli counter, it is actually the main counter and appears to be the only meat in the tiny store. The lady behind speaks no English, so I indicate with my fingers, ten slices. While she is busy slicing, I survey the two sparsely filled aisles of the shop. After a while I realise the slicer is still going and I've been in there 10 minutes, I rush back to the counter. "Whoa there!"

There is now a mountain of sliced ham where the roll used to be. Obviously 10 slices had turned into 10 kilo. I wonder, how much is this going to cost? With a smile she holds up four fingers, surely not just 400 Dinar? The huge pile of ham cost less than 4 euro. What a relief, I wipe the sweat from my brow and relax again. She hasn't finished her sales pitch... she has another trick up her sleeve to boost the day's sales. I can't find any biscuits to have with our coffee, but do eye up some Lindt chocolate on the back shelf. "Two bars please", I indicate. "Serbian better" (was that English?) she pointed to some other chocolate close by. "Ok then, two bars please", I thought it was worth a try.

Cycling back to the campsite I chuckle to myself and wonder how I will explain my shopping bag full of ham. More to the point, how we will eat it all. It turns out to be delicious, a cross between smoked ham and roasted pork. The whole of the campsite is pleased also, as I dispense slices to everybody in sight. It's amazing the uses you can find for ham....... bandages..... placemats.... fly swats... rolled cigarette substitute, to name but a few! The chocolate on the other hand, tasted of what I can only describe as blocks of weather worn tasteless muck. I think the lady at the counter saw me coming. She had probably been trying to sell it since WW2.

We spend a lovely day with Heather and Mili. They explain, they were in an area with no communication while they were visiting Mili's brother, so had not picked up our messages. I have a discussion with Mili about the bombed buildings in the city centre. He said he can't understand why NATO did such a thing. I chose to keep quiet. He also explains they hated the Turks, who had occupied them all those years ago. So much for my 'Tolerant Ottoman' theory. The afternoon soon turned into evening and we are joined by Raphael and Isabel. "More ham sandwiches anyone?"

The next day we are all up early. Heather and Mili are off to the house in Belgrade. Raphael and Isabel are launching the kayak and setting off down the Danube, and we are on the move again. We all visit the riverside to see the kayak launched into the water. They proceed to load their kit into it, and guess what, it does all go in. I give Raphael my straw hat, as he has no head cover and the sun is up and hot once again. We did get a letter off them a few months later. Thankfully, they did survive, had a fantastic time in the kayak, and my hat now has pride of place, on their hat stand.

Our young friend at reception gives us a hearty hand shake and hug as we depart. He still has his job and has now been made permanent. We are so happy for him. As we drove away, there is a glow of good feeling for our fellow travellers. Mili and Heather still had not made their mind up on where to live. We have since heard from them and they are back in Australia.

Our remaining drive through Serbia to the Hungarian border is good. We incur no problems with road signage and the roads meander through pretty countryside. The towns and cities look well kept, but nothing exceptional. We pass through the city of Novi Sad, which looks clean and modern. An old fortress sits across the river guarding the crossing. Here we stop for a brief snack in the shadows of its high medieval walls and bastion.

We arrive at the border, where there is another huge traffic queue. Here the wait is for two and a half hours. It's absolute mayhem, as cars move from lane to lane in an attempt to get through more quickly. It's swelteringly hot too, 40°, so we kept our engine running and the air conditioning on. There are lots of German and French cars among those waiting to leave. In the no-man's land between the two border stations, there appeared to be cars that have just been abandoned, as well as piles of litter everywhere. The car in front had an Austrian number plate. To our surprise, they proceeded to throw lots of litter out of the windows. A little further on, we could see the Germans were at it too, throwing a bag of rubbish into a hedge. We felt like getting out and telling them off. We couldn't believe our eyes. How strange for people who normally take such pride in themselves and who generally keep their country very clean and tidy, to do such a thing.

Serbia. Another box ticked. Would we rush back? Perhaps not, but once again we had found it interesting, all very easy going and the people very hospitable.

Chapter Fourteen

Hungary

August 5th - August 25th

Lake Balaton – Budapest

It's late in the day as we finally cross the border at Roszke into Hungary and onto the M5. We will be travelling to Lake Balaton then on to Budapest, before heading to Austria and Vienna. Our first port of call was at a roadside hut to get a vignette to allow us to travel the roads in Hungary. It was not a very pleasant experience, as the lady that served me was not helpful at all. In fact she was rude and dismissive. In the end it was a fellow traveller who helped me choose the right tariff. The size of your vehicle and how long you wanted to use the roads for, defined the tariff, but the information sheet was not that helpful. After an exasperating queue at the border to get into Hungary, it was the last thing we needed.

It was now 6.30pm in the evening and we needed to find a campsite asap, before they closed for the night We were only fifteen minutes away, according to Sheila and our ACSI book. We arrived to find it closed. Fortunately, unlike Serbia and Bulgaria, there were plenty of other sites to choose from. We had a bit of a shock when Sheila threw a curve ball and took us down a dirt track, no campsite in sight, perhaps it was ACSI who had the wrong co-ordinates, we will never know. Fortunately, we had spotted a campsite sign en route, so we turned back and made for it. Voila! There it was, 'Camping Sziksosfurdo', what a welcome sight and it was open too.

The campsite was situated on parkland, with a swimming pool and a lake that had a beach. There were hundreds of people there, most of which were now making their way home. It had been another incredibly hot day, in the forties, so everyone was out making the most of it. The staff were very pleasant, welcoming and spoke good English. We quickly set up under some tall trees and a nice quiet pitch. After what proved to be a long day, we were soon in the land of nod. We never did get to see the beach or swimming pool, as we were up and off early the next day.

Hungary. Our first impressions were good, it looked a very tidy and well-kept country, from what we had seen so far. Our drive this day was to take us to Dunafoldva, on the Danube. We did pass some more ladies plying their trade on the roadside this day, nothing new, but unexpected nonetheless. We dropped off the M5 at Keckesmet, to replenish our provisions at a big Auchan store, the first one we had ever been in. It was well stocked and very similar to our big supermarkets back in the UK. The exception being, the hugest variety of German sausages we had ever seen. The villages and towns all looked up-beat and the people were well dressed. Fields were well tended and orderly and the road surfaces very smooth to travel on. In fact we felt like we were in Germany, we were both impressed.

We found the next campsite 'Kek Duna' just a short walk from the town. It was right next to, and had lovely views of the Danube. We had the company of three ladies from England in the motorhome next to ours. The elderly mother and her two daughters appeared to be having a whale of a time, giggling and consuming cocktails. We entertained ourselves watching the river traffic on the Danube and cyclists and walkers on the tow path. Phew, it was forty two degrees again and our electric fans were on and working overtime. As dusk approached, the mosquitoes were on the war path. Our lotions and potions appeared to have little effect on the little blighters.

Our next port of call was Lake Balaton, a popular tourist destination for the Hungarians. It's the largest lake in central Europe at 230 square miles and referred to as 'Budapest on Sea', because of the many visitors from the city. We will be navigating our way almost around the entire lake, starting near Siofok on the south side. The drive over to the lake is through flat farmland at first and then on to very gradual rolling hillsides. It's all very green and lush and we pass through very pretty villages, with churches, landscaped verges and flowerbeds. Our first campsite is 'Balatontourist Lido Kemping' at Balantonszemes. The campsite was very busy, but we did manage to bag a shady pitch.

The lake itself looked very calm and was very shallow on this side. The lakeside was grassed for people to sunbathe on. People had to wade through, what looked like stagnant water, to get to the deep water and lake proper. They appeared to go half way across the lake before they were up to their midriff. It was full of the usual holiday atmosphere, with sun bathers, swimmers and children enjoying themselves. The small town itself was pleasant enough and kept us occupied for an hour.

While sun bathing outside Belle we chatted to a young couple, Peter and Judith from Budapest, who pitched a small tent next to us. They had arrived on cycles and were cycling all the way around the lake. They said this was a very popular way of seeing the lake and that there was a cycle path all the way around. We had seen many cyclists, but had not realised they were making the trip around the lake. They also recommended a few must see places on the lake for us to visit.

We stayed there for two nights before we were up and off to our next stop, the town of Keszthely and

Camping 'Casterly', on the north side. The road around the lake here only offers brief glimpses of the lake from time to time, but feels very touristy all the same. The traffic is fairly heavy, as you would expect of a tourist area in August. There are some beautiful houses, both on the lake and on the hillsides. The north side of the lake is backed by gently rolling hills that eventually become more mountainous. A striking backdrop. We also managed to find a cycle shop along the way and get a new valve for Jackie's bike (remember my fruitless attempt in Turkey?).

The campsite was clean and modern, with hedged pitches. We ate at the site restaurant, where we had our first taste of Hungarian Goulash. The ingredients included potatoes, vegetables, small pasta pieces and beef. It was very spicy and creamy in texture and very tasty. We were also able to get internet connection here, which we had not managed in Hungary so far. I began to think our laptop was on the blink. What a relief.

The enjoyable walk, twenty minutes through the suburbs, with its variety of beautifully designed houses, to reach the centre of Keszthely, was very rewarding. The houses are of all shapes and sizes, but predominantly have a gable ended roof that has a cross section of tiles on each end. There is one that looks akin to those found in Transylvania, with its two hexagonal cupola topped spires. It also brought back memories of watching 'The Munsters' years ago on the telly, as their house had the same creepy look to it. Some of the gardens are nothing short of stunning, with flower displays that would grace any affluent area in the world.

The town centre of Keszthely is so beautiful and came as a real surprise. It is the largest town on Lake Balaton and the oldest. It has the Palace of the Festetic's family, which is now a museum surrounded by English style gardens. The central street, town hall and church are a joy to behold. It's two storey buildings, in creams, and whites with their salmon colour tiled roofing and dormer windows are timelessly elegant. From the wide cobbled main street, to the narrow side streets, it's a real pleasure to walk. The water feature and statue, covered by a modern four pillared triangular shaped roof, also sit nicely in keeping with their surroundings.

The Palace, which was completed in 1754 and stands at one end of the main street, is the jewel in the crown. The buildings are of a Neo-Baroque style and have been designed in a U shape. Its fragrant English gardens are free to enter. There are humming birds and fountains. It's all a joy to see. The flowers were in full bloom, as are those in the town. Reds, pinks, whites, blues, yellows, greens, the visual display put on by man/woman and nature, is truly breath-taking. From the back of the palace, you can even hire a horse drawn carriage to take a tour of the town.

As we walked back through the main street, we visited a 'Weinhandlung Cave' called 'Pampertics Borkereskedes'. Magyar is the interesting language here in Hungary. It is Finno-Ugric and there are no friendly English cross overs to help. At this establishment, we are given an education in Hungarian wine, by a very knowledgeable young man (who fortunately spoke good English), n his early twenties. We leave clutching bottles of Tokaji, Balatonboglar and Kekefrancos, all proved later to be very palatable. Next stop was to a local restaurant, 'Bacus', recommended by the same young wine-seller. We sat outside to dine, under vine covered lattice work pergolas. The food and service was excellent. The waiter recommended some Hungarian favourites for us to try, in both wine and food, so we obliged by ordering them. We started with fish, salad and yogurt, followed by sirloin steak topped with goose liver, and finally chocolate, orange and vanilla sponge. Some of this sounds nothing special, but it all had the Hungarian slant to it, tasting slightly different to what we are used to.

The revelation of the meal was the goose liver, which had been lightly seared and was absolutely delicious. We have this long term topic about food. What is there left to discover, that one will truly like and is new to your pallet? Well, this was one of those occasions, not just a variation on a theme, but something new and exciting, both in taste and the way it had been cooked.

Our next stop along the lake was a forty-five minute drive to Badacsonylábdihegy, 4km away from the town of Badacsony, which had been recommended by Peter and Judith. 'Eldarado Camping' was on the edge of the lake and our pitch gave us beautiful views out over the water. It was an idyllic spot, with mountains to the back of us, on which we could see houses and villages nestling among the trees.

That evening, we took a stroll up the hillside, to view some of the houses and villages we could see from the campsite. It was all very pretty and the houses remind us of Tyrolean ski lodges. There were gently sloping fields of vines here and there along the way. As we walked along, we kept hearing the faint sound of music, so decided to walk in that direction. We finally arrive at a school, where there is a wine festival underway. Our little quest has paid off. The centrepiece of the festival is a beef roast on a spit, its giant carcass is now all but bare ribs. There are all types of stalls selling crafts, homemade jams and beer and of course the wine of the region.

We are soon on the wine trail, having eaten some hot beef and potatoes from the roast. There are trestle tables set out for people to eat and drink together. The music, which we had heard, and which had drawn our attention, is being provided by a large brass band consisting mainly of school children. They are playing a mix of music, from the Beatles to classic waltzes. On our way through the stalls and attractions, we bought a couple of bottles of the prize-winning local red. It was all so unexpected, but what a great night was had by all. We didn't leave too late, as we had to find our way back in the dark, with only our torch. The clear sky provided a canopy of stars. We actually saw three shooting stars as we walked along in the moonlight.

The next day finds us spending a quiet day around Belle in the hot sun. We pass the time watching swans with their signets and colourful hot air balloons floating in the distance. There were people fishing from a nearby jetty and a multitude of boats sailed past. Tall reeds rustled in the gentle breeze whilst people strolled along with children and dogs in tow. It's another perfect day in paradise. The boarded jetty juts out into the lake and provides another photo opportunity. It reminds us of the iconic 'Ikea' picture, of Ambleside, in the English Lake District.

On our third and final day at this campsite we decided to catch the 11.50am train to Balatonfüred, a 30 minute ride along the lakeside. When the train pulls in, it is a large diesel train, resplendent in red, with a thick yellow stripe down the side. There is no platform at the little whitewash single storey station, just a gravel pavement, so it is quite a step up into the carriage. The interior and seating on the train was very dated, but clean. There were very few people on board so we could sit where we liked. After a short while, a conductor came to take our fare for our return trip. The single track railway runs around the whole of Lake Balaton, snaking between houses, across roads and running right alongside the lake at times. There is no fencing to speak of. It would never be allowed in the UK for safety reasons.

The train moves at a snail's pace, pulling in at little stations along the way. Occasionally, as it is single track, it pulls onto a side track, to allow another train to pass which is going in the opposite direction. As we travel, we chat to a retired Hungarian, who is on his way to meet his son and daughter-in-law. They have come to spend a holiday with him. He is happily retired and enjoying his life. As we clickety-clack along the track, we reflect that all these experiences add up to a unique feeling and a pleasant way to travel.

Balacsony is quite a walk from the train station and there are no signs to follow, well none that we understand anyway. The town sits on the lake, is very touristy and has an extensive promenade. There is a small marina, from where you can board an old steamer for a trip around the lake. Smart wooden huts along the front offered wine tasting and goulash was being served up for lunch, so we sat at one of the many crowded trestle tables and tried all on offer. It's sheer enjoyment listening to laughter and chatter. Before we know it, another afternoon is soon gone.

Next stop Budapest, a three hour journey through the countryside, but this time on the motorway. Our home for the next twelve days was to be 'Haller Camping', a short walk and metro ride into the centre of Budapest. The busy site was tightly packed with tents, caravans and motorhomes. It's situated in a secure fenced area and is surrounded by houses and flats. It has an abundance of water taps. Electric hook-ups with connecting cables spread like spaghetti over the site. There are free washing machines and WiFi. It was full most of the time we were there, and they managed to keep the facilities clean and tidy.

Our friends were coming out to meet us again. First to arrive were Clive, Keith and Eddie for two nights and then a few days later Freddie and Alyson for three nights. All staying in hotels in the centre of the city.

Budapest is a beautiful city situated on the Danube. It has an imposing old castle on the Gellért Hill - Tabán area, which is on the Buda (western) side of the river, whilst the Parliament and central area lies on the Pest (east) side. We and our friends were stopping on the Pest side, which is the centre for shopping and hotels. After settling in, we paid a quick visit to the city. We wanted to find the hotels our friends were staying in and check out the metro times and stations. Jackie managed to get her hair cut and coloured for 25 euros (and a good job they made to), whilst I checked out the shops, restaurants and bars. We did not want to explore too much, as we wanted to do this with our friends, the first of who were arriving the following day.

We arrived at the Hotel Sofitel, where Clive, Keith and Eddie were staying. We would be staying the night, to celebrate Keith's birthday without worrying about time or getting back to the campsite. We knocked on his door at 10am. It was a total surprise for him, he had no idea we would be there. Well, they had had a corking night the previous evening and Clive was still in bed, ever so slightly the worse for wear. What was Clive doing in Keith's room and in the bed anyway?

Unbeknown to us, Eddie had bought along her friend Karen, whose husband had recently passed away, so they had asked her along to take her mind off things. This had meant they were sharing rooms, boys in one and girls in another. Later in conversation with Karen, she told us that her husband, Alan Oakley, had been the chief designer for the company 'Raleigh Cycles' at Nottingham. Alan designed the 'Chopper' bike, which was a best seller and extremely popular in the 80's, due to its innovative design.

When Clive finally appeared, he declared he would never sleep in the same room as Keith again.

Apparently, he was a light sleeper and Keith made a hell of a racket, snoring all night. Eddie just smiled and said, I have to put up with that every night of the week!

Sometime later and armed with our bottle of Hungarian Champagne and Keith's birthday cake, we all celebrated our re-union and Keith's birthday in Eddie and Karen's room. That evening, we ate out in one of the oldest restaurants in Budapest called 'Rezkakas'. Here we were serenaded in a gypsy style, by a three piece group, consisting of a double base, violin and cimbalom (a type of piano that's played with sticks rather than keys) and we have the cd to prove it. It's amazing how things don't sound quite as good the morning after. Anyway, I chose the duck liver as a starter again, which was absolutely divine. Keith paid for the meal, as it was his birthday. How kind was that? The delicious meal was followed by drinks till 2.30am, by which time our batteries were well and truly drained.

As the next day dawned we found ourselves somewhat groggy, but we still took an open top bus tour of both Buda and Pest. For some reason we never got off the bus. I wonder why? That evening, Keith elected we go for an 'all you could eat and drink banquet' for 20 euros, at a place called 'Trófea'. What an apt name, because we preceded to 'Trófea' our way through plates of food and drink, like it was going out of fashion. At one point, we ended up on the next table, with a group of young British lads who were on a fitness course for Football Coaches. We tried to get them paired off with a group of Hungarian girls, on the next table, but only managed to get ourselves into trouble, with our ladies and the Hungarian girls. Although it was noted, Karen did spend a lot of time with the lads talking fitness, among other topics!

Outside Trófea, and slightly the worse for wear again, I ask the waiter to take a picture of us all. "Press there please". We all pose and smile. "Camera no work". "Press there please". "Sorry, camera no work". After several attempts, we abandoned the idea. What a dumb waiter, he just couldn't get the hang of it. The camera was later to reveal five drunks on a video and a bemused waiter, being told to press the button. I had inadvertently pressed the video button before handing the camera over to the waiter, preventing him from taking a picture. Who was the dumb bloke there?

Well, here we are again and it's time to say goodbye to our friends, what a ripping time we all had. Eddie ("and mines a double Brandy please") always dresses so elegantly. Clive is the dapper dresser and Keith my drinking buddy. Apparently, after we had parted company the night before (Jackie and I to catch the metro and they to their hotel), they went on to another bar, where Keith and Karen polished off "just one last drink."

The next few days were mostly spent relaxing around Belle, until the arrival of our next set of friends, Freddie and Alyson. It's still very hot and both the fans were working overtime to keep us cool. We went to one of Budapest's covered shopping areas called 'The West End' for a look at what's on offer. It was empty and most of the shops were closed. I did manage to get a half decent curry and a puri, at the fast food hall there, which was a pleasant surprise. It was while we were here, we spotted a Mont Blanc shop. This is a German pen and luxury goods manufacturer. It would be Jackie's birthday in October and I was looking for something to get her. There was a lovely 'Princes Grace of Monaco' special edition pen, which Jackie liked. The shopkeeper gave us the brochure to take for free, which had Grace Kelly's life story, along with pictures of the pens and other exclusive things in. Jackie said the pen was far too expensive, so we left without a purchase.

Once outside the shopping mall and as we walked back to the metro, Jackie suddenly remembered why there were no people about, it was a public holiday, 'Constitution Day' in Hungary. We then saw a cavalcade of cars go by with a police escort. They stopped a short way up the road, at the beautiful Cathedral of St István. We walked to the cathedral, where there were masses of people and a cordoned-off area around the building, along with TV cameras and photographers. Apparently, there would be fireworks on the Danube that evening and celebrations. We, however, would give it a miss, as we were tired and hot, and our friends were due to arrive the following day.

Freddie and Alyson would be staying in the centre of Budapest, at the 'Hotel Sofitel Chain Bridge' located on the river Danube, with views over to the Citadel. That afternoon at 4pm, we caught the metro into the city as usual and were soon knocking at the door of their hotel room. Chilled Champagne was at the ready, as it was Alyson's birthday in a few days. How good it was to see our best friends again. We had so much to catch up on. They had a great view from their room, over the river and the bridge. Time flew and it was soon time to eat. We decided to eat at the 'Trofea' again, as Freddie was famished. The food and drink was just as good the second time around, which is always a relief, when you recommend somewhere.

Next day, we chose to go on the same bus tour again but this time got off at various points along the way. At one point, we got off at the Citadel, on the Buda side, with its magnificent views of the river. Here we booked a table for Alyson's birthday bash, the following evening.

The views were stunning from the restaurant by day, so we hoped for even better views of Budapest by night.

That evening we had drinks on an old boat bar/restaurant moored on the river Danube. It was a side wheeled river tramp and reminded us more of a museum, than anything else. As Alyson worried about mosquitoes, we decided to go ashore and have a meal along the river front. "Anyone for Fish and Chips then?" said Freddie. We spotted our traditional dish on the menu at one of the restaurants. All up market of course, it was a simple dish, but as delicious as ever. We all like battered fish and as Jackie and I had not had any for so long, it was a treat for us. Much later, as Fred and I walked along the promenade, taking in the views, our ladies following short distance away, we were accosted by two ladies of the night. "You like good time gents?" "Err, yes thank you we do, but only with our good ladies, who are just behind us!" It formed an entertaining topic for the rest of the evening.

The next day was Alyson's birthday, so we booked to stay in the hotel we had stayed in previously (much cheaper than theirs). It was only a short walk to where Freddy and Alyson were staying and so meant we could enjoy the whole evening with our friends again. We also pre-booked the 'New York Café, as our treat for Alyson. We had spotted it earlier, on our previous bus tour and the guide had given it a very good review. Today would be a taxi only day, as we had a lot to pack in, no metro or buses. It all felt so unusual for us.

The grand building was built in 1891 and is now the 'New York Palace' Hotel. It is a place of opulence. The beautiful interior consists of high vaulted ceilings, bedecked in frescoes and animated sculptures, surrounded by gold inlay. Marbled floors and pillars reflect the globed lights adorning the walls, whilst crystal chandeliers hung gracefully from the high ceilings.

Paintings by Gustav Manneheimer and Karoly Lotz grace the walls. Rich burgundy, white and gold add to the tapestry of opulence. The Neo Baroque style is pleasing to the eye and there is a feeling of grand wealth to the place. The cacophony of sound from the guests eating and drinking at the tables adds to the wonderful ambiance.

From here you can send a letter for free, on the headed note paper and envelopes provided, which we of course take advantage of. For a few moments we felt like royalty, as we ate in these very plush surroundings. The meal was very good and quite expensive, as one would expect. As a one off, it was well worth it, if only for Alyson's 'Happy Birthday' cake, with a huge strawberry on top. We didn't leave a tip, as a 10% service charge was already added to the bill, not normal for us. We believe in leaving a good tip, when one is deserved, if only to give us Brits a good reputation abroad.

Well-fed and watered, we set off for our cruise up the river, which was included in the price we had paid for the bus tour of the city. It was pleasant enough, although the boat was a bit basic and nothing to shout about. The views along the river, especially of the Parliament building, were well worth the effort and made up for the boat being a disappointment. A river boat trip always reveals different sights and feels a bit special, this was no exception.

Back to our hotel, for a well-earned rest and recharge our batteries. Then early evening, it's more Champagne and cocktails in Freddie and Alyson's room, before taking a cab to the Citadel restaurant, with its magnificent views over the river. It was even more spectacular than in the daytime, as the evenings soft lights turned into night and the sun slipped over the horizon. It was a wonderfully warm barmy evening. We had an entertaining meal spent in laughter, reflection, celebration and of course good company. A fitting end to our friend's stay in Budapest. They were leaving for the airport early in the morning.

So, I hear you ask, "What about Budapest?" Well, we were there for twelve days in total, so we had a lot of time to become acquainted with the place. Food and drink was very reasonably priced, you could get a pint of beer for as little as one pound, if you looked around. There is plenty to see and do, from grand buildings to magnificent views. The bus tour of the city, with its boat trip included, is a must for capturing the complete picture.

For us the views around the Danube were magnificent, either from the Citadel looking down, or looking up from Pest. This was especially wonderful at night when all is lit up to dramatically emphasize the features on show. The Houses of Parliament and The State Opera House are architectural masterpieces. The interior of the Opera House is nothing short of beautiful. The central pedestrianized shopping area is pleasing to browse around, with its cafés and ice cream parlours.

Further afield, a visit to 'Heroes' Square', with its dominating statues and half circle of pillars, is very imposing, as are the gardens and baths. Budapest is very famous for its 'Thermal Baths'. These are mineral rich waters, where people go to treat their ailments, in the belief that the waters have beneficial effects. There are several of these baths in Budapest, but the most impressive is the Szechenyi Baths. A walk around the back streets here will reward you with many fine buildings.

So "Yes," we liked Budapest very much and we liked Hungary as a whole, it was for us the surprise package. Everywhere was so well kept, the people were friendly and the countryside well-tended. It also had a feeling of prosperity. We really enjoyed our stay and feel even more educated about central Europe, and where Hungary sits as a wealthy nation. But now it's time for us to move on, Vienna was calling and the other seat of power in the once mighty Austro-Hungarian Empire.

On the budget front, two nights in a hotel and with two sets of friends visiting, had taken us over the top, but not by that much. Still, it was well worth every penny, we had had such a great time.

Chapter Fifteen

Austria

August 26th – August 31st

Vienna – Durstein – Melk- Linz

This was to be one of our very few full days travelling, as we moved from Budapest to Vienna. We took the M1 motorway for most of the way, because of the distance we needed to cover. The views over the rolling countryside of Hungary, soon turned into the mountainous valley of the Danube, as it runs into Austria. Our views here are some of the most rewarding of our tour, the river, the small villages with church spires and roads winding along the river side. The weather had been incredibly hot for weeks on end. Today, it decided to rain, just as we passed through the border and into Austria. We plan to visit Vienna and Linz, with a stop off at Pochlarn and then on to the Czech Republic. Pochlarn is where Jackie's auntie Hermine was born and raised, and of which Jackie had heard many stories.

We were heading for camping 'Aktiv' a metro ride into Vienna, once again found in our ACSI software. Our routine before setting off is one of studying the maps and tour guides for where we want to go, then looking for a campsite to suit. We follow this, by entering the co-ordinates into our sat nav, to see if 'Sheila' can find the place. On this occasion she took us straight there, with no difficulties whatsoever. The campsite and facilities were very clean. Once again, at the campsite, we study our tour guides, to plot a route for the sights and places we want to visit. We have a printer/copier in the motorhome, so will sometimes copy the map from our tour books and mark out a route.

The next day, after a short walk to the metro and a twenty minute ride, we were in the centre of Vienna. We were so excited. Vienna was one of the places we had always wanted to visit and it was not to disappoint us. It's a bit like London in many ways, most of the 'must see' sights are in a compact central area and all within easy walking distance. We had dressed up for the occasion and were looking forward to taking in the sights and having a meal.

Where to start? There are so many grand buildings and statues to see, such as the Hofburg complex, which was the former Emperor's residence, with its splendid gardens and famous Spanish Riding School. We wander on through cloisters and courtyards with magnificent arches, stucco angels and the odd twin headed eagle perched on high. We gaze about in awe at the Neo-Gothic Rathaus, the Burgtheater and the Café Landtmann. The magnificent parliament building, modelled on the Palace of Athena. Mark Anthony's Statue, the Opera House and the Secession Building. The Karlskirche, the tallest Baroque church, with its twin columns. The Belvedere, two summer palaces linked by formal gardens. The list goes on and on.

We amble our way around buildings, down each 'Strasse' and through gardens, each with its own 'wow' factor. Vienna is truly a magnificent city. For us, the beautifully set out and scented rose garden, across from the parliament building, provided a moment of reflection and tranquillity, from the hustle and bustle of the tourists.

There is a music festival taking place at the Hofburg complex, with food tents, local craft stalls, and the obligatory trestle tables. The food smelled so good and Jackie had spotted some bacon and beef filled potato dumplings, just like auntie Hermine used to make, so we decided to partake of the food and eat at the trestle tables, instead of our planned treat meal. I had smoked pork served with sauerkraut. The place was heaving with people making merry in the sunshine. Beer and wine were served in plastic cups.

As the day wore on, we decided to do a bit of window shopping. We missed the opportunity to buy a nice bust of Beethoven, due to us dithering about. We then spotted an antiques shop selling clocks, of which, I wish I had at least one or even two. Well, we walked in and were both immediately taken by the very elegant 'Three Graces' limited addition clock, under a glass case. It stood about 50cm tall in white marble and consisted of a plinth, with three naked ladies standing on it, supporting a dome shaped lidded urn. Around the lid, so not a clock face, were two discs of numbers, which rotated around the urn lid. You were able to tell the time from where one of the ladies fingers was pointing at the roman numerals.

The young guy at the counter came over and told us it was an annular clock and was a replica, made by the same company as the life size model in the Louvre, in Paris. He put on white gloves and then removed the glass covering for us to inspect the clock. It had a price tag of 1107, not bad thinks I, about £1000 pounds converted from euros. Well we umm'd and ahrrr'd. By this time, a capper dressed, large bespectacled, very old gentleman (looked like Woody Allen's father) appeared. He said if we wanted the clock, he could ship it to Christies in London and they would authenticate it, before we bought it. All for 1107 euros, not bad, both Jackie and I thought. I did notice the look of horror as I touched the clock, no white gloves for me.

Finally, I said, "We would like to consult with a friend of ours (our close friend Freddie loves antiques and is quite knowledgeable) and I need to think about it, as it is a lot of money", he agreed. I continued, "money is not the problem, as both Jackie and I do like nice things, it's just we need to be sure". He fully understood. He said, "Take the fact sheet on the clock and here is my mobile number, I will also write down the price for you". The alarm bells had started, Was 1107 not the price? Well of course not, it was £22,000. 1107 was the lot number in the shop's catalogue. Bless us both, we never missed a beat and carried on as if we could afford it. After all, if one has money you don't need to ask the price. We wave goodbye and say we may be in touch.

Outside, and nonchalantly having walked around the corner, we burst into laughter and nervous relief. We could both imagine the embarrassment, if I had got my credit card out to pay, before we knew the actual price. "There's not enough money on the card sir". What do you mean there's twelve thousand on there?" "Well, the clock is twenty two thousand". Still to this day, we both muse over the clock. We have since looked it up on the internet, as we would buy a modern day replica, if we could find one. But alas, there are similar replica clocks, but not the 'Three Graces' in white marble.

We continue on and soon come across a Mont Blanc shop. Now, I believe in providence, and this was one such moment. There, gleaming in the shop window was the 'The Princess Grace of Monaco' pen I had tried to buy Jackie in Budapest. There was also a pink diamond studded one, at around sixty thousand pounds, but it's not that one! I badger Jackie into going in and having a look. We were treated like celebrities (including a coffee) and both the assistant and I convinced Jackie, as it was close enough to her birthday, to warrant a purchase. What we have discovered since Budapest, is that I already had a Mont Blanc pen, which had been given to me as a gift years ago, and which I had been completely unaware of the value.

Later in the day, and to top up to keep us going, we had a bratwurst and roast potatoes, from one of the many street vendors. You certainly won't go hungry in Vienna.

Well, that was Vienna, what an experience for many reasons. We will be going back one day, as we both would like to go to the opera, dance a Viennese Waltz and perhaps even have a meal in a good restaurant. Back at the campsite that night, we were still chuckling over the clock incident. I also found a place in Belle to hide Jackie's pen until her birthday.

The weather continues fine and warm with clear blue skies. We are following the Danube and journeying towards an overnight stop in Durstein. We plan to follow the roads as close to the Danube as possible, so Jackie is armed as usual with the map. The Danube is a very wide river at this point and we have to criss-cross it many times, in order to stay close. It's all very rewarding. To begin with the scenery is made up of gently rolling hills with views of mountains in the distance. Soon we are into the river valley. Everywhere is lush and green, with picture postcard villages littering the way.

Our first stop is at Krems, for a snack and a quick stretch of the legs. It's a pretty place with its cobbled streets and houses painted white, cream, pastel blue and pink. Their tall windows, some with flower boxes and some with high peaked roofing are typically Austrian. A short distance along the road we arrive at Durstein, another pretty riverside town. It is very touristy, with river cruisers and large groups of Americans and Japanese visitors. It was here that Richard the Lionheart was kept in prison, as Prince John would not pay the ransom. He was discovered by his squire, who played his lute below the battlement walls, which are still there to this day. The place really is quite stunning, a mediaeval Baroque eclectic mix, with its prominent blue and white painted church.

Some of the hills are now covered in vines and we pass river boats, of all kinds, plying their trade along the river. We hand over to Sheila, to find our campsite at Melk. The location is ideal as it is right beside river. The booking office/reception is more like a local pub, serving alcohol and snacks. The adjacent field is for campers. We have views of the river over the hedge and are soon talking to a German couple, Carl and Rosemary. We spend an interesting evening with them. Carl was retired from the air force and they were from Cologne. Their English was very good.

The next day we walked into Melk. The small town is dominated by the enormous Abbey, perched on a rocky hill, above the town. The walls are painted yellow with white stripes so as you can imagine it is an amazing sight, set against a powder blue sky. This latest incarnation, was built by the Benedictine monks in 1702, to replace the one destroyed by fire in 1297. It was a bit too Teutonic and austere for our tastes. The town below is very quaint. We walked around the streets, had a coffee and peruse the shops, all in one hour. There was a lady street vendor, selling pumpkins with painted faces and other vegetables, some shaped like a man's turnip. We found this very strange for a religious setting, perhaps they like growing these phallic vegetables for other reasons. The walk back to the campsite also had its drama, as we came across a metre long black snake, sunning itself on the tow path. Fortunately, it disappeared into the undergrowth as we approached.

We left the campsite the next morning, shortly after Carl and Rosemary, who kindly left us a bottle of wine and a note of thanks, for our company the previous evening.

We were now travelling towards Pochlarn, accompanied by mile after mile of beautiful scenery along the Danube. No other words for it, speechless for once.

The visit to Pochlarn, was a homage to Jackie's auntie Hermine, who always spoke well of the place (in her lovely Austrian accent) of her birth, and rightly so. It was very picturesque and relaxing. Hermine had married Barry, Jackie's uncle, just after the war. They had met while he was stationed there. Hermine and Barry had been early mentors in our life together, being extremely kind and always having a positive happy outlook.

The small town is a few streets deep and runs behind an earthwork embankment on the river. It's typically Austrian, with clean lines and pastel coloured two storey buildings. It had an ornate pillared well in a little square. We visited the church in the town centre, with its plain but pristine interior, which matched the town's immaculately clean streets.

We then drove across the river and up to a place called 'Maria Taferl'. This hilltop village has a magnificent Basilica. The beautiful structure has black onion domes that cap two pale yellow towers. It was one of Hermine's favourite places. We could see why. The church is free to enter and is bedecked in gold with a fresco painted ceiling and an abundance of ornate statues. It oozed ecclesiastical wealth and opulence. Outside, the terrace offered stunning panoramic views over the river valley. After exploring the church and village, we ate in Belle, overlooking the countryside and golf course. We could now understand why Hermine always had that 'lost in thought look', whenever she talked of her home town.

Onwards to Linz. It started to rain as we entered the campsite late in the afternoon. That night, one of my rear lower teeth started to ache and by morning it was unbearable, and I mean unbearable. I am not one who suffers with my teeth, so this was a very rare occasion. Jackie went to the camp reception at 9.00am to enquire about a dentist. They kindly recommended one, phoned on our behalf and made an emergency appointment for later that morning.

A short taxi ride took us to Ebelsberg, a suburb of Linz. I was in Dr Flohberg's chair by 11am. Thankfully, he spoke perfect English, having studied in the UK. He said he could not use anaesthetic (don't ask me why?), but would chill the affected area with a lotion and then drill the tooth to release the pressure from the abscess that had formed. Well, I was in so much pain, anything sounded good at the time. The procedure was soon over and it was amazing how quickly the pain disappeared. He did not fill the hole he had made and told me to see my dentist, as soon as I was back in the UK.

It's at times like this, our ability to get access to near instant medical cover, really comes home. I was so grateful to Dr Flohberg, who gave me a near immediate cure and the campsite receptionist, who took the trouble to phone on our behalf. I was also grateful to my quick thinking wife, who had conjured up a solution for me in no time that morning. There was also a chemist shop involved, as we could not locate the dental practice when we got out the taxi. One of the shop assistants rang the dentist to ask directions for us. My relief and gratitude to all involved was immeasurable.

It was raining quite heavily, but still warm when we came out of the dentists. Rather than go back to Belle, we caught the tram into the centre of Linz. So, with a scarf covering my mouth and a packet of Ibuprofen tablets in my pocket, we made our way into town. We had quick cup of tea at a McDonalds en-route, as we had not had a drink or breakfast in all the rush. McDonalds, is one of the few places you can get a good cuppa, no matter where. Linz was very nice, but perhaps due to my trauma that morning, we did not appreciate it as much as we should. Lunch in Linz consisted of a dish of soft pasta, which surprisingly I was able to eat in such short a time after all the trauma that morning.

So that was Austria, it is an extremely picturesque place and lived up to its top billing as a tourist destination. We found the people very friendly, kind and helpful. Our tour along the Danube in particular, had been one of the very best, almost dreamlike. At times we felt like we were in fairy-tale land.

Next stop… the Czech Republic.

Chapter Sixteen

Czech Republic

September 1st – September 5th

Prague

As we crossed the border we were a bit apprehensive again, we didn't know what to expect, on a personal security level. We are always vigilant, no matter where we are on our tour, but all was to prove well here. Surprisingly, there were no border controls. Sometimes, we wonder why we get worried, and where we get the apprehension from, particularly about certain countries.

Within a few miles of driving further into the Czech Republic, the landscape changed, it looked more like the English countryside. We were heading straight for Prague. We were also looking forward to another visit from our friends, Paul and his lady friend Jackie, who we had last seen in Barcelona, earlier on in the tour. It rained for most of our four hour journey, only relenting as we approached Prague. Pretty scenery all the way, low rolling hills, mainly farmland, with crops in the fields. It really did remind us of England, although the houses were different, being more of an Austrian style with high peaked roofs. Everywhere was tidy, but not quite up to the clinical Austrian and Hungarian standard. The roads were good, which is always a bonus, when travelling long distances.

Our campsite overlooked the Danube, but we had difficulty accessing it as there were cars parked everywhere. There was a disco/rock concert in progress in the next field along, as well as a festive boat regatta along the river. There was another campsite at the end of the road, just past ours, which I reconnoitred. We decided to stay in the first one we had come to, as it had better views over the Danube. The area in which both campsites were located, was all a bit run down. It was situated just across the river from the Nové Město (new town) area of the city.

The facilities were acceptable, but the shower block had communal changing areas (separate for male and female of course). Fresh bread was available in the morning, from the site shop and a mini café area. We were lucky to get a good spot, as the campsite was full. Just as we arrived, a motorhome pulled out of a prime position, which had views looking down onto the river. There was a mix of mainly German, some Italian and one French motorhome, on the site when we arrived.

That afternoon, the regatta provided amusing entertainment. Colourful boats and occupants, raced along the river. On the riverside someone was beating on a drum, to give the oarsmen a regular rhythm. The growing crowds were giving vocal support. One boat contained men dressed as yellow chickens, while another had green and orange vegetables as crew, obviously a very serious race. Amazingly, the disco ended at eleven that night, so we had a peaceful night's sleep.

We visited the campsite reception the following morning and the lady there, who spoke good English, gave us instructions on which trams and metro to catch, to reach the city. The tram and metro system were to prove very efficient, cost effective and always on time, as we traversed to many city destinations during our visit. We only managed to go the wrong way on a tram once, which is not bad going for us.

Our first trip into the city, started with a short walk along the pathway from the campsite (not lit up at night) to the tram stop. The tram was crowded, but we did get a seat. About 20 minutes later, we were deposited right in the Nové Město area of the city. From here we had to take a short metro ride into the Náměskí Republiky, a large cobbled square, in the centre of Prague. Just off the square and down a little side street 'Truhlářská', was the hotel where our friends would be staying.

First impressions of the city were good. It had a nice friendly feel to it and the people looked well dressed. There was a shopping centre just around the corner from the hotel, so we went in for a little look, to pass the time, until our friends arrived. Jackie bought a jumper, some leggings and a scarf from M&S. There has been an M&S store in just about every capital city we have visited. Although it's still warm in the day, the nights are turning colder, as autumn approaches. Jackie said she needed some warmer clothes and as the new season's clothes were in the store here, thought it a good idea to make a purchase.

Our friends arrived at around 8pm that evening. We were soon in the restaurant 'La Boca' on the same street as their hotel. It was so good to see them and we had so much to catch up on. We had a lovely meal there and all agreed the steaks were some of the best we had tasted anywhere. By 11.15pm we were back on the metro and on our way to Belle.

Prague really is a lovely city, with some of the finest old architecture, as well as modern city living. It is split by the river Danube and has three districts. Hradčany and Malá Strana which has the Castle, Palace and Cathedral on one side of the river. The old town area of Staré Městro, Josefov, and the more modern Nové Město are on the other side. All this splendour is connected by several bridges. The jewel in the crown is the very ornate Charles Bridge. If Vienna felt clinical then Prague feels more antique, but is just as majestic, if not more so.

The first part of our city tour with Paul and Jackie, took us to Wenceslas Square, in the Nové Město area. It was quite a walk from Náměskí Republiky to get there. We passed through a colourful street market, selling fruit and veg. The pavements were packed with people and the roads were wide in places with trams trundling along. It was a very busy part of the city. However, it was not quite as nice or as historic as we had expected it to be. Wenceslas Square is really a long street, with a central pedestrian walk way, flanked by a road going up and (wait for it...) one going down the other side. At the top end, is the National Museum and State Opera building, along with a statue of guess who? St Wenceslas. It all left us somewhat wanting.

That evening we ate out at a place called the 'Black Elephant' a hotel restaurant. The hotel is also called Cerny Slon 'Black Elephant', simple really. It's on Týnská Street, just off the old town square, at the side of the church of Our Lady. The restaurant area was simply furnished and had a vaulted ceiling. Once again our three course meal was excellent and very reasonably priced.

We met up with Paul and Jackie the next morning, for the second part of our walking tour of Prague. This time it's the Staré Městro and Josefov area and then over the river to Hradčany and Malá Strana. We started from the Náměskí Republiky again, first taking in the Powder Gate. Then down Celetná Street, an old trading route to Bohemia, named after plaited bread, then into the wonderful old town square Staroměstskě Náměstí. We pass ornate entrances, three, four, five and six storey buildings, some modern, some very old. There is a street café culture. The weather is warm but overcast, so people are dressed in a mix of tee shirts and short skirts, jackets and jumpers. Who knows what the weather will do?

Staroměstskě Náměstí Sqaure heaves with tourists. It is so picturesque. Cameras are clicking everywhere you turn. To one side, and nestling behind some six storey decorative facaded buildings, stands the imposing twin Gothic steeples of the church of Our Lady. On the opposite side is the elaborate Old Town Hall, with its famous astronomical clock on one side. On the hour, mechanical figures perform above the zodiacal signs, to the crowd's amazement. Alongside the Town Hall, is the church of St Nicholas, another very elaborate domed building. The surrounding buildings are painted in pastel colours, creams, reds and blues, nothing short of stunning.

We deviate off the straight path, to take in the Jewish Quarter and the cemetery established in 1478. This was the only place in Prague where Jews were allowed to be buried at the time. We did try to get a photograph of the Old Synagogue, but were beaten to it by about fifty Japanese tourists, who (teleported in) and just wouldn't move out of the way. It is fascinating to think it was bult in 1270 and is the oldest synagogue in Europe. We are soon back on track and making our way to cross over the famous Charles Bridge. We, along with the masses, pass through the Malá Strana Bridge Tower, at one end and are greeted by a procession of statues either side of the bridge, representing the Saints and Madonna. I loose count after thirty five life size statues. It must rank as one of the most ornate bridges in the world. At the other end is the Staré Město Bridge Tower, which we pass through and begin our ascent to the castle.

The streets and gardens on the way up to the castle are a pleasure in themselves. At one point, we sat and watched as one of the new technological remote lawn mowers, cut a large rectangle of grass. It all seemed quite bizarre among the historic buildings. It was at this castle, in 1618 that Bohemian Catholics threw the then Emperor's envoys out the window, thus starting the Thirty Years War. Jackie said she has thought of throwing me out the window on many occasion! Onwards and upwards, the imposing castle wall houses the Old Royal Palace, the President's office, the Cathedral of St Vitus (who apparently liked to dance) and St Georges Basilica, to name but a few. The castle is one of the most grandiose we have ever visited.

We pause for thought and a drink of water, in the Royal Gardens, on the other side of the castle, before our descent. We are presented with a magnificent panoramic view, over the Charles Bridge and the rest of the city. There is also a large silver hot air balloon continually ascending and descending, offering sightseers' spectacular views of the city. The backdrop is the cream and terracotta mosaic of the buildings against a hazy grey sky. A well-earned rest is needed, as our feet are now throbbing with all the walking. The rain did keep off and it was a very warm day.

After a pleasurable walk back down from the castle, we caught the tram back directly to our campsite, to freshen up, while Paul and Jackie walked back to their hotel. We would meet up that evening for dinner. Our venue is the old town square again, as it does all look rather gorgeous, when lit up at night. It's amazing how places take on a whole different atmosphere when the sun goes down.

Paul and Jackie's last day soon came and so we sat by the river Danube, having a few drinks, before we said our fond farewells. Paul and Jackie are easy-going and good company as always. They both thought Prague was one of the most picturesque cities they had ever visited.

There is one other event to report from our time in Prague. On the second night of our stay at the campsite, a large motorhome with a GB number plate pulled in next to ours. Out tumbled six young lads in their early twenties, all laughter, 'f'ing and blinding' and smoking.

Against Jackie's advice, I went out for a chat. They hailed from Manchester and so all had that unmistakeable accent. They told me that they had driven directly to Prague from Manchester and had been on the road for twenty four hours. They all introduced themselves, as did I, but somehow I got the nick name 'John'. Now, I know they were taking the Michael (who's he?), but I persevered and talked to the main man. It was his father's motorhome and had been loaned to him, on the clear understanding, that they would not wreck it. Well, all the leather seating was now out and spread around the van, as they proceeded to have a bbq. I must have got the nod of approval, as they offered me a beer and a sausage burger, but still kept calling me John.

During the course of the next few days, they were having much fun, without making that much noise. They came home drunk one day, all armed with electric anti-rape guns, for their partners back in the UK. There followed a 'who can stand the most shocks to the nipple' game. At one point their immature banter was shocking, as they discussed what, and what not to do, with their girlfriends.

When they went out on the town, they all looked out for one another. They certainly were not looking for any trouble. They continually took the Michael (could that now be John?) out of one another, over incidents that had happened, mostly chatting up girls. They were polite to Jackie. The lads left to go to Switzerland, with a wave and a "See you John" from all. I have to say I did enjoy their company and youthful bravado. Jackie had listened into all their antics, with a raised eyebrow and wry smile, now and again. The only down side was, when they left the site, there was a lot of litter on the ground and a pair of underpants that had been drying on the camp fence. I cleared it up, not wanting Brits to get a bad name. For the record, I did not touch the pants.... they may still be there to this day.

We both have to say we liked Prague very much. In parts it was the most visually stunning city we had ever visited. Our words do not do justice to the historical heritage to be found, or the pleasing architecture of the buildings, statues, paintings, gardens and ornamentation. It really has created a dilemma, over where we would choose, as the best city we have visited, it was that good. It rivalled Vienna for photos taken. I do hope we will go back again. On another note, our budget was not too far off either, as the prices in Prague were very reasonable.

Chaper Seventeen

Germany

September 6th - September 9th

Deggendorf – Munich – Friedrichshafen

Great news today. Our daughter Shelley and her husband Stewart, received the keys to their new house in Brisbane, Australia. What a wonderful start to our morning. Belle was to take us from Prague to Munich. We have not decided beyond that, the route back into France. We will take the E53 and head to our first stop, Deggendorf just across the German border. We have consulted all our books and are looking forward to staying on a few Stellplatze, which are either free, or low cost camping areas. The weather is overcast but warm, so off we set with the prospect of a good days travel ahead.

As we make our way to the border, again no border control, road surfaces are very good and well maintained. The countryside we pass through is lush and green, with gently rolling hills, forests, small villages and farmland. Some of the villages we pass through are peaceful, some very pretty, while others are in need of an uplift of sorts. We travel by the side of single track railway lines for a while. Thankfully, there is not much traffic on the mostly single lane roads. Some village streets have shops with outside stalls selling their wares, with fruit and vegetables on open display.

Once across the border we are in Bavaria and on course to Deggendorf, the capital of the same named district. It is situated by the Danube, has a Science University and a majestic ivory coloured church, with a pointed onion skin spire, that dominates the market square. It's typically German, with not a thing out of place, but actually nothing special. We easily find somewhere to park (not always the case with 7.2m) and walk around for a while. Then having spotted an Aldi, we stock up with food for the next few days.

We have located a farm Stellplatze in our Bord Atlas, which Sheila very kindly locates for us. On arrival we can only see a farmhand working in the yard. The farm house is white rendered, with a high peaked roof, typically Tyrolean. The farmhand indicates we should park up on the hill above. We parked as instructed and are immediately presented with magnificent views over the farm and river valley below. We can see for miles. It takes a few minutes to realise, after all the hustle and bustle of the cities, here we are in the tranquil countryside. With birds twittering, rustling of the trees and that wonderful fragrance of the countryside, we had quite forgotten how glorious it is. Our chairs are soon out and we have a glass of wine in our hands, ready to relax.

A short time later, a little car arrives at the farm. Soon after, a young lady in her early twenties walked up the hill to greet us. She had also come to collect the money, 12 euros for the night. We were amazed at the price and would have paid double, just for the view. Annette explained to us that she is the farm owner's daughter and her mother and father were on holiday in Hungary, which is where her mother comes from. We told her that we had recently been to Hungary as part of our tour. We chatted for quite a while, her English was excellent. It's so nice that we can relate to names and places. She then took us down to the farmhouse to show us where the shower facilities were. They were on the ground level of the house, which was their basement. Stairs off to one side of the entrance hall, lead to the main house. How trusting of folk they must be.

That evening we took turns to take photos of the setting sun, God's gift to us that evening. A giant ball of yellow shimmered on the horizon as the sky turned orange, red and then inky black, as it disappeared. I have to admit yet again, Jackie's photographs of the sunset were better than mine. That night I made 'curry in a hurry' (see book one for recipe), Jackie updated her journal and did a few crosswords, as I read my kindle. We sat outside until it was pitch black and the sound of insects had taken over from the silence of the evening.

The next morning the views were just as delightful, as we ate our breakfast al fresco. We then went down for a shower in Annette's parents beautiful farmhouse. It was so pretty, flowers everywhere, trailing out of window boxes with roses around the doors. The actual site toilets were in a little wooden hut, not far from Belle and were also very good, if a little rustic. All clean and shipshape, we are soon packed up ready for our journey to Munich. We would have loved to have stayed longer, it was that tranquil.

Our next stop was to be Passau, as we chose to travel the small roads along the Danube. Our views along the river here are very picturesque, but not quite as nice as the Mosel, where we toured the year before. Passau is famous for being at the confluence of the three rivers, the Danube, the Inn, and the Ilz. It is another smart town, with fine buildings and the imposing St Stephen's Cathedral. We wander the streets, before stopping for lunch. We ate outside, at a little restaurant along a quiet leafy street The weather was still fine and warm. We had Wiener Schnitzel (veal in breadcrumbs) potatoes and salad. The portions of the servings were huge. We would both have been full with just one meal shared. "Bavarian portions," the lady serving told us. It was the tastiest veal we have ever had.

We now did what we do best. Back to Belle, we circled three times around Passau, before heading off on the wrong side of the Danube and back towards Austria. Sheila had a sulk on and was not responding, so we were totally reliant on our sense of direction and the signage. To this day, we do not know how we got it so wrong. Jackie is an excellent map reader, while I normally have a good sense of direction. We found ourselves going back in the same direction as we came in, back to Deggendorf. Luckily, we soon picked up the motorway to Munich.

Some hours later we arrive at our campsite, near the centre of Munich. We are close to the Tier Garten Zoo, at a campsite called 'Thalkirclen'. It was a very well set out site, had good clean facilities and a shuttle bus to the U'Bhan (underground train) for a ride into the city. We had a nice chat with an elderly German couple, who were in a caravan next to us. They were from Ulm, Albert Einstein's birth place, they said it is very nice and we should visit. Needless to say, most of the Germans we meet, speak some English. We just chilled out around Belle for the rest of the day, as it had been quite a road trip.

We awoke to cloudless blue skies and warm sunshine. We were looking forward to going into Munich, the capital of Bavaria, where BMW and Mercedes have their headquarters and factories. Our friends John and Linda had lived in Munich for a time, whilst John worked for Rolls-Royce. They told us all their favourite haunts and interesting places to see. We consequently planned to go and see the Rathaus (Town Hall) clock chime at mid-day, with its jousting Knights. Our ticket on the U-Bahn cost 10.2 euro for two and the ticket lasted for 24 hours on all public transport. The U-Bahn was uber-silky smooth and modern, we were quietly whisked into the city centre. To say we were impressed, was an understatement.

We ascended the steps to the Marienplatz (market square) and found there was a music festival in progress. We are so lucky at times, being in the right place at the right time. The square, and in fact the whole city, is alive with people. There were many white canvas tents dotted around and a large stage erected at one end. On one side was the very ornate Rathaus, with its huge clock tower. The front of the building is festooned in flowers and flags. There are the obligatory trestle tables, filled with people eating and drinking. The crowd suddenly goes quiet, as the clock strikes twelve, and out of the tower below the clock emerge the mechanical life-size figures, followed by the two knights on horseback, who joust to the accompaniment of the Glockenspiel. Needless to say, the Bavarian knight wins every time.

Jackie and I sat at one of the trestle tables, having a beer. The long table was jam-packed both sides and we feel happy and relaxed sitting amongst all ages and nationalities. We ended up chatting to some Norwegian gents, who sat next to us. It was interesting to learn, that one of the groups father, had been a trawler man in WW2 and had helped soldiers, pilots and Jews escape to Scotland and also landed SOE's (Special Operations Executives) back to Norway. We comment on how brave his father was. He was rightly very proud of him. We found it quite moving to listen to. This chap also told us that he had been to Turkey in England? His friend helped him out, "You mean Torquay, which is in Devon". What a laugh we all had.

We moved on to explore this famous city. Some places trigger thoughts of its darker history, because it is here that Hitler started his rise to power. The city is a mixture of old and new, the after effects of the bombing during the war. Most of the significant buildings have been lovingly restored and are a joy to behold. It is also a centre for the arts and media, with art schools, book publishers and TV stations, all operating here as their hub.

We move from Marienplatz out along the Kaufingerstrasse, one of the oldest streets in Munich, then along Neuhauser Strasse to Karlsplatz, a wonderful square with a huge fountain. We then swung back to find the Residenz, a former residence of Bavarian Kings. It's an impressive complex of three storey stone buildings, with grand squares within. Also connected is the National Theatre, with its columned facade. It's around the area of the Feldherrnhalle, a monumental loggia on Residenzstrasse where Hitler held his first Putsch (failed attempt to seize power) in 1923, having started the uprising in the Bürgerbraükeller.

Walking around the city we come across numerous shops selling the infamous Cuckoo Clock. We also found the BMW museum, but it was closed that day. What was a find for us was a stunning vintage Porsche, parked in one of the side streets. We couldn't walk past the Mercedes showroom without going in. It is housed in a very old building on a sharp corner and as one can imagine, the place is very impressive. The two centre pieces, in the glitzy showroom that day, were a vintage two-seater Mercedes sports car along with a stunningly dressed model. We ambled on and I spied a shop with some very old Carl Zeiss cameras in the window that I would love to add my collection.

Next up, was the Hofgarten with its tree-lined walkways, leading into the Englischer Garten. Here we sat and rested our weary feet for a while and take in the aroma of the surrounding flowerbeds filled with red, white and pink blooms. We then doubled back on ourselves, for a visit to Frauenplatz and the twin spired Frauenkirche, the symbol of this Bavarian capital city. We made another much needed break to visit John and Linda's favourite Bierkella, the 'Ardeder'. Here we had a few traditional Bavarian beers accompanied by some free canapés.

We also re-visited a Bavarian clock shop on the Kaufingerstrasse, where we bought a cuckoo clock. Jackie had always wanted one. There were over a hundred to choose from. An Oriental looking lady, demonstrated the workings and the chime of each one we admired, by winding the fingers past the hour, to make the cuckoo appear. You can choose between one and two tone chimes, on the hour, also on the half hour. 12 hour or 24 hour chain pull, from traditional to modern, different sizes, designs and materials. There were too many to choose from, it took another hour to make our minds up. In true fashion, we find it difficult to make a decision. I asked "Which one do you want then Jackie?" "The one that has the most authentic cuckoo call Adrian". I must admit, a few did sound as if they were being strangled. This particular clock shop was heaving with tourists. The main customers were Americans and Japanese and they were making some very costly purchases.

We are now the proud owners of a chalet style, cream faced Cuckoo clock, handcrafted in the Black Forest. It has two windows, a little fenced front terrace occupied by a goat and a man with a chopper in his hand, which was the deciding factor for Jackie. It has a pendulum and two weighted chains, to rewind it with. It chimes on the hour and half hour. On the hour, as well as the appearance of the Cuckoo, the man with the chopper cuts a pile of wood. We insisted on opening the boxed item she fetched from the store room, before buying, much to the young ladies annoyance. Good job we did, there was a mark on the front of that one. The second one we opened was perfect, so it was another sale for her.

John and Linda had also recommended an Indian restaurant for us to try, with curries tasting close to those that we get in the UK. We were not disappointed. 'Sitar' was situated in the Lehal area, another U-Bahn ride. Jackie had Butter Chicken, while I had a King Prawn Bhuna, Madras hot, my signature dish. However, while the curry was good, they still do not make poppadums like they do in the UK. Ours are always large and very light, while theirs were small and dry, like those that come in a packet from the supermarket and cooked in a microwave.

We ate outside, as it was still warm at 7pm. On the next table we were joined by a young English couple, Lesley and Andrew. Andrew worked for Sky TV Germany, whilst Lesley worked for an on-line fashion store. They had been in Munich for a couple of years and loved it there. They said that the Germans had been very friendly to them and had made them very welcome. They planned to stay another couple of years before returning to the UK.

We also had entertainment from a little mouse, who appeared to live in a hole at the foot of a tree on the side-walk, close to where our tables were. He had his own little garden around the tree, and kept attempting to make forays to the tables. In the end I had to frighten him away, as Jackie doesn't like the little creatures at all. Perhaps he was attempting a 'Hickory Dickory Dock' to run up the Cuckoo clock!

So that was Munich. We found it very 'Uber Teutonic', with a pleasing style all of its own. We both agreed we could live here. We were impressed by the Bavarians we met. They take great pride in their city and the way they dress. They also have a sense of humour and like to tell Bavarian jokes about themselves. The place was obviously prosperous and it had a dynamic atmosphere to it. Just like most of the places we had visited in Germany, everywhere was clean, neat, orderly and tidy.

Next stop is Bodensee or Lake Constance to you and I. We had decided to stay on the German side of the lake, instead of venturing into Switzerland. There was some debate over the route for once, as Switzerland would be an added bonus to our agenda. And of course, there had been an open invite from Sasha (our cyclist friend in Montenegro and Greece) to visit him. However, in the end, the Zeppelin museum at Friedrichshafen, swung it to the German side. This would be a big win for me, as I had read much about the zeppelins and I had not realised we would be this close. I thank Jackie for spotting it whilst trawling for information on the area.

Our trip takes us along the E54 dual carriageway to Lindau, on Lake Bodensee. Somehow on the motorways you never quite connect with the countryside you pass through. It was certainly a pleasant drive and the Bavarian countryside is lush and green. Cruise control is on and our music is playing. It changes from rolling green hills and forests to quite mountainous, as we cross from Bavaria to Barden-Württemberg.

Our first views of the lake are of mirror calm waters, with ducks and swans traversing near the tree lined banks. The lake is bordered by Austria at one end with Germany and Switzerland either side. The Rhine flows into the lake at its southern most point and sits near the Alps. We have located a Stellplatze next to a campsite, 'Cap-Rotech' and decide to stay here for 12 euros for the night. It was basically a car park at the back of the campsite reception building. We are just a short walk along the lakeside into Friedrichshafen, so it's an ideal spot for us. I had a quick reconnoitre into the town, to check on the museum opening times and if it was walkable. Jackie prepared our main meal for the day 'Derbyshire Hot Pot'. She was not happy when I re-appeared with chocolate, snacks and wine, the dreaded diet busters.

More blue skies and warm air for us the following day, it was still short sleeve weather. The walk along the lakeside was very relaxing. We were accompanied by people walking their dogs and other couples out for a stroll. The zeppelin museum is situated on the lakeside and is very '60's Nuevo', with its clean angular lines. The old zeppelin sheds were demolished some time back and the new factory is further on around the lake, so we will only pass by it later in our travels.

Inside the museum we are treated to the history of the zeppelin, which only mentions in passing, its use to bomb cities in the First World War. They caused great alarm and casualties in the UK, during the war. It took our fighter planes so long to achieve the height the zeppelins flew at, that by the time they got there, the zeppelins had gone. Later in the war this would all change, as planes had greatly improved in performance. The museum housed models of all the significant zeppelins through to the present day.

The main display is a life size replica of the D-LZ 129, Hindenburg's passenger quarters, and also the command gondola. This is the famous airship that regularly crossed the Atlantic to New York and Brazil, before the devastating disaster in 1937. The New York Empire State Building's Art Deco spire, was originally designed to moor just such an airship. When the Hindenburg crash landed (caught on newsreel in 1937) the ensuing fire killed 13 passengers, 22 crew and 1 member of the ground crew. This catastrophe signalled the end of the zeppelin. The technology used to float these gigantic leviathans of the air, was hydrogen, which is highly flammable. The Hindenburg had originally been designed to take the safer gas, helium, but for some reason America would not supply it.

Zeppelins actually circumnavigated the globe in the 1920's and 30's. They were the mode of transport for the very wealthy, of that time. The passenger quarters which had brand new art deco furniture designs (due to weight restrictions) of tubular steel, must have felt very futuristic. The passenger section on display could have come out of a designer's idea of the future. Down one side there is a giant panoramic window. Here passengers could overlook the world below, as they floated by. It must have been a serene way to travel and the views must have been breathtakingly beautiful, as the airship travelled more slowly and closer to the ground, than today's modern jet liners.

The newsreel of the time, along with the pictures on the walls, of passengers enjoying the area, now replicated for us, evokes atmospheric feelings of what it must have been like. Then the tragic newsreel of the Hindenburg's demise, conjures up an altogether different picture. All in all, Jackie and I found the whole experience very moving. I am so glad we took the trouble to visit the museum. For me, it bought to life stories from 'Boy's Own' and 'Biggles', and of course my history books.

Friedrichshafen itself is a very nice little lakeside town, full of touristy shops and cafés. After leaving the museum, we stopped for a cuppa at a café, taking in the views over the lake. It gave us the opportunity to muse over the beauty of the lake. Also, what it must have been like to witness one of these gigantic airships, issuing from its lakeside hanger, out onto the lake. The event would have been somewhat similar to the launching of a ship, except this was to go into the air. For the spectators back in the early 1900's, this really must have seemed like the dawning of a new age.

As we departed for France that afternoon, there was one of the modern day zeppelins circling the lake. It was on a much smaller scale to the Hindenburg though. You can still buy a ride in this particular airship. The construction and gas used today are now totally different and it is allegedly far safer than yesteryear. Still, it provokes more thought as we watch it move slowly over the lake. The road takes us past rows of grapevines that lead down to the lakeside. The airship and lake were soon in the distance, as we headed for Freiburg.

The roads are smooth with not much traffic, nice easy driving. We wind our way through the forested valley. Little hamlets dot the hillsides where the pasture land opens out, only for the forest and hills to close in again along the way. We pass by some large, three storey whitewash farmhouses, adorned with flowerbox verandas and their herds of cows in the surrounding fields. It is indeed a picture. At times the hills become mountainous and dwarf us, as we snake our way along. At one point we are joined by a single track railway, that follows us for a while, disappearing into a tunnel, only to re-appear some time later. We skirt the lakeside town of Titisee, with its beautiful church and tall spire, before the landscape opens out again.

We had planned to stop on a Stellplatze just outside Freiburg, close by the Rhine. Unfortunately, it did not look that inviting. It was another car park, and in not a particularly nice setting, so we decided to move on and cross the border into France.

So that was Germany. It had not disappointed. Bavaria and Munich stand their billing, as one of the most beautiful areas of Germany. We have to say, that the German people we met, made us feel most welcome.

Nearly all speak English to some degree, so we never had a problem being understood. Prices for food and drink are very similar to the UK, so keeping to our budget was no problem, except for the Cuckoo Clock. Also, we felt very safe at all times and after France, Germany is the most motorhome friendly country we have visited.

Chapter Eighteen

France

September 10th onwards

Eguisheim – Chaumont – Le Mans – Moëlan-sur-Mer

Across the border, and half an hour's journey into the Alsace, lies the village of Eguisheim. What a little gem this find proved to be. It lies close to the town of Colmar in a gentle valley surrounded by grape vines, with the Le Trois Chateaux brooding on a hill above. We were lucky to get in at the campsite, as it was full, except for two places. Eager to see the village, we quickly parked up and set off to walk the short distance down the hill. This picture book village consists of streets in concentric circles, and is described as 'The cradle of the Alsatian vineyard'.

From the moment we set foot into the village, it has a 'wow' factor for us. It is all very old, with brown timbered multi-coloured houses, a mix of German and French design. Narrow cobblestone streets surround the centre, with hotels, restaurants, fountains and wine caves. We were both ready for a drink, so stopped at the first watering hole, 'La Ville de Nancy', which had a German feel to it. The village is quite small, so we have soon traversed a few of its circles. Then it was into the 'Paul Schneider Cave', to sample some of the local wine. After selecting a couple to suit our taste, it was back to Belle for fried egg sandwiches, accompanied by one of our chosen bottles of nectar. We certainly do know how to live it up at times.

As always, it was great to be back in France, so the following day we were back on the road and heading west towards our second home in Moëlan-sur-Mer

(Moëlan for short). It will take us two stopovers to get there. The first, a site at Chaumont Marina, the second a site just outside Le Mans. The only drama proved to be up a steep hill outside the marina, where my brakes started to squeal. The following day we attempted to find a Fiat dealer, only for the squeal to stop as soon as we pulled up outside the garage. Belle was obviously having a laugh at our expense. I think it was just a stone caught somewhere that must have worked its way free. Chaumont Marina was pretty, but nothing special. Le Mans and Tours are well worth a visit, but having visited a few years before, we decided to just stay on the campsite. Moëlan was pulling us like a magnet, and perhaps, there was just a little bit of travel fatigue starting to creep in.

Moëlan is a little town that lies between Quimper and Lorient, on the south coast of Brittany and its inhabitants are called Moëlanaires. So we are Moëlanaise at last! We had been holidaying in France for many years, before we decided to buy a house in this region. We fell in love with the area right from the start, perhaps initially because it had many way-marked pathways and we enjoy walking so much. Then, there are the friendly people, the rugged coastline, the coastal walks, the beaches, many places of interest and the all-important warmer weather. On average it's at least three or four degrees warmer than Derby.

However, the pretty town of Moëlan has seen better days, with some of the shops closing in the centre. The once busy place has been blighted by the big supermarkets. Thankfully, the weekly Tuesday morning market does attract the locals, as they still like to buy the fresh farm produce. It is very tranquil where we are and perfectly situated, being less than a ten minute drive to the sea. We have many old haunts to re-visit and friends to see, which is why we are drawn to get back.

For those who may be interested, the following list represents some of our favourite places in and around Moëlan-sur-Mer.

Doëlan – This is a picturesque little fishing village on an estuary with two good fish restaurants and two lighthouses. It really is a gem of a place and a typical little Breton fishing port.

Port Belon - Another pretty little fishing port. Here you can buy fresh fish as it comes in fresh off the boat. A chalkboard at the end of the road displays days and times the fishing boats come in and what catch they have. There are two bars here. One is also a Créperie and is of course an excellent fish restaurant. Looking across the estuary you can also see another wonderful restaurant 'Chez Jacky', at Riec-sur-Belon, again, the speciality is fish.

Pont Aven - Very picturesque. Gaugin lived here for a while It's a mecca for artists with its many galleries, shops, cafés and riverside restaurants. A stroll along the boardwalk over the Aven that runs behind the main street is a must. Check out the quaint toilets on the bridge, at one time they must have emptied straight into the river.

Concarneau - A large colourful port, with many fish restaurants and shops. The fortress in the harbour is full of pretty gift shops and restaurants. Be sure to drive around the headland, as there are plenty of good beaches there.

Quimperlé - This is quite a large town, with a river running through. The main shopping area is up the hill in the old part of the town and can be reached either by car, or if you park by the river, up the steps from the main road. There is a small market here on a Friday morning.

Quimper - The capital of Finistere and well worth a visit. It's a large city set on a river, lots of old buildings and a lovely Cathedral to see.

Locronan - A very quaint old Breton village that feels like you have stepped back in time.

Quiberon - Shops, bars, lovely beaches on this peninsula. Boat trips take you over to Belle Isle.

Carnac - Another popular place, lots of shops, restaurants and good beaches. If you visit the Quiberon it is worth taking a look here, as it is close by. Also here are the Megaliths (Ancient standing stones), which are a great tourist attraction.

Josselin - Beautiful Chateau here overlooking the river, cobbled streets; well worth a visit.

Bénodet - Very picturesque port and beautiful sandy beach in a bay backed by pine trees, a popular tourist attraction.

Auray & St Goustan - Pretty little port, very old with lovely restaurants by the river. Walk up the hill into Auray for shopping.

Vannes - Really lovely walled city. Well worth a visit. Nice by the Marina.

This is just skimming the surface of the area, there are so many rewarding places to visit and sights and sounds. Then there are the Bretons themselves, a very friendly and smiley people, who do like their Celtic music. Be sure to visit a Fest Noz if you are in the area, this is a fete where Bretons go to dance and enjoy themselves in the traditional Breton fashion. Ooh la la!

Chapter 19

The End and Conclusion

Back in Derby, just a few loose ends to tidy up before our adventure is well and truly over.

Our first stop is Leisure Kingdom, to see what they will offer us for Belle. It had always been our plan to sell Belle at the end of the tour, as we had a lot of our money tied up in her. It had not quite been two years since we bought her for £43.000, excluding the fittings we had put on, such as satellite TV, alarm system and a bike rack. To begin with they wanted her in for a service and inspection, which revealed the floor had de-laminated, but they didn't mention it to us. This only came to light when a second dealer looked at Belle to give us a valuation.

When we bought Belle, the salesman told us that motorhomes don't lose money like cars do. Well, now came the moment of truth, they offered around £28,000. This was mainly down to the VAT, which he said would be lost as soon as it was taken off the forecourt. It came as an almighty shock as we had expected 17.5%, not 35% reduction. They gave the reason that it had 20,000 miles on the clock, which was high for its age. Normally, they do less than 7,000 a year. Also, it was exhibition time at the NEC and therefore a glut of second-hand motorhomes.

We decided to shop around and were offered various methods and prices for selling Belle. The lowest price was by an agent in London, who offered £26,000. The highest was £32,250, which we would only receive when it was sold off the dealer's forecourt. We did give this long and hard consideration, but did know of a motorhome that had taken six months to sell, in a similar deal. You may recall in part one, we had budgeted for a price of £30,000 when we had put all our costing's together.

We then contacted 'Oaktree Motorhomes', a dealer at Awesworth, near Nottingham. One of their salesmen came over to Leisure Kingdom while Belle was being inspected. It was he who said immediately on entering Belle, that our floor was de-laminating. He asked how much I wanted, I said £30,000 minimum. To my amazement he said, "Get the floor fixed", (which was done under warranty) "and I'll give you £30,000". So that was it, deal done. Belle was in excellent condition, inside and out. He went on to sell her for £36,000 two weeks later with one year's warranty and a part exchange deal.

Now you can get upset over these money related things. He perhaps made £4,000 on the deal, but I said good luck to him. The way I look at it is, if we had been able to wait, perhaps we would have secured £32,250. On the other hand £28,000 was the figure offered by quite a few dealers and £30,000 was what we had budgeted for anyway. In life you have to move on. All told, it was a very sad day when we took Belle into Oaktree Motorhomes. The day of the sale, Jackie followed me up in our new (to us) car, which went some way to take the sadness away from saying goodbye to Belle.

The next thing on the agenda, was to decide exactly where Jackie and I were going from here? We had originally planned to both go back to work, having taken two years out. Neither of us looked forward to this option as we were now used to not working. It was as simple as that. Yet we were not in a financial position to retire completely. Trust me, it had been one of the continuous topics of discussion on our tour. We both agreed that we would prefer to retire if possible and try living in France for longer periods. We had a few months grace before we needed to start to earn a living again.

We have always said that we believed in fate, even our tour had been put down to fate. Amazingly, an event happened almost immediately, which was to alter our plans dramatically. I went out for a drink with a couple of my old pals from printing. Brian became a good friend of mine, who I had known since we were apprentices at college. I also became friends with his brother Gordon. Brian worked with me at Bemrose (latterly BemroseBooth) but had taken redundancy two years before the company closed, due to personal reasons. Gordon had also worked at Bemrose, several years before, but had left to form his own plastic welding company, which he had since sold and retired. Brian, Gordon and their mother moved to the Isle of Wight. They liked it there so much it had been their dream to live there one day.

One day, I had a call from Brian to say that they were back in Derby for a few days, so we arranged to meet up for a drink. During the course of the evening Gordon, who's very financially astute said, "Have you taken your pension yet?" "No," I said, "Well you should, or at least get the figures." He said. Brian backed him up and told me what he had received as part of his deal with BemroseBooth. Suffice to say, I took their advice and made enquiries the next day. To say we were pleasantly surprised by the figures, is an understatement. It was a hell of a lot less than I would have got if BemroseBooth was still in existence, but it was still a significant sum.

Our calculators and spreadsheets went wild with all sorts of permutations. If we did this and that, we could also do that and this, which made it quite possible to retire now. We soon had a plan, which meant that we would not have to go back to work immediately. This was not an as easy decision as it at first may appear. It will be a close run thing financially, until we receive our state pensions, but we are a determined pair when we set our minds to something. We drew up shortlists of what we both wanted to do and at the top, for both of us, was our wish to retire and spend more time in Brittany. One of the biggest things we had to factor in, was how long we thought we would require money to travel with. This has another big assumption attached, how long will you be fit and healthy, and more importantly, alive. We have set our limit at seventy-five, if we are lucky enough to achieve that.

Jackie was once again far more positive about doing it and anyway, if it doesn't work out, we can always go back to work. This time I took far less persuading, as I wanted to start writing part two of our adventures. Where better to do it, than in the tranquillity of Moëlan-sur-Mer.

So there it was. Another fateful meeting and a momentous decision made. Although we both believe in fate, you still have to be able to recognise it when it arrives and also make the right decision. More than that, it has to be right for you. For us it felt right. But, whoever is looking after us, had given us another opportunity to make the best of our situation. We immediately looked for ways to make it work, not reasons why it would not work and to keep that positive outlook...."my cup is half full, not half empty". Time will tell.

Conclusion

As we draw a curtain on such a major event in our lives, we cannot begin to tell you how privileged we feel, to have been able to go on such a tour. We covered over 20,000 miles and came home only slightly over budget. We now feel we have a good appreciation of most of Europe. In our opinion, Europe has got to be one of the most historically rich places in the world. That very rich stream of diversity is a beauty to behold. All you have to do is cross a border, or even go from one region to another in a country, to get a great difference in architecture, language and accents.

I think the question most often asked since our return from our second outing is, "If you had to pick one place to go back to from part 2, where would it be?" It's extremely difficult to answer, as there were so many memorable experiences and wonderful places which we had seen. Thinking of one invariably conjured up another. In answer, once again, we took out the whole of France, because we just love the place. We would include Italy in this category as well. However, not being ones to sit on the fence, we chose to put it into four categories:-

	Jackie	Adrian
City:	Istanbul	Prague
View:	Metéora	Delphi
Emotional:	Haghia Sophia	Topkapi Palace
Restaurant:	Arsenal (Dubrovnik)	New York Café (Budapest)

We are both supporters of the European Union for one very big reason. Unity should be the opportunity for peace, no more wars between us all. The closer we work together, the less chance there is for a dictator to rise to power. If we could get the balance right, then perhaps the European Union will survive and peace will reign.

Looking back now, the rich experience we have gained from the people and places of Europe, will stay with us for the rest of our lives. The dark days of the closure of BemroseBooth are now long behind us, although it has left a scar. It comes into thought less and less. Time is a great healer. We even have to ask ourselves, "How did we hesitate over doing it?" Well... perhaps me more than Jackie, on the hesitation.

We both agree that the later you are in life, the more difficult it gets to give up the things you have accumulated. Possessions and money are big obstacles, as well as loved ones. Possessions: because they have been gained through your wish to have them and one is loath to give them up. Money: because it will have been hard to earn and even harder to accumulate. Friends and loved ones: because they occupy the space in your life and so stop you getting bored. If you are working: as well as providing money, this can also be the main thread of your life, if you enjoy your job that is. The combination of all these things, make up the tapestry of life, which to some extent you can control.

Your health is something else, along with your mind. We are both glad to have carried out one of our life's dreams, while we are still both fit and healthy. The fact we had enough drive to do it, which even then, took the event of me losing my job, to make it happen. Our dread even now, is that an illness of one kind or another will prevent us from fulfilling our dreams. As age creeps up on you, you realise a fit body may not always be there to rely on.

On life itself, through travel, we have learnt that underneath it all we are basically the same. In our opinion, the saddest thing about humanity is that we don't appear to be able to live together, without hurting one another. Most of it is about lines on a map, religion, colour, money and possessions, all divisions created by man. Add to this the intolerance whipped up by the media, politicians and some religious leaders and we have a perfect recipe for unease. Will we ever learn from the past and eradicate greed and the associated poverty pits, where disillusionment and exclusion, are happy hunting grounds for conflict?

As we sit here tapping out these lines, reflecting on memories and what we have achieved, we don't regret a minute of it. If you have even an inkling of wishing to have a 'life adventure', then explore it fully There should be a time and a place for everything. We certainly found out about ourselves and how much lust for life and adventure we have. Europe is a truly amazing place to visit and even our lengthy trip has made us realise, we have only just scraped the surface.

"Au revoir", we do hope you were able to get some enjoyment from our ramblings.

Adrian & Jacqueline

Appendix i - Campsites

List of Campsites, Aires and Stellplatze in order of our route

Where sourced, and our opinion.

France 1

St Gilles Croix de Vie – Aire – All the Aires in France – Small parking area on a busy side road.

Bourcefranc le Chapus – Aire – All the Aires in France – Good.

Biscarosse Plage – Aire – All the Aires in France – Good.

Ondres Plage – Aire – All the Aires in France – Good.

Spain 1

San Sebastian – Aire Paseo de Berio – All the Aires in Spain and Portugal – Very busy, good for one night stopover.

Oracain – Camping Ezcaba – ACSI – Excellent site, nice area, bus route/cycle path into Pamplona.

Navarrete – Camping Navarrete - ACSI - Very good, clean facilities, walk/cycle into the small town.

Burgos – Fuentes Blancas Camping – ACSI – Nice campsite, bus stop into Burgos at site entrance.

Salamanca – Regio Camping – ACSI – Ok for a night, facilities could have been better. Bus stop for the city at site entrance.

Madrid – Camping El Escorial - ACSI - Ideally situated for visits to historic monuments. Good clean facilities. Pleasant 20 minute walk to the bus stop for Madrid.

Toledo – Camping El Greco – ACSI - Very well-kept site, ideally situated for walking into Toledo.

Caceres – Aire – All the Aires, Spain and Portugal – Very busy. Ideally situated for walking into Caceres.

Portugal

Guincho, near Cascais – Camping Orbitur Guincho – ACSI – Nice shaded site, good facilities, bus ride then train journey into Lisbon.

Quarteira – Camping Quarteira – ACSI – Nice site, good facilities, easy walking into Quarteira.

Spain 2

Seville – Camping Villsom – ACSI – Basic facilities, well shaded pitches. Bus stop across the road for trips into the centre.

Cadiz –Roche Campsite, Conil de la Frontera – ACSI – excellent facilities, lovely area.

Torre del Mar – FKK Naturista Camping Almanat – ACSI – Not just for Naturists. Excellent facilities. Beachside location. High hedged parking pitches for privacy.

Granada – Camping Alto de Viñuelas – Baes de Granada– ACSI – Small but very nice campsite overlooking the Sierra Navada mountains. Good clean facilities. Bus stop outside campsite for trips into Granada.

Guardamar del Segura – Marjal Camping – ACSI – Superb campsite, spotlessly clean facilities and great swimming pool area for families.

Benidorm – Camping Armenello – ACSI – Excellent location with good pitches and clean facilities.

Valencia – Coll Vert Valencia Camping – ACSI – Basic facilities. Bus stop outside campsite for trips into Valencia.

Peniscola – Camping Eden – ACSI – Lovely campsite. Perfect location, two minute walk to the beach. Good clean facilities.

Tarragona – Torre de la Mora Camping – ACSI – Very nice campsite on the beach, with good clean facilities and beautiful pool areas. Bus stop a short walk away for trips into Tarragona.

Barcelona – Camping 3 Estrellas, Gavà, Barcelona – ACSI – Very nice campsite by the beach, good clean facilities. 20 minute walk (alongside a busy motorway) to the bus stop for trips into Barcelona.

France 2

Ceret – Camping Municiple – ACSI – Small campsite, a short walk into the centre of Ceret. Basic clean facilities.

Sète – Aire - Parking 3 Digues – Large purpose built parking area for motorhomes situated at the back of the beach. Extremely busy in high season.

Sète – Aire – Not in books, recommended by other campers. Located in a large industrial carpark near the train station. Good location for walking into the centre of Sète. Felt safe only because other motorhomes were there.

Arles – Pont de Crau Camping – ACSI – Nice campsite with basic facilities. Bus stop for trips into Arles just a short walk away.

Port Grimaud – Prairies de la Mer Camping – ACSI – Great campsite. Excellent facilities. Situated opposite the entrance to Port Grimaud and just a few steps onto a beautiful beach. Bus stop outside for trips to St Maxime, St Tropez etc.

Cannes – Camping de la Ferme, Mandelieu-la-Napoule – ACSI – Lovely campsite. Basic facilities. Ideally situated for walking into Napoule. Bus stop outside for trips into Cannes

Italy

San Remo – Camping Villaggio dei Fiori – ACSI – Nice large campsite. Good facilities. Could be difficult to access the site due to very steep entrance road

Ciriale – Camping Baciccia – ACSI – Nice campsite, some small pitches. Good facilities

Torriglia – Aire – Reise Mobil Bord Atlas – Large parking area located on the edge of a small mountain village. Used by heavy municipal vehicles.

Peschiera, Lake Garda – Bella Italia Camping – ACSI – Extensive campsite with excellent facilities. Perfectly located with many views across the lake. Easy lakeside walk into Peschiera.

Lido de Jesolo – Parco Capraro Campsite – ACSI – Lovely large site with excellent facilities. Woodland walk to bus stop and beaches.

Camping in the Balkans

From the link below you can download a PDF which includes campsites for Bosnia-Herzegovina, Serbia, Montenegro, Albania and Macedonia. This includes an English translation.
www.camping-balkan.net

Croatia

Novigrad – Camping Sirena – ACSI – Large site, ideal location for walks into Novigrad. Good clean facilites.

Rovinji – Camping Amarin – ACSI – Nice site. Great location for short boat ride over to Rovinji. Good clean facilities.

Pula – Camping Village Stoja – ACSI – Large site set in woodlands. Bus into Pula at site entrance. Good clean facilities.

Medjeva – Autocamp Medjeva – ACSI – Lovely campsite set at the back of a picturesque bay. good clean facilities.

Senj – Camping Skver – Passing by – Strange little campsite/tarmac parking area. Very basic facilities.

Nin – Campsite Zaton Holiday Resort – ACSI – Beachside. Extensive grounds with excellent facilities. Shaded pitches. Close to Nin. Bus to Zadar from campsite.

Split – Campsite Stobrec-Split – ACSI – Beachside. Extensive grounds with good facilities. Shaded pitches. Short walk to the bus stop for trips into Split.

Dubrovnik – Camping Solitudo – Good campsite. A short walk to the beach. Bus stop for trips into Dubrovnik 15 minute walk.

Montenegro

Herzeg-Novi – Camping Zelenika – *Website – Camping - Shätze des Balkans*. Very basic facilities. Easy walk to the beach and shops.

Budva – Camping Avala – Recommended by other campers. Busy site across from the beach, but very basic. Some workers caravans. Bus stop for trips into Budva, a short walk away.

Ulcinj – Camping Safari Beach - *Website – Camping - Shätze des Balkans*. Lovely campsite, directly on the beach. Good clean facilities.

Albania

Karpen,Kavajë – Camping Pa Emer – Recommended to us, but is also on the Website - *Camping -Shätze des Balkans.* Lovely campsite on the beach. Good clean facilities.

Himarë – Camping Himara – *Website – Camping – Shätze des Balkans*. Very small campsite. Very basic facilities. Located across from the beach. Shops and restaurants close by.

Greece

Igoumenitsa – Kalami Beach Camping - ACSI – Lovely site overlooking a shingle beach. Good clean facilities.

Meteora – Campsite Vrachos, Kastraki – ACSI – Ideally situated in the pretty village. Good clean facilities. Bus stop opposite the site for trips to the Meteora Monaster es.

Stylida – Camping Interstation – ACSI – Large campsite. Basic facilities. Situated on a shingle beach.

Delphi – Campsite Apollon – ACSI - Beautiful terraced campsite with stunning views. Good clean facilities. Ideally located for short journey into Delphi.

Athens – Camping Athens – ACSI – Good campsite. Shaded pitches. Clean facilities. Public transport close by for trips into Athens.

Paralia – Campsite Venezuela – ACSI – Lovely little campsite across from the beach. Good clean facilities.

Methonia – Camping Agiannis – ACSI – Extremely busy campsite. Basic facilities.

Sarti (Sithonia) – Camping Armenistis – ACSI – Very large busy campsite. Good facilities. Mostly shaded pitches backing a beautiful sandy bay.

Kavala – Batis Multiplex – Camping Terra – ACSI – Good campsite with basic facilities.

Alexandroupolis – Camping Municple – ACSI – Nice campsite situated on the beach. Good clean facilities. Pleasant 20 minute walk into the city.

Turkey

Selimpasa – Istanbul Mocamp, Ovayenice Yolu – ACSI – Lovely campsite. Basic clean facilities. Quite a distance from Istanbul but transport details in English at the reception.

Edirne – Grand Ömür Camping, Kirklareli Caddesi – ACSI – Very basic facilities. Bus stop outside the site for trips into Edirne.

Bulgaria

Plovdiv – Hotel Park St Petersburg - We came across this and were able to stay overnight in the hotels secure car park for 17 euros. You should report to the reception on arrival to ensure they still offer the same 24 hour parking.

Sofia – Camping Vrana – Friendly staff but very run down site. We didn't use the facilities. Ideally situated close to the centre of Sophia.

Serbia

Belgrade – Camping Dunav – Recommended. Basic campsite. Friendly staff. Clean facilities. 15 minute walk to the bus stop for trips into the centre of Belgrade.

Hungary

Szeged – Sziksósfürdö Kemping, Széksósi – ACSI – Large campsite. Basic facilities. Set beside a large lake which attracts many day trippers.

Dunaföldvár – Kék-Duna Camping – ACSI – Basic but clean facilities. Pleasant riverside setting. Short walk into the town.

Balatonszemes – Balatontourist Campsite Lido – ACSI – Large lakeside campsite. Basic but clean facilities. Short walk into the small town.

Keszthely – Campsite Castrum – ACSI – Great campsite and location. Nice walk into the lovely town of Keszthely.

Badacsonylábdihegy – Campsite Balaton Eldorado – ACSI – Large Lakeside campsite. Good clean facilities.

Budapest - Haller Camping – ACSI – Very busy campsite. Basic but clean facilities. Ideally situated for metro ride into the centre of Budapest.

Austria

Vienna – Aktiv Camping Neue Donau – ACSI – Small, well-kept campsite. Good clean facilities. Metro station 10 minute walk away for trips into the city.

Melk – Camping Fährhaus Melk – Caravan Club – Nice little riverside campsite. Good clean facilities. Short walk into Melk.

Linz – Campingplatz Linz am-Pichlingersee, Ebelesberg – Caravan Club – Good campsite. Clean facilities.

Czech Republic

Prague – Caravan Camping Prague – ACSI – Basic campsite and facilities. Riverside location. 10 minute unlit walkway to tram stations for trips into the city.

Germany

Deggendorf –Stellplatze Bord Atlas – Farm camping site not many places. Very nice people. Good clean facilities.

Munich – Campsite Thalkirchen - ACSI – Large campsite. Good clean facilities. Close to public transport for trips into Munich.

Friedrichshafen – Aire - Stellplatze Bord Atlas – Car parking area at the back of a campsite by the main road. Ideally situated for a 20 minute lakeside walk into the small town and the Zeppelin Museum.

France

Eguisheim – Des Trois Chateaux – ACSI – Good campsite with clean facilities. Short walk into the pretty mediaeval village of Eguisheim

Chaumont – Aire – Chaumant Marina – Stellplatze Bord Atlas – Parking area by a river.

Yvré-l'Evêque - Le Pont Romaine – ACSI – Very nice campsite. Good clean facilities.

Appendix ii – Guides & Memberships

The Books & Memberships

This is a list of the books and memberships we used and how helpful we found them.

Rough Guides - Very good for information including prices. We used two, one which was called 'Europe on a Budget' and the other 'France'. The former proved very helpful in planning our visits to cities and advised which museums and gardens were free entrance.

Michelin Guides - We used the one volume 'Europe', which we found of limited use and very brief.

DK Eye Witness - We found these very inspirational, and had one for just about every country we visited. While they are a bit limited on entry price information, they are excellent for illustrations of buildings, places and scenic routes to see. Also a good read for a potted history of each country. Excellent for what they are.

Caravan Club also Camping Card International – Membership to both from Caravan Club gets you a card(s) which give you discounts on a range of products and services as well as at some campsites. The book 'Europe Part 2' is full of useful information on each countries traditions and requirements. The campsites listings are good. We relied on this for information and campsites.

ACSI – Membership gets you big discounts on campsites listed, low season. We used both books which were included in the price along with membership. We also purchased the software disc for our laptop. We rate this as our number one resource for reasonably priced campsites and ease of finding locations. The software version is excellent and contains sites not in the books such as Estonia, Latvia and Lithuania. The off season discounts were brilliant. *Available from 'Vicarious Books'. Paid for themselves in four stop-overs.*

Bord Atlas - Reise Mobil – There are two books: one Reisemobil-Stellplatze for Germany and one for the rest of Europe. It is printed in German, but once you get your head around the way to use it, it is excellent. We used it extensively for Germany and our later trip through the Loire. *Available from 'Vicarious Books'. Paid for themselves in two stop-overs.*

Planet Earth - We had one book only. While it contained good information, it was little used, being outplayed by the 'Rough Guide'.

MMM Magazine – We found this magazine and its web forums most helpful, with plenty of useful information and advice on all aspects of Motorhoming.

Appendix iii - Playlist

Played on random setting

Newton Faulkner	Dream, Catch Me
Nat King Cole	What A Wonderful World
Nat King Cole	When I Fall In Love
Nelly Furtado	Powerless
Nirvana	About A Girl
Nirvana	Come As You Are
Nirvana	Silver
Norah Jones	Chasing Pirates
Orson	No Tomorrow
Pixie Lott	What U Do
Public Image Limited	Warrior
Pussycat Dolls	Don't Cha
Snow Patrol	Shut Your Eyes
Snow Patrol	You Could Be Happy
Sonny & Cher	Then He Kissed Me
Sugababes	New Year
White Lies	Death
Al Green	Sexual Healing
Amy Winehouse	Tears Dry On Their Own
Amy Winehouse	He Can Only Hold Her
B52's	53 Miles West of Venus
B52'S	Planet Clair
Basement Jaxx	Oh My Gosh
Cake	Building A Religion
Canned Heat	Going Up The Country
Charles Trenet	C'est Si Bon
Cheryl Crow	Baby Don't Go
Dean Martin	Blue Moon
The Supremes	Stoned Love
The Supremes	Come See About Me
The Supremes	Reflections
Duffy	Mercy

Duffy	Well, Well, Well
De La Soul/Gorillaz	Feel Good Inc
James Blunt	You're Beautiful
James Morrison	The Pieces Don't Fit Anymore
John Denver	Annie's Song
John Legend	Number One
Kaiser Chiefs	I Heard It Through The Grapevine
Kanye West	Jesus Walks
Kayne West	Gold Digger
Kasabian/Stone Roses	Waterfall
Kasabian	Processed Beats
Kasabian	Where Did All The Love Go
Kings of Leon	I Want You
The Kooks	See the Sun
The Kooks	Shine On
Kraftwork	The Model
Kraftwork	Computer Love
Loving Spoonful	Happy Together
Luciano Pavarotti	O Sole Mio
David Byrne	Like Humans Do
Rebecca Ferguson	Nothing's Real But Love
Rebecca Ferguson	Mr. Bright Eyes
Rebecca Ferguson	Shoulder to Shoulder
Omar Faruk Telibilek	Sounds of Istanbul (Album)

Appendix iv

Budget

Exchange rate 2012 £1 = 1.20 euro or $1.60 US $1.55 AU

It would be fair to say that analysing our budget has proved very difficult yet again and has relied on recollection rather than actuals for the small detail. There were two things working in our favour, the exchange rate was slightly better and we paid far less for diesel in Europe.

The headline spend is good as we kept records of totals rather than every last detail on each spend. The other difficulty is in true *'Rigg'* style when we were in the countries that where expensive for us to live in, we lived down to our budget and when we were in countries that were cheap to live in, we lived up to our budget. We did indulge in some luxury items this time, mainly clothes, hotels and mementos. However, even taking these into account, we did end up approximately £1000 over budget this time, mainly spent on eating out and hotels. This made up for being £1000 under budget on the first part of our tour.

I have split the analysis into two parts, 'The Budget' and 'The Countries', for ease of recognition.

The Budget 2012

£150/180 euro per week for food
£75/90 euro per week spending money (mainly for eating out)
£150/180 euro a week for campsites
20,000 miles worth of petrol
£1000 motorhome insurance

£1000 contingency plus some other ancillary costs

FOOD
We managed to stay in budget throughout all the countries and if we had set our minds to it, could have lived on far less in most of the countries we passed through. But then this was never about living frugally, more about enjoying ourselves. There was some cross over with eating out.

SPEND
This was mainly used for bus/train/ferry fares into the places we wanted to visit and eating out. In the more expensive countries we ate out less and so some of this spend would then go on the food shopping bill.

SITES
This was an area of big saving for us with most campsites costing 16 euro (using ACSI discount sites) low season and 34 euro high season. Plus, as we were more confident this time, we used more Aires (France) and Stellplatze (Germany) which cost us little or nothing to stay on. We decided for security reasons not to use these in the other countries, the exception being the one time in Italy. Our average weekly spend on campsites would be £120 overall, a saving of £30 per week.

PETROL
We had allowed for 20,000 miles worth of diesel for the total tour at £6.36 gallon or £1.40 litre (1 imperial gallon = 4.546 litres) at the then UK pump price. Most countries were cheaper for diesel than the UK and by managing our fill ups, we filled to the max in the lower priced countries, we averaged around 1.27 euro a litre. Our motorhome averaged 30 miles to the gallon or 6.6 miles

per litre. Our saving against budget here was around £1000.

INSURANCE/CONTINGENCY
The motorhome insurance cost just under £500 again, so we stayed on course for our two years. We had allowed for £1000 of contingency costs for emergencies and the like. This got eaten into when Jackie had to fly back to the UK last year. Other than this, there was a service cost on the motorhome when we returned to the UK, so we were still on course here also.

The Countries

We have split the countries we travelled through into three categories, the cash neutral, the more expensive and the less expensive. These are our opinions only based on what we purchased in those countries. Albania and Bulgaria were by far the cheapest countries we visited, while Austria proved the most expensive.

Cash Neutral
France, Spain, Portugal, Italy, Hungary, Germany

More Expensive
Austria

Less Expensive
Croatia, Montenegro, Albania, Greece, Turkey, Bulgaria, Serbia, Cheque Republic

Summary
Without going into every detail, we were about £1000 over budget at the end of part two of our adventure. This included all the savings on petrol and

campsites. To be fair, because we were £1000 under budget from part one, we did let things slip in part two. Plus the exchange rates had moved in our favour (1.16eu to 1.20eu/£), giving us a feel good factor. It had been a great relief to know that overall we were in budget, as this was an important aspect of remaining relaxed during our travels. We did know that it was possible to be spending far less, as we witnessed others we met along the way, who were doing it on a shoestring. Then there were those who were spending far more and for whom money appeared to be no object. The most important thing is that we are all enjoying our own route to happiness.

Appendix v

History Reading Books

I have made a list these for those who may be interested, as for me they provided a historical backdrop to the paces we passed through. They tell of the Christian ejection of the Moors from Spain. Then of the Jews, who had financed the war and who the Spanish could not pay, so ejected them as well. How the Ottoman Turks welcomed these Jewish financiers, artisans and intellectuals (as second class citizens). One of whom would allegedly help them build the mighty canon, that would bring down the walls of Constantinople. The momentous struggle with the Ottoman Turks and the sieges of Constantinople, Malta and finally Vienna. How fellow Christians first sacked Constantinople ensuring its downfall 100 years later by the Turks. The heroic defence of Malta by Valetta, which I think should be made into a movie. The 100 Year's War which desolated large tracts of France and also the 30 Year's War that tore apart central Europe.

Finally, on the history front, during our tour, I also read about the Spanish Civil War. Some of the atrocities during that period equalled the violence of the Second World War and are still felt in Spain today. For perspective I would also like to add that I have read many books on the First and Second World Wars and about ancient Greece and Rome. All of which have left their marks on the landscapes and its peoples.

Empires of the Sea – Roger Crowley – *Excellent.*
Constantinople – The Great Siege – Roger Crowley – *Good.*
The Great Siege of Malta 1563 – Ernle Bradford – *Good.*
The Enemy at the Gate - Andrew Wheatcroft – *Good.*

The Last Crusaders – Barnaby Rogerson – *Excellent.*
Hundred Years War – Volume One – Jonathan Sumpton – *Good, but heavy going.*
A Brief History of the Hundred Years War – Desmond Steward – *Good.*
Europe's Tragedy – Peter Wilson – *Good, but heavy going.*
The Battle for Spain – Anthony Beevor – *Excellent.*

As a footnote, thank goodness for the electronic age of e-books, for the constant traveller, they are a huge boon. To be able to purchase and read books on the move, added significantly to our enjoyment of the tour. It would have required a trailer on the back of the motorhome to house the books we consumed. The above books are just the tip of the iceberg, as I am an avid science fiction and fantasy reader while Jackie likes her historical romances and humour. We are both very sad for the printer's and book store's whose revenues are being eroded, but needs must. It will be a sad day indeed when the book store disappears from our high streets.

11370016R00159

Printed in Great Britain
by Amazon.co.uk, Ltd.,
Marston Gate.